KINGS ISLAND

KINGS ISLAND

A RIDE THROUGH TIME

EVAN F. PONSTINGLE

Rivershore Press

Published by Rivershore Press. Visit us at www.rivershorecreative.com.

ISBN: 978-1-7321210-8-9

Cover design by Paul Bonifield

CONTENTS

Part V
CEDAR FAIR

ca's Family Entertainment Center

RIVERTOWN

HAPPY LAND OF
HANNA-BARBERA

THE JACK NICKLAUS
GOLDEN BEAR GOLF COURSES

FOREWORD

I was the first General Manager of Kings Island when it opened in 1972—forty-eight years ago! I oversaw design concept, construction, and its first season of operation following the merger of Cincinnati's Coney Island and Taft Broadcasting in July of 1969. The purpose of the merger was to move Coney's operation out of a flood plain and limited space, shed its aging "amusement park" label, and become a modern "theme park," a term inspired by Disneyland when it opened in 1955. Coney Island and Taft shared a vision to build a new theme park in Warren County utilizing Coney Island's management and Taft's financial backing. Taft also brought to the merger the resources of its newly acquired Hanna-Barbera division on the west coast.

My on-site responsibility at Kings Island ended in September 1972 when I moved to Richmond, Virginia to build a sister park, Kings Dominion. But the prior years of research and planning, I believe, produced a unique theme park with the inclusion of its iconic International Street, the Hanna-Barbera characters, and the re-emergence of the wooden roller coaster, *The Racer*. A new wooden coaster of this magnitude had not been built for decades in the United States.

I was responsible for keeping the project on budget and on time. But I did not succeed in keeping it on budget, the final cost being thirty million dollars. I felt, however, it was a big bang for the buck. I did succeed in opening the park on time—May 27, 1972. This was a critical objective. The park functioned well and was a success from the beginning.

It is interesting that Kings Island never experienced the external challenges that Coney Island did. There was no Great Depression, no 1937 flood, no World War II, no devastating *Island Queen* steamboat explosion that ended the park's main source of patron transportation, no 1950s polio scare, and integration of the park. Kings Island, by contrast, faced a different challenge, that of adjusting to five different ownerships. One of these owners, Paramount Parks, was in my opinion detrimental to Kings Island. Paramount Parks' west coast philosophy did not relate to the park's Midwestern culture.

Kings Island's present owner, Cedar Fair, parent company of Cedar Point and several other amusement and theme parks, clearly understands the business, providing hands-on care and direction from exceptional on-site management. Kings Island is restoring its original values, including distinguishing each themed area, re-emphasizing live shows for more balanced entertainment, restoring International Street, and bringing back family rides such as the popular *Antique Cars*. This team gets it!

When asked what I am most proud of, I would say Kings Island's reputation as one of the last bastions of clean, safe, wholesome family entertainment experienced by well over a hundred million visitors. I am also proud of the unique employment opportunity for hundreds of thousands of young people who enhance their interpersonal skills putting smiles on the faces of millions of patrons. They will talk about their summer at the park for the rest of their lives. Finally, I am proud that Kings Island is returning to its core values established by Coney Island and Taft Broadcasting.

The future? The new 300-foot giga coaster, *Orion*, says it all—the sky's the limit!

Gary Wachs

PROLOGUE

*I*n 1867 a man by the name of James Bell Parker bought a portion of farmland on the banks of the Ohio River near Cincinnati that belonged to the late Thomas Whetstone. Parker began growing apples and strawberries and raising hogs on the property; within a year people began holding picnics in Parker's shady apple orchard. Word spread and the popularity of the picnics in Parker's groves increased, especially after steamboats began bringing excursion parties from Cincinnati. Over the years concessionaires began setting up sideshows, theaters, and games to entertain those picnicking in the orchard; by the 1880s a mule-powered carousel and dance platform had been added.

James Parker sold his grove in 1886 to steamboat captains William F. McIntyre and Jacob D. Hegler, who focused on transforming the daytime picnic excursion into a large summer resort. On June 4 ownership of the property was passed to the Cincinnati Steamboat Excursion Company, with Hegler named as president and McIntyre appointed as secretary-treasurer. Hegler decided that Parker's Grove should be a showplace and named the new resort Coney Island after the famed amusement center in New York. The new Coney Island officially opened June 21 with rides and a shooting gallery. The park's first roller coaster was added soon afterwards, a switchback railway called the *Hegler Coaster.*

Just two years later Coney Island was sold to William E. Hutton, who transferred the park to the newly formed Coney Island Company. Levi H. Brooks was named the new president. Brooks made several changes to the property, including an expansion of the roller coaster. Rides, attractions, and restaurants were added over the years, including new coasters that were introduced in 1902, 1911, and 1913. In the 1920s the large *Skyrocket* coaster was built, designed by the famous coaster designer John A. Miller.

The 1920s were an exciting period of growth for Coney. In 1924 Rudolph Hynicka and George Schott formed Coney Island Inc. and purchased the park. The second *Island Queen* boat that served as transportation between downtown Cincinnati and Coney Island was christened on April 18, 1925, replacing one that had burned in 1922. Until 1947 when the ship was destroyed in an explosion, the *Island Queen* was a popular and iconic ship that set the scene for the Coney Island experience. One of Coney's most famous features, *Moonlite Gardens*, was added in 1925. *Sunlite Pool*, which still to this day is the world's largest recirculating pool, opened on May 22 of that same year. Two Philadelphia Toboggan Company-designed coasters, the *Wildcat* and *Twister*, opened in 1926; that's when Coney Island gained its famous tagline "America's Finest Amusement Park."

After the sudden death of George Schott in 1935, his son Edward was named park president, overseeing Coney's continued rapid growth and popularity. 1947 saw the addition of the park's signature attraction—the *Shooting Star* roller coaster, a radically altered and redesigned version of the 1937 *Clipper* coaster.

By the 1950s Coney Island had such a tremendous reputation that even Walt Disney stopped by while he was researching ideas for his Disneyland project. Walt was extremely impressed with Coney's cleanliness and landscaping, two features that would become staples at his own park. He also found encouraging support for his ideas from Coney's management, a welcome change from the naysayers that had dominated his quest thus far.

Following the death of Edward Schott, Ralph Wachs, the son-in-law of George Schott, was named Coney Island's president in 1962.

Coney Island was a tradition. It was a tremendously popular park and had become a signature staple of Cincinnati's culture. It was also widely recognized as the greatest traditional amusement park in the United States. No one could have guessed that a flood in 1964 would change the course of Coney Island and Cincinnati's amusement park scene forever.

PART I
TAFT BROADCASTING

WE'RE GONNA MOVE THE PARK

*S*ituated along the banks of the Ohio River, Coney Island was especially prone to flooding. In 1964 the fourth highest flood in the park's history struck, cresting at 66.2 feet. Gary Wachs, vice president of Coney Island and son of park president Ralph Wachs, went out and surveyed the damage the flood had wrought.

"I thought, 'I don't want to spend the rest of my career pushing flood mud and trying to stay competitive with the industry and other parks,'" Wachs recalls. "Every time we made improvements, it became more vulnerable. I used to have an expression, 'You can stand the flood in your basement but not your living room.' And we were a living room!"

Another issue Wachs started thinking about during the recovery from the flood was expansion. Coney Island was not only flood prone, but landlocked as well. "We had maybe 160 acres, but we were landlocked by Kellogg Avenue, the Ohio River, River Downs race track on one side, and California, the community, and homes on the other. We couldn't really grow any larger." This was a significant issue as the age of the family-owned traditional park was giving way to the new wave of theme parks following the opening of Disneyland in 1955 and Six Flags Over Texas in 1961.

"They really spruced up the industry and frankly, as much as I love and adore Coney Island—and it was the top of its peer group—we were all practicing habits that were dying out and getting old. And here came Disney and he said, 'Hey, I want to refresh this industry. I want clean parks, I want well-landscaped parks, I want to use refreshing, wholesome college kids.'" These two issues weighed heavily on Wachs' mind in the days and weeks following the flood of 1964. Gary Wachs knew that Coney Island could not keep operating as it was. Coney had to move.

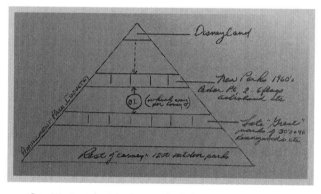

Gary Wachs drew this diagram depicting where Coney Island (circled in middle) was in comparison to the evolving amusement park industry. Courtesy of Gary Wachs.

Wachs recalled, "I started thinking, 'How do I go about this? How do I talk to members of our own little family corporation, including my own father? How do I sell this idea to our own company? Because if I can't get our company behind me, I can't do this.'" Gary figured he would have to sell the idea of relocating the park to the heads of each division in the park, his father, as well as the chairman of the board, Charles Sawyer. Sawyer, who had been President Harry S. Truman's Secretary of Commerce, was the largest single stockholder of Coney Island.

He began developing a presentation to persuade the board and his father to move the park. "Obviously, we should move because of the floods and the fact that we have no land, but the third major reason we should move is our competitive market," argued Wachs. Coney Island fed off the markets of Cincinnati, Dayton, Columbus, Indianapolis, Lexington, and Louisville. "We owned it [that market] at the time, but what if a competitor comes into our market? We're in trouble."

First, he laid out the basic concept of the new park. Wachs knew it had to be a heavily themed, immersive environment to compete with any potential modern theme parks that could be built in the region. Gary roughly mapped out a children's area, an historical area inspired by Cincinnati's heritage as a river town, a representation of the Coney Island of days gone by, and a grand entrance of a European boulevard, influenced by a 1963 trip to Europe. The entire park would adapt Disneyland's "hub-and-spoke" design into a "four-leaf clover."

Wachs next contacted a friend who went to Wharton Business School to assemble a financial report estimating projected attendance and cost for building the new park. "I had the concept down, I had the dreamer side down, and I had the financial side down," Wachs recalled. "Then I had to have the rationale side down and the support side; why are we doing this? I literally developed a two-hour presentation." Gary first tried out his presentation on Coney Island's department heads, without his father. "When I got up in front of everyone, I had two easels that I showed my renderings on and some other things, and I go through this whole thing of here's why we have to move," Wachs said. "I went through the history of Coney Island, I went through the history of our old industry and the coming, new industry. I got into our market area and I said, 'We're vulnerable and we've got to [move].'"

"They looked at me as a young guy and I thought some of them rightly thought, 'Wait a minute Gary, we're doing damn well. We're successful. Every time we put something in new, the park's growing.' But the more I talked about that [moving the park], the more I sold them on the idea."

Gary next convinced Ralph Wachs, Gary's father and president of Coney Island. "I'd sold my father enough that he let me keep going on this project," continued Wachs. "He didn't place any restrictions on exploring moving the park. Somebody else could have said, 'Gary, you just stick to running the park' or assisting or whatever. I was fortunate."

With both the department heads and the park president on board with the idea of building a new park, the last person Gary had to convince was the board chairman, Charles Sawyer. "He was a guy we had a great relationship with. As long as we were successful, anything we wanted to do he would rubber stamp [it]. He said, 'Keep going guys, I think you're doing a great job.' He would say that board meeting after board meeting after board meeting. So you couldn't ask for a better chairman of the board. If we wanted to put in nineteen new roller coasters, he'd say 'Do it!'" Sawyer loved Coney Island the way it was, and Gary Wachs knew that selling the idea to him would be the toughest obstacle up to that point. "I said, 'Mr. Sawyer, let me put you in a plane. I want to show you the future of the industry. I want to show you what's coming and if we don't do it, we're going to be in serious trouble.'" So Wachs and Sawyer flew down to Six Flags Over Georgia during its opening year of 1967.

"[I] took him to the first real live show Mr. Sawyer had ever seen," recalled Gary of their trip to Atlanta. "They had five standing ovations; it was Americana at its best. I thought it would make a lasting impression on him...I took him down there and he processed the whole thing, but never seemed to get excited. Then I got him back to Cincinnati and gave him my two-hour presentation."

Wachs got Sawyer up in his office, set up his easel, and began his spiel, talking about "the effects of floods on Coney Island; I had a whole section on all the floods from 1925 up to that point. It's a thesis about that thick [gesturing with his hands], why we ought to move! I went through the whole thing with him. 'Here's our market area Mr. Sawyer, here's where we're successful in Indianapolis and cities like that. We're ahead of our game, we now control our own destiny. But Mr. Sawyer, what happens if somebody knocks on the door?'"

"Well I go through this whole thing, and I'll never forget his first reaction. Two hours of me talking, and when I was finished I said 'Well?' And he said, 'If we move, what happens to my dividend?'"

"I knew at his age that Coney Island was his playtoy, and he didn't want anything to happen to it! I had this expression, 'Old men don't look down the road. Young men look down the road.' So I understood I was talking to an old gentleman. The future didn't seem to concern him."

Wachs felt as though he was at a dead end. Charles Sawyer was not going to give up his "playtoy," no matter how the amusement industry was changing and no matter how many floods Coney Island had to weather. Wachs decided the next step would have to be drastic.

"I was on the board too; I was going to call a meeting of everybody, including my father [and] Mr. Sawyer, and go through this presentation—which the board had not yet seen—and that was going to be a showdown," Gary remembers. "Are we moving or not? Let's vote on it. I talked to my cousin who had Coney Island stock. I went through this with some of our key stockholders and they all thought, 'Gary, let's move, let's do it.' Now, that board meeting would have been...I don't know if I would have still remained with the company after that. It was a big risk. But I didn't care, I had been working on this for four or five years and had gone this far, so I was going for broke. And guess what? That board meeting never happened. Why? Because out of the blue, like a lightning strike, [came] Fess Parker."

FRONTIER WORLDS

On September 9, 1968 Fess Parker, the famous actor who played Davy Crockett and Daniel Boone on television, announced he would be building a massive theme park called Frontier Worlds in Boone County, Kentucky, a short drive from Coney Island. The 360-acre, heavily themed $13.5 million park would feature "20 super attractions" and themed areas representing "frontiers from the past and future," according to the *Cincinnati Post*. While the initial development was for 360 acres, Parker had optioned 1,400 acres where I-71 and I-75 split, with the remaining land designated for hotels and shopping. The park was scheduled to open in 1970. Wachs knew at once that Parker was serious.

"I panicked," Gary admitted. "I knew it was do or die time. I went to my father and said, 'Dad, if that guy opens that park, Coney Island is either out of business or we're going to become a second-rate amusement park, because we won't have the funds to do all the wonderful things [we want to do]. I don't want to live like that.'"

Ralph suggested to his son that he should consider working for Six Flags Over Texas. Gary instead decided to search for a large, corporate partner to provide financial backing. And he knew just where to look for one.

TAFT BROADCASTING ENTERS THE PICTURE

Coney Island ran many promotions and special events, one of which was called WKRC Day. WKRC was a Cincinnati television station owned by Cincinnati-based media conglomerate Taft Broadcasting Company.

Taft Broadcasting "got the idea that they wanted to do Pops concerts in the afternoon at *Moonlite Gardens*. We would set up card tables on the dance floor with checkered tablecloths and candles, and famous concert people like Arthur Fiedler would come in from Boston. They'd have many wonderful people come in and give these Pops concerts," Wachs explained. "They were successful and very popular, and we'd go up on the balcony of *Moonlite Gardens* and enjoy the concert."

Wachs always sat with Lawrence "Bud" Rogers, president of Taft Broadcasting Company. "I got to know him, and because of that I thought I'm going to contact him. I'm going to call this guy, tell him who I am, and say I'd like some time with him."

"I said, 'Bud, I want to come see you. Do you have some time?' He's a nice fellow and responded, 'Sure Gary, come on down.'" Rogers, who was on a call when Wachs arrived, assumed Gary wanted to discuss doing a fundraiser for the Cincinnati branch of the United Appeal charity. In reality, Wachs was hoping to sell Taft Broadcasting on the idea of helping him to build a new Coney Island. Gary laughed, "So I go in his office and I'm bringing all my stuff for my presentation. And he got wide-eyed; he didn't know what the hell I was peddling!"

"I'm setting up this stuff, getting ready; he hangs up, looks at me and says, 'What can I do for you? Why are you here?' 'Bud, how much time do you have?' He said, 'Well, I don't know, go on, start to tell me.' 'Bud, I am here to talk to you about a merger with Coney Island to build a new theme park.' 'Tell me about it.' Two hours later I was finished. I gave him the whole thing. He didn't jump up and down, he didn't say you're crazy. Again, this is a lot to process! So he said, 'Alright. Let me get back to you.' That was about the extent of his remarks. It wasn't get out of here, it wasn't you're crazy, it wasn't oh, let's go tomorrow, it was a process kind of thing. I said okay and I thought that was—you know, I'll take that for the first meeting."

Two weeks later Rogers asked to meet with Wachs for lunch at the Netherland Plaza Hotel in downtown Cincinnati. "He said, 'Gary, the first thing I want to ask you: how does your father feel about this?' I said, 'I wouldn't have talked to you, Bud, without my father's blessing.' Okay, that's important. We didn't have a long lunch because I had given him my pitch."

In that two-week interim, Rogers had spoken to Taft Broadcasting's new CEO, Charles S. Mechem, Jr. As it turns out, Mechem, who was Taft's attorney prior to the sudden 1967 death of Hulbert Taft, had been interested for several years in building a theme park.

CHARLIE MECHEM'S IDEA

Mechem recalls, "After we had acquired Hanna-Barbera [cartoon studio in 1965] and after I had become CEO, I began thinking of how we could leverage the Hanna-Barbera characters—involve them and simply put them on a bigger stage, even bigger than they were on TV. Obviously, the roadmap was Disney and the way they used their characters in their amusement parks."

Through a friend in Los Angeles, Mechem was able to meet Roy Disney for lunch to discuss the amusement park industry. "We had a lovely lunch; I asked him a lot of questions. And he was most encouraging about the amusement park business even though he knew that anything we might do would be a regional park, not a full year-round park. He liked the business and he explained why he liked the business.

"As we were leaving, I said, 'Mr. Disney, is there anything we haven't touched on?' He smiled and said, 'You know, it's ironic that you would come out here and ask me about the amusement park business, because you have the finest small amusement park in America right in your backyard, Coney Island! It was the first park that my brother Walt and I visited while we were starting to think about going into the park business. You ought to go back and buy that park and use that as your springboard to go bigger if you choose.'"

And wouldn't you know it? Now Coney Island was asking Taft about a possible merger!

TAFT BROADCASTING IS CONVINCED

Following Rogers' and Wachs' meeting at the Netherland Plaza, Rogers asked Gary to meet with him and Mechem at Cincinnati's renowned Maisonette Restaurant. Mechem and Wachs had not previously met, so Wachs knew he had to introduce something to fully persuade him to merge Coney Island with Taft Broadcasting. "The Six Flags parks were bought out by a company called Great Southwest Corporation. Their stock was going through the roof because of these parks. I went down with a stockbroker friend of mine, and I got all the numbers for the Great Southwest Corporation."

"About halfway through the lunch I said, 'Charlie, let me show you the financial success of the Six Flags parks which were acquired by the Great Southwest Corporation located in Dallas, Texas.' I showed him the financials; the graphs were going like this [upward]. He picked it up and looked at this, and he backed up, almost knocked over a waiter! I knew at that moment Kings Island was born. They were going to do it. The vaccination had taken."

One obstacle remained—Charles Sawyer. Luckily, Sawyer and Mechem had previously worked together in the same law firm. When

Mechem asked about Sawyer, Wachs said, "'He very well may have a change of heart [because of Fess Parker], but he doesn't know I've been talking to you.' Charlie said, 'I'll take care of Mr. Sawyer. I know Mr. Sawyer, let me talk to him.' I said, 'Great!' The next thing I know, I get a phone call from Charles Sawyer. 'Gary, come down to my office. We've got to call some banks! We've got to stop Fess Parker! We can't let him do this deal!'"

Sawyer had many connections in Cincinnati. "He knew everybody, he knew bankers," Gary reveals. "Now he became a great asset on our side of the fence because he could go to banks and say, 'Hey, we're doing this thing with Taft Broadcasting, we've got Coney Island behind us, we're going to do a theme park.' So he literally ended Fess Parker."

And so the noble, crazy big idea of moving a park had finally taken root. Throughout the holiday season of 1968 and into the beginning of 1969, Coney Island and Taft Broadcasting negotiated terms of the merger while determining the location for the new park.

"There were really only two options," explained Charlie Mechem. "We knew that it had to be on an interstate to have the egress and ingress necessary. [Interstate] 75 even then was crowded, clustered, it still is! 71 had virtually nothing between Montgomery and this area. We wanted to get far enough out so that we could acquire the land at a price that wasn't formidable. We tried to buy in too close; couldn't do that."

Another issue that arose was the amount of acreage. Once again, a memory from the Roy Disney-Charlie Mechem meeting came flooding back. Mechem remembered, "One of the things he [Roy] told us when we met was, 'One bit of advice: figure out how much land you need and then buy five times as much. We didn't do that in Anaheim and we've regretted it ever since.' So when we went looking for land for Kings Island, we ended up buying over 1600 acres. We associated ourselves with a really wonderful man named George Henkle of the real estate firm Henkle-Schueler. George Henkle was one of the most delightful and skillful men I've ever met, and he managed to acquire those 1600 acres for us without one leak at all, which made it a lot easier."

The two companies finally settled on a massive parcel of land twenty miles north of Cincinnati in Kings Mills, a town within Deerfield Township in Warren County.

Dennis Speigel, the assistant park manager for Coney Island at the time, recalled, "When I saw the land for the first time, actually Gary Wachs and I went out to look at the land and walk it and it was a cornfield! Just open space. Nothing there. There was a road [Columbia Road] that went right through the middle of [what would be] the parking lot at that time. He and I went out there, we walked the park, and we said, 'Hey, this would be a great place for the *Eiffel Tower*, this would be a great place for *The Racer*. Went back in the backside of the property and found this big gorge and we said, 'Wouldn't that be wonderful, take the train across that gorge?' That day, that's about as far north as I'd ever been! Twenty-six miles outside of the city."

"We had a lot of work to do on the site acquisition because there were a lot of parcels," said Dudley Taft, vice president of corporate development for Taft Broadcasting at that time. "It was mostly one parcel that was controlled by a real-estate guy in Lebanon, George Henkle. We actually acquired part of that for stock and then had to pick up the other pieces. We had one holdout we finally were able to get just before the park opened which was right in the middle of the parking lot."

With the merger details and location of the park ironed out, it was now time to officially unveil the plans to the public.

BUILDING A NEW THEME PARK

On March 28, 1969 Lawrence Rogers and Charles Mechem of Taft Broadcasting and Ralph Wachs and Charles Sawyer of Coney Island announced the new park in a joint press conference. Plans called for "an entire leisure-time complex that will combine a giant, family-oriented amusement park with the recreational use of the natural beauties of the woods, hills, and streams of the area." Wachs assured everyone that Coney Island "would continue to operate as usual" for the next two years while the new park was developed.

While the presentation indicated that Coney and Taft would be working together on the new park, Taft Broadcasting publicly announced that they would be purchasing Coney Island outright on April 21, 1969. The deal reached by both companies was that Taft would acquire all assets of Coney for $6.5 million in Taft Broadcasting stock; the sale was completed July 14. Even though a new company now owned Coney Island, all of the staff at the park remained the same. Taft Broadcasting almost immediately began using their new asset, including filming portions of the Hanna-Barbera *Banana Splits* television show at the park.

Meanwhile, planning of the new amusement park had begun. "My father…turned to me and said, 'Alright, you've been pushing this thing for four years,'" Gary recalls. "'Now I want you to get out of Coney Island, you get your group together, you get this concept settled. You get architects, you get engineers, you get out there and build this damn thing and we'll run Coney Island in 1970 and 1971.' And figuratively speaking he said, 'I don't want you back here! I want you on that job!' I said, 'Yes sir, we're doing it!'"

With Gary Wachs named general manager of the new theme park, he and his Coney Island team would meet throughout the rest of 1969 to fully hammer out the new concept. "We had a pretty smart group and it was imperative to have Kings Island conceived by operators laying out the conceptual part of the park. Crowd flow, queue lines, all of these things, and then after we got it the way we wanted it from an operational point of view, we called in the architects for the window dressing. That was very important. Six Flags didn't do it that way."

Planning the park was "a lot of fun, a lot of meetings!" according to Dennis Speigel, who was now the assistant general manager for the new park. "We had a lot of meetings with that team of sixteen guys [Coney Island officials], a lot of it was seat of the pants. We were working with a couple of local architecture and engineering firms, Savage, Shepalear and Schulte was one of the engineering firms. Dusty Daniels was our architect. And then as we were planning International Street, it just needed more pop, more oomph. And Gary brought in a fellow by the name of Bruce Bushman, and his father was a very famous silent movie star in the 20s, Francis X. Bushman. But Bruce Bushman was the one who, we had an idea and a conception for International Street, but he's the one who solidified it and brought it together for us."

Charley Flatt, the director of the *Sunlite Pool*, would be the project manager for the new park's construction, serving as the liaison between Coney and the general contractor, C.V. Maescher.

Developing the new park meant fleshing out Gary Wachs' original four themed areas into fully immersive environments with rides and attractions.

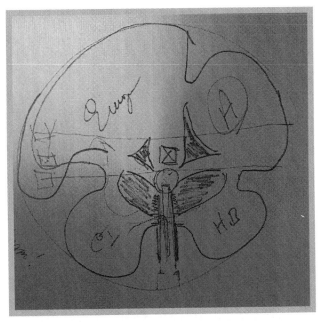

A very early sketch by Gary Wachs of the layout for the new park. Courtesy of Gary Wachs.

INTERNATIONAL STREET

"I went to Europe in 1963, and I became so impressed with what I saw...it was just beautiful," Wachs remembers. "Then I saw the real *Eiffel Tower*, and I saw these fountains around the tower...I took hundreds of slides...I visited Tivoli Gardens, the oldest amusement park in the world. I went to Oktoberfest in Munich. I was smitten with Europe. So I knew we wanted International Street."

In particular, Gary was impressed with what he called the "Three F's: flags, flowers, and fountains. All over Europe. Flags, flowers, fountains, it was just beautiful." After his trip to Europe, Wachs immediately began integrating these ideas into Coney Island park, including adding flags of many countries and a fountain on the midway. For the new park's entrance, multinational buildings would sport the flags of their country, surrounding a long fountain (inspired by the *Fountain of Warsaw* in Paris) ensconced by lush landscaping.

The magnificent Royal Fountain. Photo from the 1978 employee yearbook. Courtesy of Perry Denehy.

Taking a page from Disneyland, the park would have a visual "weenie" (a Walt Disney term meaning something that draws your attention) serving as the centerpiece and icon of the park. For the new Coney, it would be a 331-1/2 foot, ⅓ scale replica of the *Eiffel Tower*.

Originally, Wachs had wanted the *Eiffel Tower* at Coney Island to replace the *Lost River* boat ride. "There was a company in Pittsburgh called American Bridge," Wachs recalled. "They were famous for building big bridges around the country. I'm thinking sort of erector sets, bridges and *Eiffel Towers*. Obviously, I had a million pictures of the original *Eiffel Tower* in Paris. I worked my way up on these phone calls, and I got a vice president on that phone and told him what we're doing. He's in Pennsylvania and he's never heard of a theme park, you know. I'll never forget, he said, 'Son, we don't build towers. We build bridges.' That was the end of that conversation!"

Still, Wachs wanted an *Eiffel Tower* for Coney Island. "We had some connections with ride people in Europe. There was a company in Europe called Intamin AG, and it was run by a guy named Reinhold Spieldiener. I called him up and said, 'We need an *Eiffel Tower*. A ⅓ scale *Eiffel Tower.*'" Intamin said sure, they could do that. Yet, "In the back of my mind, I knew that was wrong. We didn't want to build it in Coney! We wanted to move, we wanted to get out of there." So it was put on hold and repurposed for the new park.

Throughout development, many attraction ideas were either scrapped or relocated to different areas. The kiddie *Turnpike* attraction was relocated to the Happy Land of Hanna-Barbera, while a building representing England was scrapped altogether. A German beer garden and an Intamin *Drunken Barrels* attraction would later become a fully fleshed-out themed area, Oktoberfest.

The Hanna-Barbera characters on International Street.
Courtesy of Tom Kempton.

THE HAPPY KINGDOM OF HANNA-BARBERA

The idea of using Hanna-Barbera characters in theme parks a la Disney was one of the main reasons behind Taft Broadcasting's initial desire to build a park. So naturally the children's area would be themed to the Hanna-Barbera intellectual property. Initially named the Happy Kingdom of Hanna-Barbera, it became Happy Land of Hanna-Barbera by late 1971. "We had a children's land in Coney Island; it was called the Land of Oz, but it was nothing like Hanna-Barbera," Gary explained. "But I knew even back in Coney days the

Land of Oz was very popular. People could take their children there, watch them ride the rides, have a great time. Hanna-Barbera was a huge extension of that. It was a good fit, a good merger, a good corporate fit."

Many rides from the Land of Oz at Coney Island would be relocated to the new property, although re-themed. *Galaxi*, a coaster added to Coney Island in 1970 with the intent of moving it to the new park, was originally slated for this area. When Oktoberfest was developed, the coaster was moved there instead. A planned Hanna-Barbera carousel would not become a reality at the park until 1982.

The star attraction of the Hanna-Barbera section would be a dark ride called the *Enchanted Voyage*. "What we wanted was something like [It's a] Small World, only built around the Hanna-Barbera characters," recalled Dennis Speigel. "We created this layout of this ride that went back and forth and around through the channel in a flume boat, a big flume boat actually. The story was going to be about the cartoon characters who live in the television. So originally, when you went into that building, it had like a television screen with 'rabbit ears' on it."

Speigel became the liaison between the park and Hanna-Barbera. "I was going back and forth to California, and we were working on the dark ride and Bill [Hanna] dropped by. 'What are you doing this weekend?' 'Well, I'm just here to work in the studio.' 'Why don't you come out on the boat with me and we'll go over to Catalina.'" On Hanna's yacht, the *Galatea*, conversation drifted to the theme song for the *Enchanted Voyage*. "He and I sat out there, we had a couple of glasses of wine and we were watching the buffalo, the bison over on Catalina Island. He could play the organ, he started a melody and everything, so we wrote a song called 'All in My TV,'" with Speigel writing the lyrics and Hanna doing the melody!

"So we worked on that and got the words down, and when we did that Paul DeKorte, who was the musical director [for Hanna-Barbera] invited me to come down to a studio in Los Angeles called Glen Glenn that was famous. They did all the recordings for the movies and singers and everything. It was a pretty neat place. So we went down in the studio, and we had different sections within the dark ride. There was a hillbilly section and a scary section...But I had the orchestra, so we wanted to have the same song playing throughout the ride, just like Small Word played in Disney, and it would change, the melodies and things, but the song never changed. So I had them take apart their horns and trombones and do things to make it sound like scary and hillbilly, play like bluegrass stuff. So we recorded it over a few days and it really came out right. I mean, we didn't even have to go back, it was good!"

The Enchanted Voyage facade resembled a gigantic TV set.
Courtesy of Tom Kempton.

FRONTIERLAND

Most theme parks built during the 50s and 60s included an historical or Old Western-themed area, such as Frontierland at Disneyland and Frontier Town added to Cedar Point. For the new Coney Island park, the historical section would not be Western-themed, but instead have a local twist, themed to Cincinnati's pioneer days. Some ideas never made it to fruition, such as an Arrow Mine Ride coaster and a museum walk-through of Ohio Valley history. The park's main live show venue, originally slated for Frontierland, was relocated to International Street.

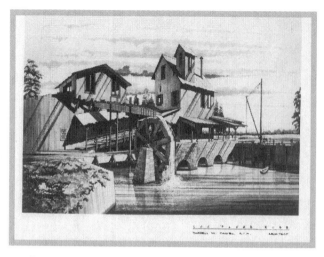

Concept rendering of the transplanted Kings Mills Log Flume.
Courtesy of Tom Kempton.

Frontierland *would* become home to the relocated Arrow Log Flume and two canoe attractions from Coney. The main attraction of this area of the park would be a train ride, inspired by the train at Coney Island that was added in 1964. "We built this miniature train ride and a wonderful causeway over Lake Como, and it would travel underneath our western entrance road where you'd drive, and it would go out in the nearby woods," Gary described. "We set up this animation of Indians attacking a fort...It was kind of crude animation, it was just two-dimensional where they're pulling back the bow and arrow. It wasn't audio-animatronics like Disney did where you have variable cams and the figures look human; this was kind-of 'click, click, click.' But the public didn't know the difference. They'd never seen animation. They went crazy. They'd go back in that woods and we'd have pioneers firing their guns out of these log cabins, and on the other side of the tracks the Indians are firing at them. I think we had a ridership on that train that year of over 400,000 people. It was almost half of our park attendance. It drove the company to great revenues, great profits, so we were doing great things along the way."

As with everything at the new park, the train would be larger and expanded upon. The attraction would feature two full-sized, steam-powered Crown Metal Products locomotives, compared to Coney Island's much smaller, diesel-powered Chance Manufacturing trains.

The Kings Island and Miami Valley Railroad featured employees in conductor uniforms to add authenticity. Photo from the 1978 employee yearbook. Courtesy of Perry Denehy.

The name Frontierland was eventually changed to Rivertown by late 1971, reflecting the local historical tie-in.

CONEY ISLAND

Naturally, the new theme park would feature a section themed to Coney Island's famous mall as it would have looked in the 1920s. It would become home to many of Coney's relocated flat rides such as the *Monster*, *Scrambler*, and *Dodgem*. Ironically, an area themed to tradition would become the most radical departure from the modern theme park.

Gary pointed out that "the Six Flags parks did not have games. That was sinful in their minds. That was the image of the old park...Coney Island made a lot of money off of games: *Fascination*, throwing the basketball, *Fish Pond*, whatever. We had to have games in that park. So we had our excuse because we were going to theme the old, traditional park."

Another old park favorite not included in modern theme parks of the time were large roller coasters. These represented another "unbecoming" image of the traditional amusement parks—too carny for modern tastes. Most parks built in the 1950s and 60s included smaller steel coasters, typically Arrow Mine Trains. But for the new Coney Island park, "I knew we had to have a new [large] roller coaster, and I knew the *Shooting Star* at Coney Island was wildly popular," Wachs said. "It wasn't one of these circular, old wooden roller coasters. This was an out-and-back negative gravity ride where you felt a sensation of floating on the way back. People loved that. I thought, we just can't put that up there, we've got to do something different....I had researched this and had an idea. Back in the 1920s, they had what they called racing roller coasters. Side-by-side, out-and-back racing coasters, dueling coasters. I said, 'That's what I want. A racing roller coaster. That'll be the best of our old *Shooting Star,* but it will be something new and different! Nobody around here has ever raced side-by-side.'"

At that time, the only reliable company building roller coasters was the Philadelphia Toboggan Company, which boasted the famous coaster designer John Allen as their vice president. "I went to John Allen and said, 'John, can you build this for us?'" Wachs recalled. "He said, 'Gary, I've been trying to retire for three years. I'm going to retire. I'm sorry, I can't do it.' I went to my father and he said, 'You know, we're going to see John Allen at our [amusement park industry] convention in Chicago.' I said, 'Dad, great idea! We'll meet with him!' So we met with him in the Sherman House hotel in late November 1969, and they had a bar in the basement of that hotel called the Well of the Sea...So we got John Allen there and we started drinking martinis. At the end of that lunch, John said, 'God damn it, I'll build the thing for you, Ralph, Gary!' And he was key, we needed his experience. We got him on board, he designs it, our team builds it, and that was a key thing in that park, that coaster."

The Racer under construction. Courtesy of Tom Kempton.

The Coney Island section was probably the area that changed the least from initial concepts and development up to the park's opening. There were only three major attractions originally intended to go in this area, but moved elsewhere as plans continued to evolve: *Rotor*, relocated to Oktoberfest once that section was developed, the *Sky Ride*, now running between Oktoberfest and the Happy Land of Hanna-Barbera, and the *180° Theater*, which was scrapped altogether but resurrected for the 1986 season.

OKTOBERFEST

This was the fifth themed area and came later during the design phase, incorporating a few ideas that had been targeted elsewhere such as the beer garden, *Drunken Barrels*, and the *Rotor*. The *Galaxi* coaster from Coney was relocated here and renamed *Bavarian Beetle*. Providing a bird's-eye view of the park, the *Sky Ride* landed here from the Happy Land of Hanna-Barbera. By early 1971 this small section was added into the lower-left "clover-leaf" of the park's layout.

The grand plan included much more than just a large amusement playground—the entire project would be designed as a resort destination with hotel and camping facilities. Altogether, the park was initially budgeted to cost $16,325,000 with a $3,000,000 cushion to cover any potential additions or overruns to the operation.

GROUND IS BROKEN

June 15, 1970 was the official groundbreaking ceremony. Guests were loaded into buses and driven around the park site; afterwards they gathered at the future location of the *Eiffel Tower* for the official ceremony. The major participants were:

- Bill Hanna, president of Hanna-Barbera Productions
- Charles S. Mechem Jr., CEO of Taft Broadcasting Company
- Lawrence Rogers, president of Taft Broadcasting Company
- Dudley Taft, Taft Broadcasting vice president of corporate development
- Gary Wachs, vice president and general manager of the new park
- Ralph Wachs, president and general manager of Coney Island
- Hanna-Barbera characters Fred Flintstone, Yogi Bear, and the Banana Splits

"It is a tremendously exciting new development in the entertainment field in the Cincinnati area," Cincinnati mayor Eugene Ruehlmann proudly proclaimed at the ceremony. "We think of Cincinnati's future development not in the confines of the city itself. This will have tremendous impact for total growth in our area." Other local officials in attendance included Mayor Menard Sensenbrenner of Columbus and Mayor Donald Mollman of Mason.

BACKLASH

Surprisingly, the public's reaction was not entirely favorable. "When the public heard that Coney Island was closing, they couldn't believe it because everybody in Cincinnati loved Coney Island," Gary remembered. "I can't tell you how many thousands of people met their husbands and wives at Coney Island. In *Moonlite Gardens*, people would fall in love and get married later. We had a big steamboat, the *Island Queen*, people fell in love on the world's largest floating dance floor. When they heard we were building this *something* up on I-71, they didn't know what the hell it was. Back then, only a handful of people had been to a theme park. We had a public relations battle on our hands, oddly enough."

Charlie Mechem confirmed the challenges that lay ahead. "When it became known what we were doing, whenever I would go places or whenever my wife and I would go to a cocktail party or that kind of thing, there were two comments that were made over and over again. One was, we decided to go the pay-one-price policy which Disney had promoted. Coney, you paid 50 cents to get in and then you paid for each ride. People were used to that and when we announced, and this will blow your mind, the original pay-one-price was six dollars, people said, 'No one's going to pay six dollars! What are you talking about?' And we said, 'Well, that remains to be seen!' That was one of the bits of skepticism. The other was, 'Nobody will ever drive that far.' Those two supposed negatives, nobody will pay six dollars and no one will drive that far, I've looked back and laughed many, many times about."

"We had a tremendous educational job to communicate what Kings Island was all about, why it was being done, an entirely new pricing structure going to pay-one-price from ticket books and general admission and pay by the ride. That was a huge undertaking to educate people on the value of pay-one-price," said Tom Kempton, manager of public relations during the park's development. "A lot of other policies that were in place at Coney that we wanted to alter. Example, [for] a lot of people, it was traditional at Coney, you could bring picnic baskets into the park. The last thing we wanted to do was to build this beautiful new park with lots of restaurants and have people bringing food in. So you had to educate the market. When you start, there's zero awareness, so your challenge was to build awareness up and then to build trial and usage. Traditional marketing and that's called ATU, awareness, trial, and usage, and we were very successful at doing that probably within 300 miles of the park."

Others viewed the massive new theme park with a more positive lens. "I remember standing at a construction fence line with my family and another family watching the earthmovers and bulldozers and dump trucks move around Kings Island," recalled Rob Decker. "We drove down there because they were changing farmland into an entertainment destination...I just remember growing up on Sunday nights watching the *Wonderful World of Disney* in color on a color television and how great that was...and I knew I would never go to Disneyland. I would never make it. It's Disneyland California; I'd never go to California! When news broke in the late '60s that they were going to build a Disneyland-like park just an hour and a half down the road on I-75, I lived one block off of I-75 [in Sidney, Ohio], and it was going to connect me all the way down near this park. It was just mind-blowing that someone would have the genius and the guts to do that development."

Decker would go on to be the senior vice president of planning and design for Cedar Fair. Thirty-five years after he and his family stood at that construction fence, Kings Island became Decker's sandbox when it became part of the Cedar Fair chain.

LET'S SEE...WHAT TO CALL IT

Throughout 1970 construction continued on the new theme park. But one issue remained—a name. Internally, names such as Twin Oaks and Kings Mills Park were being considered. "We had a debate. What are we going to name this park?" said Gary. "Nobody had a name for it. I think I threw in something like Tivoli [Gardens], I was so enamored with the one over there, and Charlie [Mechem] said, 'No, there's already a Tivoli.'"

Executives wanted the name to be "distinctive, but easy to say." Unable to think of a name that stuck, Taft Broadcasting decided to hold a public contest. In August of 1970 the winner was revealed as Rebecca Richards, 13, of Carroll, Ohio. She coined the name Kings Island, taken from the "Kings" in Kings Mills and the "Island" in Coney Island. Interestingly enough, Richards was one of forty-five people who also turned in the name Kings Island out of 45,000 entries. Out of those forty-five, her name was drawn randomly, and she won a trip to Hollywood. The other runner-ups received free tickets to Coney Island.

The Oktoberfest section of the park under construction.
Courtesy of Gary Wachs.

CONSTRUCTION CONTINUES

Construction continued throughout the rest of 1970 and through 1971. Unfortunately, the project was running over budget. "I was trying to keep the price down for Taft Broadcasting, so I was thinking we might do International Street the second year," said Gary Wachs. "We would do the fountain and the *Eiffel Tower*, but maybe the buildings we'd do the second year, and Charlie Mechem was right. He said,

'Gary, I want to do the buildings the first year.' So I had to go back to Charlie two or three times going over budget, and that was a hard problem for him because he had sold his board of directors on this move. I didn't sell the Taft board, he did. His credibility was at stake, just like mine was at stake, because he did the financing. I was on the design and building side, and he was responsible for financing the project. His credibility with banks and his board of directors was very important. So I went back to Charlie and Dudley [Taft] one or two times with going over budget and I said, 'You know, this takes guts and vision, but I think every penny you spend on this park is going to pay off handsomely.' They did it; it turned out to be obviously hugely successful."

Coney and Taft were also busy heavily promoting Kings Island in the Cincinnati area. The two types of antique cars to be featured on the Arrow antique car attraction were exhibited at Kenwood Mall. Coney Island opened for the 1971 season with a Kings Island preview center, featuring a scale model of the new park and a film of the park's construction titled "Fun in the Making."

The Eiffel Tower rises above the under-construction International Street. Courtesy of Tom Kempton.

The *Eiffel Tower* was topped off May 26, 1971. "It was built in Graz, Austria, and it was pre-assembled," Gary explained. "They put it halfway together, disassembled it, and shipped it over here. The erector out of Dayton, a company called Sofco, they told me, 'Gary, we only had to rout out twenty-six bolts that weren't designed right in the whole project. It went up perfectly.' That thing lock, stock, and barrel, painting it, lighting it, it was a million six. I don't know what that would be today. Ten million maybe."

For the park's most elaborate attraction, the *Enchanted Voyage* dark ride, park officials leased out space in the old Peters Cartridge Company factory in Kings Mills to assemble the large set pieces. "Then we put them in the *Enchanted Voyage*," Wachs continued. "And... we locked [park art director Dick] Harsley in there for about a week... We sneaked food into him, he slept in there, he was a hell of a guy. He put that damn thing together by himself."

Kings Island Drive, created to service traffic to the new park, officially opened for motorists on August 2, 1971, complete with its own ribbon-cutting ceremony.

Time was running short with the grand opening scheduled for May 27, 1972. "I was so concerned about opening on time, I had thirty calendars printed, the ones where you rip off a page each day," Wachs recalled. "I had these calendars printed in reverse order! It was like, 300 days 'til opening, 299, 298, and I gave them to all the department heads. I made sure everybody ripped one of those off every day. I said, 'We're going to open on May 27, 1972,' and I had an old expression, 'If you wait 'til you're ready to open, you'll never open.'"

SAYING GOODBYE. HELLO KI

"All good things must come to an end, so after 85 years of successful operation, Coney Island will close with tonight's operation, September the 6th, 1971. Coney Island has played a part in the lives of several generations; the memories and good times you have enjoyed here will last a lifetime. Now we must look to the future, a new park, a new home, Kings Island. I promise you it will be more than you could ever dream an amusement park could offer."
Ralph Wachs' closing speech, 1971

Don Helbig, who would become Kings Island's public relations area manager in 2007, grew up in Anderson Township and remembered Coney's final season. "I remember the last year, my parents talking about how Coney had been sold, it was going to close, they were going to move it 'out in the boondocks' was the word that my dad used for it. So when we'd go up that last year, you'd see the signage for Kings Island with the logo, 'Coming next year, 1972.' I remember by the *Shooting Star* this rendering that they had of *The Racer*. It touted it as the biggest, longest, fastest roller coaster in the world, so I was intrigued by that."

Coney Island closed September 6, 1971. "Coney became a symbol of all that is carefree and good and fun in life," wrote the *Cincinnati Enquirer*. "Problems and worries waited outside as the people danced and swirled and laughed." 20,000 people attended Coney Island's last day. It rained, ironically the same weather the park suffered on its own opening day in 1885. Half a year later, Kings Island would open in the rain in April 1972. Coney closed in style with a spectacular fireworks display.

It was an emotional night for longtime guests and employees. "I remember the fireworks on that last night. It rained that day from what I can recall, and then Ralph Wachs giving his speech and just talking about how Kings Island's going to be beyond your wildest imagination," Don Helbig recalled. "That don't be sad, be happy for the years you had here, but look what waits for you kind of a message. So I remembered that part of it with Coney Island. It was part of what we grew up with. That was our big thing that we did as a family every year. A lot of people went on vacation to Florida and everything...our vacation was going to Coney Island."

"We had a siren that we used to blow every night in the park at Coney Island that told everybody it was closed, let all the ticket sellers and everybody know and all the employees," recalled Dennis Speigel. "I was the guy who blew the siren the last night on Coney Island on Labor Day 1971, and then we started the move right after that, and then we all moved up to Kings Island." (Half of the Coney Island officials had been working at the new site for the past year while half of them remained to operate the park through its final two seasons.)

Coney Island officials wasted no time relocating salvageable attractions to the Kings Island site. "I, along with [park manager] Ed McHale, we were responsible for moving everything from Coney Island to Kings Island," said Speigel. "We did that in basically one month. That was everything from the *Sky Ride* and the flume ride to the knives and forks that were in the cafeteria. We took all of the rides that we could. Some we tore down—*Shooting Star* was left and demolished, *Teddy Bear*, the small coaster. But the carousel and the *Sky Ride*, and the *Monster* and the Italian coaster [Galaxi] and

Dodgems, things like that, we took everything that we possibly could."

Even the iconic thirty-five gingko trees that lined Coney's mall were transported and replanted at the new park's Coney Island section. As a matter of fact, when it came to landscaping, just thirty-five bushes from Coney Island were the only landscaping pieces *not* transported to the new park.

"We were genuinely surprised to find how easy the rides were to tear down," Jim Figley, Kings Island maintenance director, told the *Cincinnati Enquirer*. "To date [October 18, 1971], we have moved most of the rides, and by November 1 we plan to have the old rides installed."

"Moving things from Coney really was not a problem," explained Charlie Mechem. "All those rides at Coney were relatively small rides, if you know what I mean. They were easily moved, and we basically just rebuilt the coaster from Coney [*Galaxi*]."

The two Crown Metal Products locomotives for the *Kings Island and Miami Valley Railroad*, named the *Tecumseh* and the *Simon Kenton*, arrived in late 1971 and took their first test ride around the track on December 15. Other aspects of the park were being finished. The *Royal Fountain's* 106 jets and 306 lights were done by the Fountain Specialist Co. of Milford and were ready by December.

Park executives tapped the talent at the University of Cincinnati College Conservatory of Music to develop Kings Island's entertainment lineup. Jack Rouse, the professor of UC's opera and musical theater program, became the park's first entertainment director. "I got approached by a fellow I worked with at CCM, a guy named Carmen DeLeon; he's been the conductor for the [Cincinnati] ballet since time began. And he said there's these people that wanted to build a theme park. I didn't have any idea what the hell that was! I'd been spending my life with Mozart and Puccini and Beethoven. So anyway, they packed us off to Six Flags Over Texas, which was really the first theme park after Disney, and it was a summer gig and my wife's going back to work on an advanced degree. I decided what the hell, what's to lose? In those days, the entertainment program was massive, it's nowhere close to what it is today. In time, we hired probably 200, 250 singers, dancers, magicians, jugglers, clowns, the usual."

"The entertainment department was almost an afterthought," said Keith James, who was hired in late 1971 as a stage manager. "We came in quite late and were primarily focused on putting entertainment all over the place, filling the park. In the early days, the entertainment in Kings Island was everywhere. There were stages on the bandstand and smaller stages up and down the Coney Mall, and we had a musical group on the porch of the general store. In Rivertown, we had a melodrama out across from the train. I guess it's not appropriate to say [nowadays], but we had cowboys and Indians on the train ride. There was entertainment everywhere!"

With the dawn of 1972, the park was right on schedule. Two opening dates were set, with "preview weekends" beginning on April 29 and a grand opening May 27. In January, Ralph Wachs was named Chairman of the Board of Taft's new theme park division. Construction was finishing up, and *The Racer* was ready for test riders. John Allen, who designed the coaster, proclaimed "It rides like a baby coach!" after his first ride. "There's been a lot of sensation built into this ride," Allen told the *Cincinnati Enquirer*. "We [Philadelphia Toboggan Company] think this is the finest coaster ever built, one of the largest ever built, and certainly the largest we've ever built." *The Racer* took more than 600,000 board feet of lumber to build and 6,000 gallons of paint.

For the *Salt Water Circus* show, the four porpoises arrived at the park April 22.

PREVIEW WEEKENDS

Time was running out—the park's first day open to the public was a preview weekend on Saturday, April 29, 1972. "We were up all night; we didn't sleep," recalled Dennis Speigel. "I remember being in the dark ride in Hanna-Barbera [*Enchanted Voyage*] working on some sets and things, and I lost my radio, my two-way radio, and it was in a boat. I found it somewhere in the middle of the night. I was calling, using somebody's to find it, and somebody was in there and heard it in the boat. It was kind of crazy because it was curtain up, show goes on! We were ready, there weren't many things that were not open and available at that time."

That Saturday, it poured rain.

Although the day started out sunny in the lower 60s, the rain arrived at 2 p.m. By 4:00 only 4,000 people had entered the park. Finishing touches still had to be applied. Signage remained to be installed, and landscaping work wasn't yet completed. The most popular rides, judging by the number of people waiting in line, appeared to be *The Racer* and the *Eiffel Tower*. In spite of a soggy start, reviews were generally positive.

"Nearly everyone did agree that the park is big and beautiful, with lots of potential," wrote the *Cincinnati Enquirer*. "And everyone agreed that the weather was lousy. Certainly no kind of a day to open a new amusement park."

The park's most favorable early review was printed in the *Cincinnati Enquirer* by Jim Knippenberg. "If you plan on taking a few hours and dashing up to Kings Island to see what the place is all about, you can forget it," Knippenberg wrote. "If you plan, on the other hand, to take a day or two to look the place over, well, that's more like it. Because you need that much time. Kings Island is that big. And there are that many things to do and see. And each attraction is, in one way or another, worth all the time."

Frank Weikel of the *Enquirer* wrote, "After visiting the park two words will describe it...IMPRESSIVE and FUN."

THE GRAND OPENING

Finishing touches continued to be added ahead of the May 27 grand opening. "We were working up until the very last night," Dennis Speigel recalled. "We were pouring blacktop the day before! The blacktop was going like this back in Hanna-Barbera Land [waving his hands to describe it], it was still on wet land and it was still moving."

A spectacular grand parade opened Kings Island on May 27, 1972. Courtesy of Tom Kempton.

"In hindsight, it was clear that a lot of people said, 'It's going to be a mess. We won't go right away. We'll wait until later when everything's shaken out,'" Taft Broadcasting CEO Charles S. Mechem Jr. said, referring to the low attendance throughout the preview weekends. "Well, I had never had a second thought about the wisdom of the investment. But on the opening day, I remember going up to the 50-foot level of the *Eiffel Tower* where there's a walkway, and I stood there by myself and for the first time *ever*, I remember thinking, 'My God, suppose nobody shows up?'"

The grand opening began promptly at 10:00 a.m. with an employee parade representing the different themed areas in the park, accompanied by a dozen Hanna-Barbera costumed characters and five marching bands. A ten minute fireworks display lit up the morning sky at 10:40 a.m., complete with skydiving clowns and floating American flags. Following the dropping of the flags, four Air Force jets made two low-level passes over Kings Island as the bands played the National Anthem. 30,000 helium balloons were then released, signifying the official opening of the park. Earl Wilson, the *New York Times* columnist, was the Grand Marshal of the day.

Kings Island's grand opening on May 27, 1972. Courtesy of Gary Wachs.

"I was in charge of the opening day festivities. That was one of my assignments, and we had planned this wonderful parade with the release of a lot of balloons, hot air balloons, and we had the best bands around, and we did a parade coming in the front gate and winding around International Street," said park public relations manager Tom Kempton. "We had Miss America and Miss Ohio and Miss Teenage America. Miss America and Miss Teenage America were also from Ohio, so all three were Ohio ladies! We had Bill Hanna and Joe Barbera, the executives from Taft, and of course a lot of good political friends. It was just a celebration. It was a culmination of years of planning and lots of working getting it built and just a very festive occasion."

By 8 p.m. 18,000 people had entered the park, a respectable

number that was very encouraging to all involved. Reviews from park guests were extremely favorable.

"I was blown away," said Don Helbig. "When I first walked in, the first memories, you saw the fountain and you saw the buildings going down International Street, the *Eiffel Tower*, you had the *Sky Ride* going across in front of it. Pulling up on Kings Island Drive, you just approached the parking lot and you saw the *Sky Ride* and the tower and all that going there, but then as you walked through the front gate, because you couldn't see it from the outside, it was like you entered a whole new world. Coney didn't have that whole new world feel. It [Coney Island] was great and it was a lot of fun, but this seemed like you were in another place and it was just so magical. Just right then and there, I was hooked on it."

WORD-OF-MOUTH SAVES THE PARK

Gary recalls the aftermath of getting the park open. "We couldn't get through to the masses what we were doing. I said, 'You just wait when they come in the entrance,' and we built this entrance kind of low...because we wanted people to go in there and not quite know where they were going. And then they'd pop out on International Street and I can't describe their reaction! It's like going to the best movie you've ever seen. You know how you go to a great movie and tell ten friends? 'Harry, you gotta see this park, you won't believe it.' It was word-of-mouth that saved us. That clicked in. We could run a million dollars worth of advertising, but the first people that came in there, they went crazy. I'd stand by that front gate and I'd just watch people come in, and they'd come under that thing and they'd look at International Street and I knew, given enough time, it was going to work."

"From opening day up through July, the crowds were about the same as they were at Coney Island [the year prior]," said Speigel. "We were starting to wonder, 'Uh oh.' Charlie Mechem, the chairman of the board, he said to me in a meeting, 'What if you threw a party and nobody came?' We were starting to think, 'Should we have just stayed where we were?' Well, on July 4th, 1972 the spigot was turned on, the floodgate opened, and we did over 40,000 people! From July 4 through closing, we did between 35 and 40,000 people a day."

At Taft Broadcasting's annual meeting, held at Kings Island July 11, Taft officials announced that the company's earnings had jumped 25%. Coney Island drew 332,000 people in forty-five working days while Kings Island drew 501,026 people. Most importantly for Taft Broadcasting, earnings at Kings Island totaled $1.062 million, while Coney Island's earnings totaled $498,579 during the same period. Kings Island was shaping up to be a success. In fact, on July 31 Kings Island saw its one millionth visitor, only three months after opening!

Å

They could finally breathe a bit knowing their dream was going to survive. It wasn't cheap, though. Kings Island ultimately cost $31,012,000 to build. "It turned out that I went over budget, but I opened the park on time." Gary certainly had reason to be satisfied, having brought a successful project all the way from that fateful flood oh so many years before.

The Clown Band was a popular Kings Island attraction for many years. Courtesy of Tom Kempton.

A WALK THROUGH KINGS ISLAND
IN 1972

*Authentic gas lamps on International Street. Photo from the 1977
employee yearbook. Courtesy of Perry Denehy.*

*I*f you had attended Kings Island in its inaugural year, you would have entered through International Street, with its magnificent view of the *Royal Fountain* spraying 10,000 gallons of water into the air, leading up to the 331-1/2 foot tall *Eiffel Tower* replica. Lining International Street were five buildings representing European countries:

Auld Suisse Haus (Old Swiss House)
Kahn's Sausage Haus, Rainbo Backeri, Hanna-Barbera Shop, and *Mod Laden* ("for today's kids"), complete with two chandeliers from the Cincinnati Music Hall.

Gesellschaft Deutschland (German Company)
Munchen Cafe (meats and cheeses from around the world), *German Menagerie Shop* (ceramic and china figurines), *Spielwaren* (stuffed animals), the *Schmuckwaren* (glassware), *Kerzen* (candles), the *German Lock Shop* (rings, bracelets, and earrings), *Hute-Hemden* (hats and shirts), and the *Schnell-Imbiss* refreshment stand that faced outward toward the street.

Fiera Italiana (Italian Fair)
Fotomat Fotografia (film and cameras), *Toys Internationale, La Fiera Pizzeria* (LaRosa's Pizza), *French Bauer Gelato* (ice cream), and another toy shop in *Fiera degli Animali* ("animal fair").

La Tienda Espana (The Spanish Store)
Confites de Coffelt (candy), *La Tienda Espana* (Spanish imports), *La Luces* (more candles—must have been quite the thing in those days), *Expresion de Carino* (jewelry), and the *Cristaleria* (glassware).

Bazaar Francaise (French Bazaar)
This was the smallest of the International Street buildings, featuring the *Bijouterie* (French jewelry), *Les Poteries* (pottery), and the *Cafe Parisienne* (soft drinks, pretzels, and potato chips).

Guests could be entertained by the roaming musicians Silly Sousas Marching Band and the Strolling Guitars. The inflatable Kings Island Theater featured "Something New!!," a musical representing the themed areas.

HAPPY LAND OF HANNA-BARBERA

Towards the right from International Street was the Happy Land of Hanna-Barbera, filled with several rides and attractions geared toward families and children.

- Small attractions from Coney Island included *Motor Mouse*, a small revolving car attraction, *Kikky Kangaroo*, *Winsome Witch's Cauldron* spinning tea cups, the revolving motorcycles and cars of *Autocat*, the *Funky Phantom* kiddie whip, and *Squiddly Diddly* miniature turtles.

- More elaborate rides included the *Enchanted Voyage* dark ride, the John Allen-designed *Scooby-Doo* wooden roller coaster, *Gulliver's Rub-a-Dub* boat ride, and the Marathon Oil-sponsored *Turnpike* car ride. One of the two stations for the *Sky Ride* was located here; it utilized ride supports and mechanical parts relocated from Coney Island, but with additional new gondolas.
- Live entertainment at *The Happy Theatre* featured the Hanna-Barbera Character Show. Guests would also encounter roaming entertainers such as jugglers and magicians.
- *Yankee Doodle's Pigeon Popcorn* and *Granny Sweet's Treats* kept you going until lunch (or dinner).

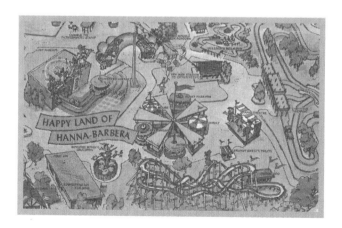

RIVERTOWN

Continuing counter-clockwise around the park, guests next found themselves in Rivertown. Intended as an homage to Ohio's great rivers and related trades, the entire area was centered around Swan Lake, a massive scenic pond.

- The two major attractions were the *Kings Island and Miami*

Valley Railroad and the *Kings Mill Log Flume*, relocated and renamed from Coney Island.

- Two canoe attractions were featured as well, *Shawnee Landing* and *Kenton's Cove*.
- One of the two tracks of the antique cars could be accessed from Rivertown, the *Ohio Overland Auto Livery*.
- *Wheel of Fortune*, a Chance Trabant relocated from Coney Island, was also here.
- For freshly-cooked fried chicken, shrimp, and French fries, guests could stop at the *Columbia Palace Dining Hall*, designed to resemble a rustic saloon.
- *Whistle Stop*, next to the train station, served popcorn and snow cones.
- *Barrel-n-Bun* served hot dogs out of a barrel structure relocated from Coney Island.
- *Humble Pie* served French fries and hamburgers.
- *Balloon Drink Stand* sold soft drinks diagonally across from the *Ohio Overland Auto Livery* station.
- For souvenirs, guests could pick up "unusual gifts and novelties" from the old fashioned drug store *SupeRx General Store* (whose porch was home to "The Fudge is Done" melodrama). *Great Rivers Outfitters & General Merchandise* provided trading post type items.
- For those with skills (or lack thereof), park visitors could try their hand at the shooting gallery or the *Age and Weight* game booth.
- Live entertainment included *Salt Water Circus*, featuring Skipper and Dolly, the two dolphins from Coney Island. Their theater was situated on the path between Rivertown and International Street.

CONEY ISLAND

Next was Coney Island. Referred to as "Coney Island" on the 1972 map, but "Old Coney" in the 1972 guidebook, this area paid tribute to the grand old park that got the company to this stage.

- Most of Coney's relocated rides were in this area: *Monster, Dodgem, Scrambler,* the 1926 *Grand Carousel, Flying Scooters, Cuddle Up,* and *The Flying Carpet* slide. The *Tumble Bug,* also from Coney Island, was built in 1925, making it the oldest ride at Kings Island (although it received new track). The only new rides in this section were *Les Taxis, Halley's Comet,* and *The Racer.*
- Just like at the previous park, this area featured games like *Age and Weight* and *Skeeball.*
- Refreshments included *Sweet Tooth* (ice cream), the *Lunch Basket* (hot dogs and chili), and two unnamed refreshment stands selling hamburgers, popcorn, and soft drinks.

- Kings Island souvenirs could be purchased at the *Coney Emporium.*
- A vaudeville *"Show Wagon"* provided entertainment along with roaming barbershop quartets and Dixieland bands.

OKTOBERFEST

Oktoberfest, the last themed area, is still to this day the smallest. In 1972 it featured the following:

- The *Rotor* from Coney Island.
- The *Bavarian Beetle*, an S.D.C. Galaxi coaster from Coney.
- *Der Spinnen Keggers*, a brand new Intamin Drunken Barrels ride.
- The second station for the *Sky Ride.*
- *Der Alte Deutsche Bier Garten,* overlooking a pond and serving metts, bratts, potato salad, beer, and other German foods.
- Polka dancers, who roamed throughout Oktoberfest with a German band.

THE RACER IGNITES A RENAISSANCE

Incredible as it may seem, *The Racer* "was the first roller coaster [of its scale] that had been built since 1947," according to Dennis Speigel. "Kings Island's *The Racer* was the renaissance of the coaster! And really, that's owed to Gary Wachs; he's the guy that really started that. A lot of people in the industry think that Six Flags did it, but they didn't. We knew the Six Flags guys, they were very nice and helpful to us when we were planning Kings Island; we'd go down and study their park and try to learn as much as we could. Again, they didn't have any [large] roller coasters. When they came to see Kings Island when it opened, they went 'Oh my God, what is this thing?' And they went back and since they were so good to us, Gary offered to help them. One of their general managers wanted to do a coaster so they put *The Great American Scream Machine* in Georgia. I sent two of my guys...down to help him because Gary Wachs had said, 'Let's go and help them.' People thought, 'Oh, Six Flags was the progenitor of coasters.' It really wasn't; it was Kings Island."

Wachs recalled, "I'll never forget when [Six Flags Over Georgia general manager] Errol McKoy came in the park. There was a line going around the corner and he said, 'Gary, what's that? Where does that go?' I told him, 'You come with me!' He sees that line to the

[*Racer*] coaster and it was just like Charlie Mechem when I showed him the stock numbers. Boom! It was like Mr. Sawyer calling all the banks, boom! I knew all these steps, and I knew when Errol McKoy saw that, I knew Six Flags [would soon also have large-scale] roller coasters."

The Racer had a red, white and blue color scheme from its opening until it was repainted all-white for the 1992 season. Courtesy of Gary Wachs.

"Prior to *The Racer*...the fledgling theme parks were more about the smaller steel family coasters than large thrill machines that traditional parks were known for all along," wrote American Coaster Enthusiasts Historian Dave Hahner. "*The Racer* was the first large coaster—wooden or steel—to set the bar higher, if you will, at the newer theme parks."

The installation of *The Racer* proved to the amusement park industry that large roller coasters were still a viable form of entertainment in the modern theme park era. *The Racer's* installation prompted a worldwide renaissance of the roller coaster—one that hasn't slowed down nearly a half-century later.

PIZZA? IN A THEME PARK?

In an interesting sidenote, Kings Island was also responsible for bringing pizza to the amusement park culinary scene!

Dennis Speigel recalled, "We had two spots up on International Street, and we didn't have the money to fill them, and the chairman of the board, Charlie Mechem, was not going to give us any more money! So we went out and found our project superintendent, Charley Flatt. His fraternity brother Jack Pancero was in the meat-packing business. Not in the pizza business; he had never made a pizza in his life! But he said, 'He'll take that spot maybe and do something in there,' and we needed another restaurant. 'He'll make pizza.' So Pancero and his son Greg, they put a pizza parlor in the Street. Well, it became the most popular restaurant in the park and number one, they had never made a pizza in their life, number two, LaRosa's had nothing to do with it other than they sold the product to the Panceros. So they sold them the pizza dough, the meat, the cheese and everything, and because it was their recipe, it became known as LaRosa's. But Buddy LaRosa and the LaRosa organization had nothing to do with it! I've always said that we put LaRosa's on the map! And the reason is because while LaRosa's was prominent in Cincinnati, not like they are today, but they had a few places at that time, we sold more pizza in Kings Island in one day than they sold in a week at their pizza parlors! So LaRosa's sold the product to the Panceros, the Panceros made their pizzas and sold it to the people.

"So at the end of the first year, we were watching this, it was amazing how much pizza they were selling. It was beating everything else in the park, and it was a concession. They were making more money than we were! Really! So I did a study for management. I was assistant general manager, and they said in this one meeting we had, 'How much pizza did they sell?' And I said, 'Look out the window at the *Eiffel Tower*,' because I measured this and figured it out. I said 'See that tower? If you took all the pizzas they sold, stacked them, that one plus another one and a half! Two and a half times the height of the *Eiffel Tower*.' That's how much pizza was sold. Two and a half times the size of the *Eiffel Tower*. That lasted for a long time, then they opened the *Rivertown Pizza*, which was equally successful. But I think the important part of that is, we were the first theme park that ever sold pizza. Nobody else had done it. Disney, Six Flags, nobody had sold pizza in the parks at that time. It was all hot dogs and hamburgers and that kind of food, finger food."

THE PARTRIDGE FAMILY COMES TO KINGS ISLAND

On June 29 it was announced that the popular television show *The Partridge Family* would film an episode at Kings Island. "Taft Broadcasting was a movie, television, cartoon company, [and] radio and television, and it came through them to our marketing team, like *The Partridge Family* and *The Brady Bunch*; they were always looking for places to go and do remotes and things like that and make it fun," explained Dennis Speigel. "They came to our marketing department at Kings Island, and Phil Dempsey was our marketing director at that time. He's gone now, but he worked very closely with them."

The group arrived on August 7, 1972 to find a park packed with *Partridge Family* fans who had traveled from Cincinnati, Texas, and anywhere in-between. Fifty extra bodyguards were hired to protect the show's cast from their hordes of admirers; in spite of all the attention, the cast reportedly had an enjoyable time at the park. David Cassidy, the star of the episode, rode *The Racer* ten times in a row while taping the show. This didn't hold a candle when compared to his co-star Danny Bonaduce, who rode it twenty-two times.

Speigel laughs when talking about helping out a certain *Partridge Family* fan. "I got a call from a fellow who worked at the [television] station, WKRC, and he said, 'I know they're going to be out there and my son loves this group. Would you care if he came out and was there and watched them when they're filming?' I said, 'No, bring him on out.' This little guy was ten years old, I think, at the time. It was George Clooney! He was running around, getting into everything, messing around. If he comes to Cincinnati someday, I'm going to go up to him and say, 'Hey George, do you remember when you came out to KI and you were running around with *The Partridge Family* driving us all nuts?'"

The episode, titled "I Left My Heart in Cincinnati," aired on January 26, 1973.

GENERAL MANAGER #2: EDWARD J. MCHALE

Gary Wachs was appointed to be the general manager of Kings Dominion, Taft's second park planned for Virginia, in August of 1972. Wachs was immediately replaced at Kings Island by Edward J. McHale. McHale had started at Coney Island in 1952 in the group sales department and became assistant to the park manager in 1959. In 1962 he was promoted to vice president and park manager of Coney. McHale was instrumental in the planning and design of Kings Island and supervised the relocation of the rides from Coney Island to Kings Island. McHale became a manager at Kings Island and was promoted to the job of general manager on August 29, 1972. McHale oversaw the rest of the 1972 season, which continued daily through Labor Day and then operated weekends-only until October 29.

YEP, WE CALLED THAT ONE

"We did a study [before the park opened]. We commissioned a guy, kind of an old hand named Thompson in the theme park business, and did a study that projected we would draw two million people," said Dudley Taft, executive vice president of corporate development. "The amazing thing is that we ended up drawing two million, twelve thousand people! [The initial estimate was] pretty close." Kings Island would be the first theme park outside of Disney to draw over two million people in its first year.

Dennis Speigel chuckled, "The Six Flags guys, we'd had a call the year earlier, and they said, 'How many people are you going to draw at that place?' We said two million; they laughed on the phone. We had a call with them after we opened, they said, 'How did you guys do?' and we said 'Two million twelve thousand.' They didn't talk for about thirty seconds! They were shocked because they hadn't done anything like that at their three parks; they hadn't broken two million."

Overall, Kings Island was a drastic step up from its predecessor. Speigel continued, "[The] last year at Coney Island, we did about one million one in people, first year at Kings Island we did two million twelve thousand. Employees at Kings Island, we had 400 [employees at Coney Island], Kings Island we had, first season, [between] fifteen [hundred and two thousand]. We went from 155 acres to 1500 acres; we went from $5 million in revenue the last year at Coney Island to $35 million at Kings Island. Everything was just straight up! You couldn't even graph it, the lines all going up like that. And people loved it! It was just an enormous success."

MOVING FORWARD

For 1973 Kings Island received $6 million for expansion. Nearly all the major additions were items that were either planned during the park's first year, or had originally been intended to open with the park, but were cut for budget reasons.

In Rivertown, a new Arrow Hydroflume, *Kenton's Cove Keelboat Canal*, took the place of the *Kenton's Cove* canoe ride. *Powder Valley Nature Trail* was added to the back corner of Rivertown. An Intamin Flying Dutchman was added to Oktoberfest along with a Schwarzkopf Bayern Kurve.

A larger arcade was added to the Coney Island area. Space was carved out in the stroller rental location at the main gate for an additional souvenir shop, and a new building selling LaRosa's Pizza was added to Rivertown. Perched above the front gate with a spectacular view of International Street was the *International Restaurant*, a new fine-dining location. Unique for the park, it was intended to be open year-round for Kings Island patrons and non-patrons alike.

For entertainment Kings Island added "Saturday in the Park," a big band show on the International Street bandstand. Also new was the "Give My Regards to Broadway" musical revue in the Kings Island Theater (replacing "Something New!!"), and the Barbershop Quartet and Dixieland Band played from the stage behind the *Lunch Basket* stand instead of freely roaming about the park. A new melodrama, "The Family Jewels," was presented on the porch of the *SupeRx General Store* in Rivertown, replacing "The Fudge is Done." A new skydiving exhibition team was also featured.

Kenton's Cove Keelboat Canal under construction. Courtesy of Richard Fussner.

Kings Island opened for 1973 preview weekends on April 28. For the start of daily operations on May 26, the park celebrated with the Human Fly scaling the side of the *Eiffel Tower*, a dozen high school marching bands, four fighter planes, and the release of 7,000 balloons.

With the success of Kings Island and the construction of a second park underway, Taft Broadcasting created an Amusement Park Group in July 1973, with Dudley Taft elected as executive vice president. That same month the company's annual stockholder meeting was held at Kings Island's picnic grove. "We have just completed the most successful year in the company's history," proclaimed Charles Mechem. Kings Island saw a 30% increase in attendance from the year prior for its first 44 days of the 1973 season and a 38% increase in revenue. The park's three millionth visitor, Gregory Sharp of Batavia, arrived July 26.

Concept rendering of the International Restaurant. Courtesy of Tom Kempton.

THE BRADY BUNCH

The stars of television's *The Brady Bunch* set up shop at Kings Island August 20, 1973 for a week of shooting. The episode, "The Cincinnati Kids," aired November 23.

Dennis Speigel said it was "Pretty much the same thing [as the Partridge Family event], one did it and then the other one had to do it. Similar shows, the family and the music and all that stuff. Yes, so it was the same thing. It was a lot easier for the second one, I remember. But they came in, brought their whole production and we had to shut down rides and sections of the park to get the shot and do that. But it wasn't that bad, as I remember. It was exciting, too, to see Hollywood come out and do that! That was kind of fun."

Kings Island closed for the 1973 season October 28. Children twelve and under got into the park for free that day if they came in their Halloween costumes. The park hosted 2.4 million guests that season, an increase from its inaugural year.

*Hordes of people came to Kings Island to catch a glimpse of
The Brady Bunch. Courtesy of Richard Fussner.*

In December 1973, a new division was added to Taft Broadcasting: Kings Productions, which would be in charge of design and entertainment for the Taft parks. "Primarily, it was because the company was expanding and going to build multiple parks," explained Keith James, who became assistant director of Kings Productions. "We had Kings Island in Cincinnati, they had plans to build Kings Dominion in Richmond, Virginia, and decided to put the design and the entertainment producing group together, basically any of the creative forces together, and we created something called Kings Productions...Since there was some ability and benefit in duplication, they [Taft Broadcasting] wanted to have one creative entity. We produced the shows for both parks [Kings Island and Kings Dominion] and eventually the third park [Carowinds] and the fourth park [Canada's Wonderland] and the fifth park [Australia's Wonderland], and we did the design work for the parks as well."

KINGS ISLAND GOES WILD IN '74

The largest addition to Kings Island in its history (in terms of acreage) was Lion Country Safari in 1974. "Wild animal parks were becoming the rage, and we had a lot of excess land and decided we would do it," said Charlie Mechem.

"There was a company called Lion Country Safari that was building free standing, drive-through lion safari projects, and so we actually made a deal with them to supply the animals, consult with us," explained Dudley Taft. The deal with Lion Country Safari, Inc. and Taft Broadcasting was announced September 14, 1972. Lion Country Safari would provide animals and management for the preserve, while Taft would provide financing and construction.

As the concept developed, it was decided that the preserve would be accessed via monorail instead of the typical drive-through. "We had huge gorges we needed to go across with the monorail, and it just wouldn't have been practical to do a drive-through," said Jeff Gramke, who was an assistant engineer for the park at the time. "The terrain was just too rough to do it that way."

The entire safari area would be added to the park adjacent to Oktoberfest. The monorail attraction would be accessed from this section and take guests through the preserve, which spread over 100 acres into the woods behind *The Racer*.

Site preparation and construction lasted throughout the 1973 season. Laying out the monorail track proved to be a tricky task for the Kings Island staff. "We had to put electricity [in the train's track] where the animals could not get to it," Lion Country Safari manager Warren Taylor told the *Cincinnati Enquirer* magazine. "We wanted some animals to be able to step across the rail but had to elevate it in other places so some could go under it."

The first animals, sixteen zebras, arrived at the park September 25, 1973. Throughout the fall and winter more and more animals arrived to fill out the menagerie at the park, from rhinos to giraffes. The animals were strategically placed within the preserve so that they would never be over 125 feet away from a monorail train.

The monorail was a unique feature for the safari. Photo from the 1978 employee yearbook. Courtesy of Perry Denehy.

The Lion Country Safari preserve was divided into three sections. *Umfolozi Reserve*, the first section on the monorail tour, was home to rhinoceros, hippopotamuses, giraffes, and antelopes. Section two, *Serengeti Plains*, was home for the namesake lions. The final section, *Tsavo Park*, was home to additional antelope, zebras, and ostriches.

In the actual themed area, guests could visit the *Nairobi Nursery Hut* and landscaped islands featuring monkeys and macaws. *Kafe Kilimanjaro* served up sandwiches and soft drinks. The area came with its own gift shop, *Congo Curio*, offering African imports. The total cost of Lion Country Safari was nearly $7 million, making it the most expensive addition to Kings Island up to that time, and a record that would stand all the way until 1996's *Flight of Fear* attraction.

Not everything went smoothly that summer for the safari. A power failure on June 25 on the monorail's track led to a lioness named Daisy escaping into a different section of the preserve. Three days later Daisy was tranquilized and brought back to where she belonged.

Kings Island opened for the 1974 season on April 27 with other additions throughout the park, including the *Chapeux* (hat) shop in the *Bazaar Francoise* on International Street. The new show in the Kings

Island Theater was titled "Make Your Own Kind of Music." Another new show, "The Bash," debuted in the Happy Land of Hanna-Barbera.

The iconic hot air balloon from the Firestone International Air Show. Courtesy of Tom Kempton.

One of Kings Island's most well-remembered shows debuted on opening weekend of 1974—the Firestone International Air Show. "Firestone at that time would look up in the sky and see the big Goodyear blimp, and they were envious of it," explained Bill Price, Kings Island director of corporate sales at that time. "So we developed an international air show for them that consisted of a hot air balloon that took off from in front of the turnstiles. That area there, we put down some astroturf and the hot air balloon would go up, and then a World War I vintage fighter plane would fly on the back side of the park, do some aerobatics, and then an old DC-3 would fly over the park and three or four parachutists would jump out and land right where the hot air balloon had taken off. That was wildly successful, and we got huge crowds for it every night during the regular season. That air show also traveled, too, and that hit the objective of Firestone and for the park, trading awareness of that."

As another part of the 1974 festivities, the internationally famous high wire walker Karl Wallenda broke the world high wire walk record on May 25. Wallenda walked a length of 1,800 feet while sixty feet above the ground while also performing two handstands on the narrow tightrope.

Following the end of daily operations on September 2 and the final operating day on October 27, Lion Country Safari remained open on weekdays from 10 a.m. to 5 p.m. The attraction by itself had an admission price of $3 for adults and $1.75 for children. Despite being intended for it to be open year-round, Lion Country Safari only operated through weekends in November before closing for the season as the Cincinnati area was bracing for a harsh winter. Even the *International Restaurant*, opened year-round the year prior, closed for the season on January 1.

It was indeed a tough winter. On December 1 the giant inflatable *Kings Island Theater* collapsed from heavy snowfall. About $2,000 worth of sound and lighting equipment was able to be salvaged from the structure.

Kings Island's 1974 season attracted 2.57 million guests, an increase of 200,000 from the year before. Successful from the get-go, the park continued to set new attendance records each season.

TWO NEW PARKS FOR THE CHAIN

Carowinds opened March 31, 1973 straddling the border between Charlotte, North Carolina and Fort Mill, South Carolina. However, the park suffered from poor attendance throughout 1973 and 74, and by the end of their second season the Carowinds Corporation was forced to sell the park. On January 15, 1975, Taft Broadcasting Company and Top Value Enterprises (a subsidiary of the Kroger Company), operating a joint venture called Family Leisure Centers Inc., announced they would purchase the park for $16 million.

Original concept rendering of Kings Dominion. Courtesy of Tom Kempton.

Taft Broadcasting had also been looking at options for building a second theme park in the Richmond, Virginia area since at least September of 1971. Spurred on by the success of Kings Island, Taft announced Kings Dominion in August of 1972. The park would also be a project by Family Leisure Centers, with an estimated completion date of May 1975.

Kings Dominion opened as originally planned on May 3, 1975 as a tremendous success. Tom Kempton, Kings Dominion's marketing director at that time, recalled, "In the spring of 1975 on the weekends in May, we had a very ambitious financial goal to hit for that park—attendance and so forth—and we felt that if we were going to be successful, we had to open and be very strong from the opening. We had to have great attendance early on. So with our agency, I put together a promotion with McDonald's restaurants across all of Virginia, Maryland, and even to a degree in North Carolina, that was an incentive, dollars-off to visit. When that broke on weekends in Virginia, we had traffic backed up on Interstate 95 one Saturday ten miles. It was an unbelievable success. You can imagine, living in Mason, if it were backed up past Morrow and all these people tried to come to the park! So the promotion was a huge success in that it did deliver attendance. I always felt that it hurt us because the experience probably wasn't as good as we would have liked. The park was crowded, people didn't get perhaps as many rides and shows and entertainment elements as one would hope. But anyway, our awareness skyrocketed, we had tremendous publicity, and the park was off to a very good start."

Å

1975

Kings Island opened for the 1975 season on April 26 with a $3.5 million expansion to the Coney Island section. The midway was lengthened, nearly doubling the size of that area. Guest surveys had indicated that many people wanted a Ferris wheel, so Kings Island added a Waagner-Biro/Intamin Giant Double Ferris Wheel. At 135-feet tall, the *Giant Double Wheel* was taller than the first hill of *The Racer*! Across from the *Giant Double Wheel*, the park added a HUSS Troika flat ride. Facing that was a new restaurant, the *Brass Ring*, themed to an old-fashioned carousel; appropriately, the food was uniquely served from a large revolving lazy Susan. The former *Skee-ball* building near the front of *The Racer* was converted to an arcade with a variety of games, as a new *Skeeball* building was built in the new back half of the mall. The new *Skeeball* building also featured a hat shop. A new stage was added between the *Skeeball* building and the *Giant Double Wheel* to host the show "We'll Sing in the Sunshine," and a new path was carved connecting the new back of Coney Island to Rivertown.

On International Street, *Rainbo Backerei* in the Auld Suisse Haus was replaced with the *Magic Shop*. Space was carved out of the *Lost and Found* for a hat shop. A new 2,000-seat amphitheater in Lion Country Safari played host to the "Fowl Play" bird show, while a replacement air structure for the *Kings Island Theater* played host to "Strike Up The Band." The *SupeRx General Store* in Rivertown was changed to the *Rivertown Arcade*, and *Coffelt's Candy Store* took up residence in the interior of the Rivertown train station.

Kings Island's Giant Double Wheel, later renamed to Zodiac.
Courtesy of Richard Fussner.

EVEL KNIEVEL

Taft Broadcasting had good and bad news regarding their three theme parks for the 1975 shareholder meeting. By June 30, while park attendance had fallen by 8% from the previous year, per capita spending rose two dollars. To help boost attendance for the rest of the season, Kings Island held a series of promotions and concerts. "The first performer that we brought in…[was country music singer] Conway Twitty…and we had about 5,000 people walk through the turnstiles at that time," recalled then-marketing director Bill Price. "Then we did another one with Loretta Lynn. That was very successful. Then we did another one with Tammy Wynette. It got some momentum going for big-name talent." While successful and helping to boost attendance, the singers were nothing compared to what Kings Island expected to be the ultimate attendance booster—daredevil Evel Knievel.

"He [Kings Island promotions director Jim Gruber] walked into my office one day and he said, 'I happen to know that Evel Knievel needs to make a jump before Christmas to hype the Evel Knievel toys,'" said Price. "'Well, okay, yeah. Are you suggesting that we do the jump here?' He said, 'Yeah, I think we could do it in the parking lot.' I said, 'Oh no, I think that you're crazy but we'll think about it.'"

The more Price and other park officials thought about the possibility of the jump, the more it made sense. "We started putting two and two together and said, 'By golly, we could build a place out there in the parking lot for Evel to do the jump.'"

Price and Gruber decided the next logical step would be to visit Rick Case, a close friend of Knievel's who lived in Cleveland. "We got together with him and he called Knievel and said, 'Evel, do you want to do the jump at Kings Island?'" Price recalled. "He [Knievel] said, 'Well yeah, I could do something there,' he said, 'but how am I going to get all my equipment out to the island?' 'Well Evel, it's not really that kind of an island,'" Price laughed.

Price, Gruber, and Case flew out to meet with Knievel in his hometown of Butte, Montana. After spending three days chasing a moody Knievel around his golf course, they eventually hammered out a contract for a $100,000 guarantee from Kings Island.

Ed McHale announced that Kings Island was expecting 70,000 people to attend the October 25 jump, where Knievel would jump fourteen buses, breaking a world record if done successfully. Tickets went on sale September 10. While the jump would be televised on ABC's Wide World of Sports program, the show would be blocked out in Dayton, Cincinnati, Columbus, Cleveland, Akron, Canton, Indianapolis, Lexington, and Louisville in order to drive ticket sales at the park.

Construction on the massive temporary arena began. It was designed by Jack K. Elrod, owner of Jack K. Elrod Co., the largest company east of the Mississippi that specialized in building spectator seating. The arena had bleacher seating for 15,000 people, chair seating for 20,000 people, and standing room for 35,000 people. The arena and jump site altogether covered 1500 parking spots.

Knievel arrived in Cincinnati twelve days before his big jump. "He was very charismatic, a great entertainer," said Bill Price. "Most of my days would start with a phone call from him. 'You've got a problem!' 'What would the problem be?' We resolved them all!"

To the park's loss prevention department, Knievel was a pain in the neck. "He broke every rule in the book when he was there from the standpoint of our safety stuff," recalled Richard Fussner, Kings Island's director of loss prevention at the time. "We did not want him to drive out on that road before the show, before he was actually going to do it. It was set up so he went across the buses, back down in the parking lot, and we'd build a roadway across the front ditch out there to Kings Island Drive. He was going to go across all those buses, go across the bridge and out onto Kings Island Drive, that was the finale of the thing. Darned if he didn't run a car out there or his cycle at least once when people were driving out there. He wouldn't pay [attention to] anything. He was Evel Knievel and he did what he wanted to do."

The day of the jump finally arrived—Saturday, October 25. "On the Friday before the jump, the weather was absolutely perfect," Price said. "Saturday, the day of the jump, it was terrible. The Sunday after the jump was perfect. It was one of those fronts that moved through." 30,000 people showed up at the park, not even half of the expected 70,000. Still, Knievel amazingly jumped over thirteen buses and touched down on the edge of the 14th bus.

"I hit the 14th bus, but I planned to do that," Knievel told the press. "I put in the 14th bus because thirteen is so unlucky, and I missed thirteen in London. So I cleared thirteen, making it my longest jump. And it was my safest and most successful."

While attendance at the park for the jump was poor, the overall publicity was not. The jump resulted in the highest-rated episode in the history of ABC's Wide World of Sports show. Over 52% of America's televisions were tuned in! "We got enormous publicity and exposure," Taft CEO Charles Mechem said. "It was a great television event," concluded Bill Price.

AMERICAN BICENTENNIAL

On January 26, Lawrence "Bud" Rogers announced his resignation effective April 1, 1976 as both president and chief operating officer of Taft Broadcasting. Dudley Taft would replace him. This left a vacancy in the role of executive vice president of the amusement park group, which was filled by the appointment of Gary Wachs. Wachs had formerly been general manager of Kings Island and Kings Dominion before being promoted to the job of vice president of operations for the amusement park group in 1973, which he held until his new appointment.

THE AMERICAN BICENTENNIAL

"The first year we opened, because we really ran out of money and we were going over budget, we didn't have enough money to build the *American Heritage Theater* like they did in Six Flags [Over] Texas or Six Flags [Over] Georgia, so we built this air structure, which is a hell of a lot cheaper!" said Gary Wachs. After the collapse of the original *Kings Island Theater* in December 1974, the decision was made to finally build a new, state-of-the-art theater for the 1976 season.

"The air structure was nearing the end of its life and so they had to decide whether to build a new one or not," said Jack Rouse, director of the design and entertainment production arm, Kings Productions. "Instead, they built the theater. In fact, they built two of them. The one in Virginia [at Kings Dominion] is identical, it's the same plan and everything...Because I had theater in my background, I'm not going to say was easy, but that was a natural, I knew I could get that kind of work done pretty simply and they both went up at the same time and they opened at [almost] the same time."

The *American Heritage Music Hall* cost $1.8 million to build with a colonial facade, to reflect the bicentennial. The theater was designed by Paul Shortt of the University of Cincinnati College-Conservatory of Music. For its inaugural year, it played host to the 30-minute bicentennial musical revue "We the People." The old *Kings Island Theater* played host to "Follies," an elaborate Sid and Marty Krofft puppet show featuring hundreds of marionettes and one (real) little person.

The celebration of the bicentennial extended past the theming of the new theater. Trash cans were painted red, white, and blue. The *Flying Scooters* were renamed *Flying Eagles* and got a new patriotic paint job. A new floral Liberty Bell was created.

For the bicentennial, the nationally syndicated "Great American Celebration" show came calling to Kings Island. "We had a wonderful time doing it," said marketing director Bill Price. "[We had] all the employees and their families in the park free that night, so we had a good crowd for national television. That was a major, major success."

Rock star Paul Revere, of the band Paul Revere and the Raiders, was married at Kings Island on July 4. Kings Island asked Revere's band to play two concerts at the park on the bicentennial, and Revere agreed on the condition that his wedding could be held at the park (Revere's fiancée was originally from the Warren County seat of Lebanon).

The Rivertown melodrama show was replaced with a mountaineer band called the *Hoe Down*. More shade trees and benches were added to the Happy Land of Hanna-Barbera.

Kings Island opened for preview weekends on April 24 and closed for the season October 31. Two rides were removed following the 1976 season. *Cuddle Up*, the spinning tea cup attraction, was removed and replaced with an arcade for the game *Fascination* the next season. Costly to operate, the low capacity *Shawnee Landing* was shuttered and the location left vacant—for the time being.

LION COUNTRY SAFARI TROUBLES

While a financial success and a major draw when it opened in 1974, the massive Lion Country Safari was eating away at the park's budget. For 1976, the park decided to impose a fifty cent entrance fee for the monorail in the hopes that it would help cover the safari's operating expenses. "Once you paid at the front gate everything was supposed to be free after that," said Bill Price. "As I recall, it was somewhat controversial to put a surcharge on the animal attraction over there." Controversy aside, Kings Island's first truly significant issue with the safari in 1976 came when the park's new zoological director decided that the safari needed an extra attraction—or rather, fifty of them.

"The basic idea was the lions sleep about twenty hours a day so you need something to liven up the attraction a bit," said Dudley Taft. "One of our animal experts said, 'I've got a great idea. We'll bring these baboons in, and they're very active and they'll wander around and get a lot more action going in the exhibit and get the lions going and stuff.' We actually rented fifty baboons."

The park erected two new stainless steel fences around the preserve, with a special weave that the zoological director said was impossible for the baboons to grip and climb. "There were two fences: an eight-foot on the inside and a fourteen-foot one was the outer one," elaborated Richard Fussner, the former director of loss prevention. "There's a road between them. But anyway…if they got over that [inside] fence, they have another one to go over. So they thought, 'Well, they won't get over both of them if they get out.'"

"They brought in these baboons, fifty baboons, in this one big container, big cage was what it was," [zoological director] Dietlein said. "'Well, I think what we'll do is let two of them go first. Two of the baboons first.' A fact known later was one was a male and one was a female. And they let them loose. Well, for two weeks we stood there and watched them for a little bit. Those two, they wandered around and they wandered around and all of a sudden, *pfft*, over the fence, just like that, the two of them. Dietlein said, 'I have never seen them climb anything like that before in all my life. They had never seen a fence before.' Well, that was all BS, it ended up they were from other wild animal preserves from all over, you know."

Forty-eight baboons were still in their cage, waiting to be released —and the stainless steel fence around the preserve was now clearly not enough to contain them. "They came up with the idea of electrifying the fence, make it a shocker fence," Fussner continued. "If they touched it, *zap*, because they put electricity all the way around the thing. Got it all prepared, so they called us and said, 'We're going to let them out again.' We all went back out there to watch it, and they opened it up and those forty-eight baboons came out and they looked around, and the two that had gotten out were on the other side of the fence, screaming at them; they were saying 'Come on, come on!' Next thing you know, those fifty baboons went over that fence, like a black streak just going *pfft* right over that fence. We had fifty wild baboons now roaming our woods by the river."

"One baboon gets on the electrified fence and gets shocked, and then another guy gets on top of him, and then another one on top of him, and finally they all pull each other over," Taft said. "When the press came through on the monorail, they saw the last one going over the fence!"

"We set up security parameters to try to keep them at least in an area by feeding them every day in the preserve where they're supposed to go," said Fussner. "For several days, in the evening they would go in the preserve where we wanted them, and they would eat the fruit that we put out there. That kept them in there during the night, but the next day they'd walk across the thing and get out of there."

To rope the baboons back in, officials next tried using tranquilized fruit to get them closer to the compound. "Those little suckers would come out there, they'd pick up the banana and eat it, and then they'd sit there and they'd *pfft*, go to sleep," said Fussner. "They'd sit there like that and you'd try to sneak up on any one of them, no way! I mean, there was no way. They'd get up and going, it wouldn't do anything for them...They were little guys...but they did have teeth like on a canine, bad teeth, and they could be nasty.

"The security guys were really leery, and I was out there at least on one morning just to see what was going on, and the guards were stationed trying to keep them from going up the river. These troops, you'd be standing there in the morning and it's daylight, but it's a little dark and all of a sudden this [baboon] troop would just walk out of these bushes at you. They'd stop and the male would come out, and I saw them little suckers come out and show their teeth at you and break a stick in half as if to say 'You better get the hell out of the way or that's what's going to happen to you!' It was making my officers real nervous to be out there in the morning."

Fussner's department opted to build a gigantic trap with a remote-controlled door, which managed to eventually capture all of them with the exception of the first male that had escaped.

"I would get calls every day, 'One of your monkeys is in my garage.' I'd jump in the car with one of the Lion Country rangers and we'd go hunting. I did that, I don't know, probably six or seven times over a period of maybe a couple weeks." Fussner recalled one instance in particular. "I got a call, on the other side of the river, above where the trail is, there were some people that were building a nice home up there. The lady called me up and says, "There's a monkey in our bath-room!' It's a new house, nobody's living there. She said, 'Your monkey is in our bathroom.' We jumped in our vehicles, we went up there and when we got there he wasn't in there anymore. He was gone, but a deputy sheriff had gone up there to see what it was. Wasn't one of our monkeys, it was a chimpanzee from somewhere, and this offi-cer...went in with a push broom to try to get him out of there, and the monkey took the broom away from him and broke the handle off and beat him with the handle! I'd have given anything to be there to have seen that."

Finally, Kings Island caught up with the lone renegade baboon at a camp upriver from the park near Fort Ancient. Fussner continued, "This crowd had gathered there, and there were some people who still didn't know what was what, but they said he was hitting on the camp's roofs and he would hang from the gutters and look in through the windows! There was nobody in them at the time, and I think he saw his reflection in there. That's what was attracting him...We were getting tired of chasing him and we were afraid he was going to bite some kid or something, so I'd taken my .223 along with a scope on it. We heard him go up into the woods, and I saw him. He went up there and sat on a branch out there. I'll never forget, I got my gun out, and I got by the tree where I could steady the gun next to the tree because it's pretty far up in there. I was getting ready to shoot, and this little old lady comes up and she says, 'You're not going to kill him, are you?' And I said, 'No, this is a tranquilizer gun. I'm going to tranquilize him, and then we're going to take him back to the park.' So boom, I shot and killed him. The other ranger went up in there with one of our little cages, we put him in the cage, brought him in the car and took him back. Last living animal I ever shot. I've regretted that to this day. It wasn't his fault we did it."

All but two of the baboons were shipped back to their provider, International Animal Exchange, in Ferndale, Michigan. The remaining two were locked in a cage with a sign reading, "These are the baboons that made monkeys out of us."

Just two months later on July 24, a 20-year-old Lion Country Safari ranger, John McCann, was mauled to death by the lions. McCann, a ranger for fourteen months, had a history of disregarding park rules and had been injured by one of the lions just two weeks before his death. After pulling his jeep behind an earthen berm in the back of the preserve to relieve himself, McCann was caught by the lions. He tried to get back in the jeep, but failed. His parents hired high-profile lawyer Marvin Kleinman, who ordered the Warren County sheriff's office to investigate the death, but the authorities came to the same conclusion that McCann was the only person responsible.

New signage was added to reflect the name change to Wild
Animal Safari. Photo from the 1978 employee yearbook. Courtesy
of Perry Denehy.

"The problem again relates back to complacency on the job," said
Fussner, who was the chief investigator from the park on the incident.
"If you do the same job every day, day in and day out, eventually
you're going to break some kind of rules. You're going to do something you shouldn't do and it's because you get complacent. We had
letters from those who rode the [monorail] train and said they saw
rangers riding on the backs of lions because they'd been playing with
them and knew them; maybe there was a lion that let them get close
or something. Of course, we never saw it because they never did that
stuff when we were around, but I had no doubt that they were. Every
incident that we had [with the safari rangers] was a matter of complacency or a lack of following the rules, something like that."

Those two incidents led Kings Island to terminate their contract with Lion Country Safari Inc. before the start of the 1977 season and take over operations of the safari themselves. "I think it was a good business decision," said former park marketing director Tom Kempton. "We had the knowledge and expertise, and it was a smart business decision. The monorail system that we implemented was a tremendous means for the guests to really see the animals and go through the safari."

The section of the park was renamed Wild Animal Safari. For 1977, North American animals such as bison were added, and the charge for Wild Animal Safari was raised to seventy-five cents.

GENERAL MANAGER #3: WILLIAM C. PRICE

In September 1976 Ed McHale was promoted to vice president of special operations for Taft's amusement park group. McHale was almost immediately sent by Taft back to Coney Island to develop it into a non-competitive alternative to Kings Island. McHale stayed at Coney until his retirement. For his role in developing the park and being instrumental in the park's first few years, McHale was inducted into the Kings Island Hall of Fame in 2012. Edward J. McHale passed away at the age of 94 on September 19, 2017. "He was a fine fellow and a very good operations guy," said his successor at Kings Island, William C. Price.

Price had originally become involved with Taft Broadcasting in 1973 as marketing director of an amusement park Taft wanted to develop in Chicago. The land purchased for the park fell into litigation and the project was cancelled, so the company moved Price to Kings Island in 1974 as the park's director of corporate sales. A year later he was promoted to marketing director, a position he retained until his September 1976 promotion to general manager. Price said that it "was kind of astonishing because I had no experience in the theme park industry. But I did have a wealth of experience in marketing and public relations, promotions, and all that because I had worked at the great Leo Burnett Company in Chicago."

⚓

1977—THE SCREAMIN' DEMON

Kings Island's first looping roller coaster premiered in 1977. The *Screamin' Demon*, a $750,000 Arrow Development shuttle loop coaster, was announced on October 2, 1976. However, at the time of the announcement it had no name as of yet, which wasn't uncommon in that day and age.

The Eiffel Tower as seen through the loop of the Screamin' Demon. Courtesy of Richard Fussner.

The ride catapulted guests fifty feet down, reaching a top speed of forty-five miles per hour, then up through a fifty-six foot tall vertical loop before heading up a second fifty-foot incline. Then the train shot backwards, retracing its steps backwards to where it had started.

After purchasing the ride, park officials had to figure out where to put it. They finally settled on placing the coaster over the lagoon and islands in Lion Country Safari (renamed Wild Animal Safari for 1977) to attract more people to that corner of the park. The ride was painted a brownish-yellow to "give a rainbow effect," according to Bill Reed, director of ride operations at the time.

The bitterly cold January of 1977 halted construction on the roller coaster. But Kings Island had gotten a good head start and fortunately was able to finish the ride by the park's opening date of April 16. The ride's train, originally planned with four cars, was modified to five at the park to increase capacity.

"The good news was it was a new ride, it was exciting, it had a couple of thrill elements to it," Tom Kempton said. "The bad news was it had a very low capacity. On a lot of coasters, as you know, you could have two, three, four trains perhaps at any one given time and handling x number of people per hour, etc, etc, but the *Screamin' Demon* was very low in capacity, so that was the downside."

Other additions for the 1977 season included the *Chili Haus* in the Swiss Building on International Street, the *Stadium of Stars* amphitheater, *Coney Disco* in the Coney Island section, *Boulder Bumpers* kiddie bumper car ride, and a new outdoor theater, the *International Showplace*. The *American Heritage Music Hall* debuted a new show, "Hooray for Hollywood." All told, the 1977 additions cost $4 million.

Dick Van Dyke arrived to film commercials for Kings Island with the park's new tagline "Kings Island's For Everyone, Kings Island's For You."

"In tandem with Lawler-Ballard, our advertising agency, we just felt that aligning with a commercial spokesman could, I'm going to use the term, 'Interrupt the mindset,'" Kempton said. "It could get people to think about Kings Island that maybe didn't have us top of mind. We looked at commercial spokesmen and we loved everything Dick Van Dyke stood for. He was a marvelous spokesman for us; he was fully engaged and loved our business. We dedicated an outdoor amphitheater [International Showplace] to Dick...and he was in for the weekend and we dedicated this amphitheater, and we also were going to preview a new show in the *American Heritage Music Hall*. We had the governor and senators and all kinds of VIPs in the park, and we had a wonderful planned event.

Dick Van Dyke rode The Racer for one of the 1977 commercial shoots. Photo from the 1977 employee yearbook. Courtesy of Perry Denehy.

We were watching the show in the amphitheater, we dedicated it to Dick, and just before it was over we knew that the rains were coming, so we quickly got Dick and our other guests to the *American Heritage Music Hall* inside before the rains interrupted. That being said, the cast was not ready to perform. It wasn't like we could just walk in, be seated, and everything was ready. So the orchestra was getting tuned up, the cast was getting stretched and ready, but there was about a thirty minute wait inside the *American Heritage Music Hall* which was full to the gills. I was seated next to Dick Van Dyke and he said, "How much longer do you think it will be?" and I said, "Oh, we've probably got another fifteen minutes." So he stood up and walked down to the end of the row and excused himself, went to the steps going up the stage, and if you know anything about Dick Van Dyke, he is an incredible entertainer. He tripped on the steps going up purposely and the crowd just roared, he was doing it intentionally. He went up and did fifteen minutes of impromptu onstage before the show that was just absolutely marvelous. When he came back down and the show was premiered, the result was amazing.

"He was so overwhelmed by the quality of the entertainment and he said to me, 'This is like vaudeville. There is nothing like this in America today where aspiring performers can really perfect their craft. I want to go backstage after the show and meet the kids.' So he had his manager and his agent and our team, and we went backstage and he met the kids. They were thrilled, of course, and he said, 'I want to bring back my staff of my manager and my agent,' because all the kids were wanting to know about how do we view our future in entertainment? How do we work with an agent or a manager and who does what? And he said, 'Well, let me come back and we'll do a full seminar one day,' and he did it at both Kings Island and Kings Dominion. It was just a wonderful, wonderful commitment on his part. Our show people were thrilled and especially for the young performers, it was quite a treat."

Kings Island closed for the 1977 season on October 16. To close it out, the park held what was one of the more bizarre promotions in its history—the Peanut Olympics. Billy Carter, President Jimmy Carter's brother, was flown out to Kings Island to compete against Yogi Bear to see who could make the larger peanut-butter sandwich, along with other peanut-themed events. Carter won eleven of the sixteen events and was crowned champion.

"In the fall of '77, we were very close to hitting our attendance objective, but we really needed a little bit of a jump, a little bit of a spark, something to get people to think about us who had already probably visited the park, and fall season could be difficult because the kids could be back in school and lots of high school sports, college sports, it's not always the easiest time to draw attendance," explained Kempton. "So we created the Peanut Olympics and everything was peanut-themed, and Billy Carter with the Carters and Georgia and the peanuts they grew was an ideal spokesman. He'd come out with Billy Beer, and Billy loved to have a cold beer, so we created the Olympics and brought him in for a weekend of appearances and that's why we did that."

Final attendance for 1977 was down 1% from 1976 to 2.5 million, but per capita spending soared 11%.

1978

No new rides were initially added to Kings Island in 1978, but four new live shows premiered. "New York, New York" was the featured show in the *American Heritage Music Hall* along with "Singin' to the World" in the *International Showplace*. "The Flapper Dapper Dixie Band" performed in Rivertown and "A Pickin' and a Grinnin'" country show was featured in Wild Animal Safari.

Tower Gardens still remains a shady respite in the park. Photo from the 1978 employee yearbook. Courtesy of Perry Denehy.

The *Kings Island Theater* was demolished. The facility was deemed unnecessary since the *American Heritage Music Hall* had been built and the contract for "Follies" ran out. It was replaced by Tower Gardens, a lushly landscaped sitting area with a 25-foot waterfall. *Gulliver's Rub-a-Dub* was renovated to feature new Hanna-Barbera sculpted pieces.

Penguins, vultures, and cranes were added to Wild Animal Safari, with the admission fee raised to $1 a person and now sponsored by Encyclopedia Britannica. A new shooting gallery was added to Coney Island. The shooting gallery in Rivertown was renamed and renovated to *BoomBangKapowInc*, while the *Rivertown Arcade* became both the *O.K. Korral Cowboy Shop*, which carried authentic western apparel, and the *Trading Post*. Appearing later in the year was a Ferris Wheel, replacing the *Bavarian Beetle*.

Two penguins escaped from Wild Animal Safari on September 14. One was struck and killed by a car in Fosters, Ohio, while the other was caught by a gas station attendant in Loveland and returned to the park.

Kings Island opened for 1978 preview weekends on April 15, and the park closed for the season October 15. Final attendance was 2.6 million people, a record up to that time.

THE FIRST DEMOLISHED COASTER

The *Bavarian Beetle* roller coaster was a portable coaster, built to be on-the-move. It had reached the end of its lifespan mechanically and occupied a space that park officials were looking at for possible expansion space. A lawsuit from a 91-year-old man who broke his neck on the ride was the final nail in the coffin, and the *Bavarian Beetle* was quickly demolished mid-way through the season without warning, becoming the first roller coaster to ever be removed from Kings Island. A Ferris wheel was plopped into part of the space.

It was the same lawsuit that also resulted in the creation of the Fun & Safety Guide, now ubiquitous at amusement parks across the world.

"That particular incident was what prompted me to develop a sign that went on every ride that puts the responsibility of riding on the individual for making the decision," said Richard Fussner. "If you read the signs, every symbol says, 'We recommend.' We don't say, 'You can't ride it if you're pregnant,' or 'You can't ride it if you got a broken leg.' We don't say that because he hurt his [neck]...and we had a lot of discussions about this again, the operators that are operating the ride, they were all at least sixteen years old, but...a person like him, he was incapacitated, he was 91 years old, he couldn't hardly walk very good, he got on the ride and nobody stopped him. He hired a lawyer and sued us because we left him on that ride, obviously being able to see that he was old, he couldn't walk right and all that stuff, and we had the responsibility to tell him not to get on that ride. Now, we made the decision and we talked to our attorneys and everything about it, to put the responsibility on a sixteen-year-old kid to look at them people coming in and making [a decision about] one person that you think isn't capable of riding is just opening up a door for everything."

Sparks rain down as the Bavarian Beetle is demolished in 1978. Photo from the 1978 employee yearbook. Courtesy of Perry Denehy.

To solve the issue, Fussner designed the Fun & Safety Guide to be installed at the entrances of all Kings Island attractions. Nine years later, the concept was adopted for international use by the International Association of Amusement Parks and Attractions.

"That's basically where my sign originated from. There's a sign for every ride. You had the opportunity to read that sign and it tells you flat out that you're making the responsibility, not us. We recommend you don't ride that ride, but we're not telling you you can't. I've lived with that for years, everywhere I go I see that sign everywhere...I'm proud of [it]. It's all over the world!"

MARK OF THE BEAST

A reverse look at The Beast in 1979. Courtesy of Tom Kempton.

*T*he 1979 season saw much expansion to the park. *Kiddie Turnpike* car ride was added to the Happy Land of Hanna-Barbera. *The Cincinnati Reds Dugout Shop* was added to the space in Rivertown formerly occupied by the *O.K. Korral Cowboy Shop*. "The Yabba Dabba Doo Caperoo" now played in the *American Heritage Music Hall* along with "New York, New York," which returned for a second season. The *International Showplace* became home to "Rock Around the Clock," a musical tribute to the 1950s. The biggest addition, however, was over in Rivertown—an addition that would ensure Kings Island's permanent place on the coaster map.

The decision to close *Shawnee Landing* in 1976 opened up a vast amount of land for possible expansion. Kings Island's maintenance and construction department began planning for a clone of Coney Island's *Shooting Star* to go into the space, but the idea developed into building a monster roller coaster that would break *all* the records—the tallest, longest, and fastest coaster ever built.

The park initially turned to John Allen, who had built the park's two previous wooden coasters. "He was semi-retired, he was older than I am now, and you've got to remember that back then we had no computers, we had no scientific calculators, everything was done with slide rules and logbooks, manual calculators," said Jeff Gramke, an assistant park engineer at the time. "He just didn't want to take on that big of a project. We had done some preliminary topography studies of the area where we knew we were going to build it, so we all came back [to Kings Island]. There were several of us that went up there, and were kind of disappointed that he didn't want to do it and he couldn't really recommend anybody to do it."

On April 24, 1977 a forty-seven mile per hour gust of wind resulted in an empty *Sky Ride* gondola slipping off its wire. The ride's safety systems kicked in and the ride shut down, stranding all forty-five passengers as high as ninety-six feet up in the air. After eight hours and the assistance of six fire departments, the final guests were rescued. The next day, general manager Bill Price and director of maintenance and construction Charles Dinn went out to see what exactly had gone wrong.

"I told Charlie [Dinn], I said, 'This dumb *Sky Ride* has been a problem all the years,'" Price said. "'Why don't we just take it out and put something bigger in here?' He said, 'I think you're right.' I said, 'Okay, why don't we build a huge roller coaster?'" Fortunately, Dinn and his team had been working on a roller coaster for several months! "He [Dinn] said, 'If you can get the money, I'll get her built.'"

Price put together a presentation and pitched the attraction concept to Taft Broadcasting officials. "We loved wood coasters and we wanted to build the biggest, baddest one that there was," said Charlie Mechem. "The whole coaster business is a continuing arms race and we thought we'd come up with something different and God knows we did!"

Now that the coaster was officially greenlit, the park was able to coax John Allen, along with his wife, back out to the park to look at the site and try to persuade him one last time to design their coaster. "The last night he was in town, eating up in the *International Restaurant*, he took a menu from up there and flipped it over and wrote a bunch of formulae on the back of it," Jeff Gramke said. "He handed it to Al Collins, who was my crew chief, and said, 'You guys can design a coaster yourselves.' We didn't think much of it that night, but then the next day we looked at what he had written and he sent us a book, he actually sent us his book of roller coaster design stuff, so it had all kinds of stuff in it. It had wood properties, it had oil viscosity properties, bearings, all the information that he had gleaned over the years, he sent that book to us. The company [Taft Broadcasting] talked about it and we talked about it internally here, and decided it would be worthwhile to try, so the company took a chance and let what essentially were the two surveyors at the company start designing what became *The Beast*." So Collins and Gramke began designing the record-breaking coaster—without the aid of electronic calculators or computers.

Surprising as it may sound, executives left the two surveyors lots of freedom when it came to laying out the coaster. "When we started doing it, they knew we wanted to build the station where the war canoes were. We had a war canoe lake in Rivertown and that's where they wanted it to be, so we knew where the station was going to go, and from then on it was pretty much up to us to decide what we wanted to [design]," Gramke said. "We talked about it with management as we were going, to see if we were on the right track of what they were looking for."

"Al and I were actually doing the layout and the design at the same time," Gramke continued. "We were trying to save every tree out there, so we'd do a preliminary design and then go out and do some surveying, whack through the woods and cut as minimal amount of trees and branches down as we could. Both of us had poison ivy I can't tell you how many times! If there was a nice tree in the way, we'd come back and redesign the ride. Well, we did that for a while, but it got to where we'd been—every time you make a change in a roller coaster, it affects everything from that point forward. We decided not to do that and let the chips fall as they may. If a good tree had to sacrifice itself for the ride, that's what happened."

The famous double helix finale was born out of necessity. "We knew we had to get back," Gramke said. "We knew we had to go around. To get it to be the longest ride, we needed to go around it twice, so it was kind of a function of we had a lot of energy because we had two lifts, and we had to use up the energy somehow, so it worked out good doing a stacked helix."

The tunnels, another iconic element, were another "happy accident." Gramke explained, "Rather than building the structure taller to stay above the ground, it was cheaper to dig the tunnel underground and keep the structure shorter. That let us keep the wood down and the rest of the ride from then on we didn't have to build as tall of a structure for the wood. So the first tunnel wound up being an accident that turned out to be a great part of the ride! Then we had a couple other tunnels in the back of the ride by the block brake for the same reason, to get the dynamics to work right we needed to go underground a little bit."

The Powder Valley Nature Trail allowed guests to get up close and personal with the construction of The Beast. Courtesy of Alfred Freeman.

John Allen's design principles continued to come in handy throughout the design process. "John told us to straighten the train out before you change directions," said Gramke. "In other words, if you're banking to the left and going around a curve to the left, try to straighten the train out so it's level again before you go to the right. He said, 'Try to keep at least half of the train straightened out first before you make changes in directions to keep from jerking people around so much.' Well, we had so much distance, we had the luxury of so much distance on that ride, we have no compound bank angles on that ride. We bank, straighten, then bank again, then straighten, then bank again, then straighten. I think that's what's kept the ride to be so popular over the years, because it's not messing around with people's equilibrium. A lot of people can ride coasters and a lot of people can't, and *The Beast* is a ride that most people can ride because we straighten you out first. We're not constantly throwing you back and forth over and over and over again. I think that's what kept the durability of it and the desirability of it."

Constructing it in a wooded, hilly location proved to be one significant challenge. "We couldn't set up on a radius point for instance and turn angles to every one of the bends," Gramke explained of the site. "The bends are about less than nine feet in the curves' center, so we had to do a lot of deflecting. For surveyors, the way you do that, you do a deflection for points and then you set up again and then you deflect around the curve again, and because the ground was so rough it was hard to see and hard to measure, because we had to measure everything back then. Now everybody uses GPS and several years after the ride opened people were using lasers to measure with; we had to measure everything by hand. You have to pull a tape that had twenty pounds of pull and use a plumb bob because the tape had to be dead level, and we had to make corrections for temperature, because the steel tape changes length with the temperature change. We were constantly having to make calculation changes while we were doing the calculations for the ride. It was just a real, real, real tough site to work on."

The roller coaster's 110-foot tall lift hill was topped off November 9, 1978, at which point approximately 60% percent of the roller coaster was completed.

The Beast's first drop is seen here under construction. Courtesy of Dave Focke.

Throughout the coaster's development, the ride did not have a name, not even by the time the official announcement was held on July 10, 1978. Ruth Voss, the park's public relations director, frequently heard the construction workers referring to the ride as a "beast of a project." It struck her that *The Beast* would be the perfect name for the ride. Voss submitted the name and it eventually wound up on a final list of five possible names.

"We had five names we had selected, and *The Beast* was one of the five, and we were skewing towards the name called *The Great Mountain Runaway*," said Tom Kempton, marketing director for Taft's theme park group. "*The Great Mountain Runaway*, the creative [theme], and the advertising were brilliant. It was a Cub Scout leader around a campfire with a group of scouts, and there was a mine shaft behind them and he was telling them stories at night. He was kind of a Gabby Hayes, bearded, old scout leader and he said, 'Boys, let me tell you, back in that mine shaft one night, the biggest, baddest longest thing came out of that mine shaft a-roaring,' and you were cutting to the faces of the kids and their eyes are big and you kind of get the feel of this commercial, and we really loved that advertising. But we decided to do what a smart marketer should do and that is let's listen to our audience. Let's talk with the target audience, we did a series of focus groups. Focus groups are usually a dozen or so people. We did five or six of those to talk about various names, various ideas. We put all the names out there, we got the feedback from the audience. I think we did them in Cincinnati and maybe Columbus or Indianapolis, and the results were the reason we did the research. It came back and said, I think it was like 98% of the people voted *The Beast* first or second. They just absolutely loved *The Beast*."

A logo was drawn up and the name published on February 6. "It was so good and Lawler-Ballard Advertising Agency in Cincinnati designed it, one of their art directors," said Bill Price. "We sold T-shirts and Coca-Colas in the queue line of *The Beast*; it may not have paid for it [the coaster] in the first year, but it came pretty darn close."

Dave Focke, an electrical engineer from Aetna Electric, helped work on *The Beast's* control systems. "It was unbelievable to see the way it was carved into the hillside and fit the terrain," Focke said. "I couldn't wait to see it run the first time. That was a very exciting time." A few years later in 1981, Focke would join Kings Island full-time, a career at the park that would span the next twenty-one years.

One of The Beast's curves under construction. Courtesy of Dave Focke.

Construction was completed and soon thereafter testing began. For *The Beast*, the first test was a monumental moment for everyone involved in the project. "Al [Collins] was kind of a dry guy, he didn't get real excited, he wasn't the kind of guy that laughed all the time," Gramke described. "When it came around, I mean we did all the calculations and we were confident John gave us the dynamic information that we needed to do the calculations, we were sure it was going to work. But always in the back of your mind you're wondering, 'Is this going to come out of the helix and back into the station?' When it did, he almost got choked up. It was pretty exciting to see it come back for the first time."

Executives began test riding it shortly after. "We were having a board of directors meeting, we were all up in the suite, the Caprice we called it, over the front gate," said Dennis Speigel, who was general manager of Kings Dominion at that time. "We were having cocktails that night, the park wasn't open, it was April, it was like this kind of weather. Very drizzly and cool. Great conditions to get the greatest speed out of a ride! We went down, we said, 'Let's get them to light up *The Beast* for us and take us for a ride.' Nobody had ridden it! It was only sandbags at that time...They took the sandbags out, it was safe, we got on this ride *The Beast* for the first time, we're half-crocked and this thing goes up the big [lift] and down the whoopty-doos and around. It goes up the second chain, down the hill into that tunnel, it hits that tunnel, we thought we were all dead! It literally scared the crap out of us. We were sober when we got off the ride, all of us! We said, 'Oh my God, this is going to kill somebody, what have we done? It's too fast, it's crazy,' I mean, it was bananas. I'll never forget it...It literally scared us sober."

"I went down that thing, I thought we were going to flip off and go into Warren County!" said Gary Wachs, executive vice president of the Taft theme park group. "That was the wildest damn ride...I thought it was out-of-this-world."

"I couldn't believe anything could be as exciting!" said Taft CEO Charlie Mechem. "When you get on top of that first drop and look down into that [tunnel], it looks like a postage stamp. I remember thinking, 'This is just absolutely phenomenal.'"

Some executives at the park did not feel that the ride was frightening *enough*, and wanted to add a little extra "something" to the coaster, according to loss prevention director Richard Fussner. They wanted to take an old coaster train from the park's maintenance bay, paint it like *The Beast's* trains, and then damage it and put it up where the train emerged from what was then the third tunnel, suggesting that the train before yours had jumped off the track and crashed. Other executives at the park were less than fond of the idea. They felt that the ride was frightening enough without the added effect, and the crashed train was never installed.

The menacing theme even extended to *The Beast's* phone line, at least for a brief period of time. "Each of the rides had a telephone and every phone had a three-digit extension number, and somebody picked the number 666 for *The Beast*," said director of park services Walt Davis. "I saw that and a couple of other managers saw that and thought, 'Let's not!' We were picturing headlines. If something ever goes wrong, that would be on the top of the headline! It disappointed a lot of the staff but we had to change that number."

Fittingly enough, Kings Island held the press preview for their new $3.8 million toy on Friday, April 13, complete with an "unchaining" ceremony featuring the local Marines. "We had a couple of Marines on it," said general manager Bill Price. "They said, 'That's something else!' They couldn't believe it, I guess it was like going through combat!" Even though the day was rainy, the press reviews were extremely favorable.

The Beast was unleashed to the general public on Saturday, April 14. "On opening day it was Saturday. There were 6,000 people in line to ride that ride," Fussner recalled. "They weren't up in the queue lines yet; we kept them back and it's a good thing they did because it wouldn't run! We couldn't get it going. All of these people were in line waiting, and we had a guy that worked on the computer programs and that kind of stuff in the park, and something was screwed up with the program somewhere that was causing it to not want to run...I think it was almost 1:00 before we got that ride running. And I really thought I was going to get killed. I was up with the security guys, we were up there and I was up there on the front rope, and I was getting called a lot of funny names up there!"

The Beast finally opened to the public—and officials realized they had a hit. "When we first opened it, the only queue line we had was up in the station, and the line stretched halfway across the park!" said director of park services Walt Davis. "So we built more queue line areas down on the ground...and the line still stretched halfway across the park. And people were coming off that thing cheering and screaming. They don't do that on other rides. You see one or two going 'Wow, that was great,' but this was universal. And they'd go back and get back in the same line again. Four hours! They'd wait four to five hours to ride that thing."

After observing riders, park officials decided that the first curve after the first drop was pulling extremely heavy g-forces. "We went back after that first week and tore up the track and re-banked it, banked it up quite a bit," Davis said. "That's very difficult to do because that track is laminated wood and it's [extremely thick]. To do anything with it, let alone change its shape and curve was very, very difficult, but we did it. That helped it a lot, but still not enough. We had to go back then one more time and bank it again not only in that first curve, but also down in the helix."

The first ride on *The Beast* became a rite of passage for people across Cincinnati. "I was a little hesitant about it, a little apprehensive, since you couldn't see the ride," recalled Don Helbig on his first ride in 1979. "It was just out there in the woods; there was this mystique about it. Seeing all the media coverage on TV about it, there wasn't social media or anything like that, so you could only go by what you were hearing people say about it. People were saying, 'It's so fast, I thought it was going to fly off the tracks,' and that was what you would hear when you would talk to your neighborhood friends that had ridden it. It was just awesome, an awesome experience, that first ride. I can remember going up the lift and seeing how we were going above the trees. It didn't have the helix enclosed yet at that time, so it was a wild experience. Vivid memories of that, just going through there and seeing all this wood come flying at you, going through that. It was one of those rides, and I can only say this about a few rides that I've been on, that as soon as that train came back in the station, you wanted to get off the ride and get right back in line again. You just couldn't get enough of it. But I remember as soon as I got off the first train, I did run to the payphone in Rivertown to call my brother and say, 'Oh, we've got to come back next week! This thing is off-the-charts good. If you think *The Racer* is good, oh my God, you've got to come out to ride this.'"

Taft Broadcasting and Kings Island executives never thought *The Beast* would remain the world's longest wooden roller coaster over forty years after it debuted. "It's still probably in the top five [best coasters] after all these years," Gramke concluded. "That's pretty amazing, I think."

The introduction of *The Beast* had an extremely positive impact on the park. By the time Kings Island closed for the 1979 season on October 14, the park had seen 2.75 million in attendance, up 4.8% from the year prior, setting an attendance record. Per capita spending was also up 9.3%.

Many decades after opening, The Beast is still a world record-breaker. Courtesy of Dave Focke.

SEASON PASSES ARE INTRODUCED

Kings Island was built to be a resort, complete with its own motel, campground, and even a golf course. However, most of the park's visitors were coming from a close proximity. For the 1979 season, the park introduced a season pass.

"One of the driving things was we always felt strong about repeat business," said Tom Kempton. "Boy, if we could get that person that came once a year to come twice, think of the impact of that in our core market, and I'm thinking more Cincinnati and Dayton. So season pass really started to target that and back when we opened the park, a major contributor to attendance was group sales. It was major. Company outings and school groups and organizations and churches, and you've seen when there's hundreds of buses in that parking lot on Saturday. Back in the '70s, there were a lot more of those, but that business has largely been replaced by season pass. It's still there and there's still a lot of group business, but a season pass has taken some of that business away. It's a shift in how tickets are sold."

"We really weren't sure what our expectations were because no one had really tried it before," said Nelson Schwab III, vice president of corporate development at that time for Taft Broadcasting. "All of a sudden, it just took off. We got nervous that we were selling too many so we actually cut it off at 55,000. We didn't know whether they would come twice or ten times. If they came ten times, we might be in trouble because we didn't have the capacity. That was an innovation that, frankly, changed the industry. Almost everybody [today] relies on season passes as probably being their go-to ticket category."

Today, Kings Island's season pass program has grown so much that about ⅔ of the park's annual attendance currently comes from season passholders.

1980

In 1980 the park saw a number of various changes and enhancements. Now that Kings Island had another reliable and high-capacity ride with *The Beast*, park officials could finally close the problematic *Sky Ride*. The Oktoberfest station was renovated into a wine and cheese shop while the Happy Land of Hanna-Barbera station would eventually be turned into a gift shop. The Scooby-Doo children's coaster was renamed *The Beastie*, and a tunnel was added to the bottom of the first drop. The big new show for the year in the *American Heritage Music Hall* was "That's Entertainment!" "Kings Company" opened in the *International Showplace*. Elephant rides in Wild Animal Safari called *Maxi Taxi* were also added.

The notable change for the 1980 season was the joining of the second and third tunnels of *The Beast*, the addition of a tunnel over the helix finale, and steeper banking. The lack of a significant addition for the park this season was largely because it was a year sandwiched between two major investments, *The Beast* in 1979 and *The Bat* in 1981, and may have been partly responsible for the 10% attendance drop the park saw that year.

Kings Island opened for the 1980 season on April 12 and closed for the year on October 12.

GENERAL MANAGER #4: FRANCIS R. BUSH

Bill Price, who had been Kings Island's general manager since late 1976, was promoted to the position of director of corporate projects for Taft Broadcasting in October 1980. Shortly afterward he left the company to start a new business in Chicago. He eventually joined Cincinnati's Empower Media Marketing, which his wife founded, as chairman. "One of the things that I always liked about the park was we had a pretty good balance between live shows and rides," Price said of his vision for the park. "In those days, we thought that made a lot of sense because we wanted an all-family type of clientele. To have rides and really good shows, which we did have, was kind of my strategy." Price looks back at his time at Kings Island fondly. "It was a wonderful, wonderful job. To have something where you can get up and go to work every day with the objective of making people happy, it was a pretty awesome experience."

Replacing him was Francis R. "Butch" Bush. Bush started in 1974 as the vice president of finance at Carowinds. He moved to Cincinnati in 1978 when he was promoted to the position of director of finance for Taft's amusement park group, and in 1980 he became vice president of finance for the amusement park group. Just a few months later he was appointed to the general manager position at Kings Island.

The end of 1980 saw a new leader not only for Kings Island but also for Taft's amusement park group, as Taft began entertaining the notion of selling off their parks. Dennis Speigel, the new vice president of operations for the amusement park group in 1980, explained,

"Television and radio had incredible operating margins. They would operate in the 40% margin. There were some that were operated in the 70% margins, off the chart. The amusement parks, in the 80s, going into the 80s, we were still figuring out the business and how to operate it, make the most money with it. Well, we were on the launch pad! Here's the rocket, it's ready to take off and Taft, being a public company, its stock value had always been held back by the parks. Because the multiple of what you sell, a company sells its stock at, that multiple was lower than its competition. Cox Broadcasting, Cap Cities, CBS, companies like that, they were radio and television doing these kind of margins, but their value was way up here, their multiple was much higher. The analysts would always say, 'It's because of this part of the industry [theme parks], your business, it's too iffy. We don't know. It's a weather dependent business, there are a lot of things.' So Taft decided to do what's called an LBO, a leveraged buyout, so they shuffled the deck of management in 1980. They brought in a guy, Nelson Schwab. Nelson had never run anything. His job was real estate. But he knew nothing about the theme park business. Being lucky at the right time, he was very lucky! They brought him in. Gary Wachs left, he was replaced by Nelson Schwab."

Even with Gary Wachs leaving the company and Nelson Schwab III being promoted from Taft's vice president of development to executive vice president of the amusement park group, the company's parks would continue to be operated at the usual high-quality standard. However, hovering in the background over the next few years was the question of when, not if, the parks would be sold.

Å

KINGS ISLAND GOES BATTY

1981 saw an expanded live entertainment program, including the new shows "Rock Around the Clock" in the *American Heritage Music Hall*, "Grin 'n' Bear It" in the *International Showplace*, "Can't Stop the Music" and "I Believe in Country" on the International Street bandstand, and the *Caribbean Serenaders* in the Wild Animal Safari amphitheater. New roving entertainment was also added, including mimes, magicians, jugglers, and ventriloquists roaming the midways. 1981 also saw the addition of a groundbreaking new attraction for Kings Island.

Cranes assemble The Bat. Courtesy of Dave Focke.

Coaster company Arrow Development had forged a strong partnership with Kings Island over the years. They had built many rides for the park's opening and *Kenton's Cove Keelboat Canal* for the 1973 season. They had also built a full-scale roller coaster in 1977 with the *Screamin' Demon*. So when Arrow began developing a concept for a coaster with the train suspended below the tracks, it was only natural they would approach Kings Island first. "The idea came from Arrow [Development] and they approached *us*," stressed Walt Davis, director of maintenance and construction for the park at the time. "Their sales rep came by with artists' renderings."

Walt Davis and Bill Price, who was general manager at that time, were intrigued by the renderings of the suspended coaster. "That was going to be our next frosting on the cake...I thought it was an incredible idea," commented Price. "We'd follow *The Beast* with *The Bat*." Price and Davis traveled out to Arrow's headquarters in Mountain View, California to view Arrow's working prototype model of the ride. They were impressed, and Kings Island bought the ride. While buying a prototype was a risky decision, park officials had faith in Arrow Development. "We had all sorts of guarantees that it was going to work and all that," Price said. The decision was made to place the coaster at the end of Coney Island. To make room, the round-up flat ride *Halley's Comet* was removed following the 1979 season.

"There was supposed to be an element in there where the cars would swing all the way around," Davis said. The prototype was built with the inversion, but "as they got more and more into the design, they [Arrow] realized that they couldn't safely produce the dynamics that they needed to make those go over the top. So what they made were cars that would swing up sideways alongside another train on the same ride coming back the other way, and they would kind of twist against each other, and it looked like they were going to crash every time but they wouldn't, they'd pull out. Turns out that still didn't work."

Eerie costumed characters helped reveal The Bat to the world. Courtesy of Dave Focke.

Price and marketing director Dave Palmer came up with the perfect name that reflected the ride's swinging, flying nature. "I was sitting in his office and we were thinking about what to name it, and we came up with *The Bat*, thinking, you know, *The Beast*, *The Bat*," explained Price.

Since Bill Price left Kings Island in late 1980, the official announcement of the ride was done by his replacement, F.R. "Butch" Bush, on October 29, 1980, fittingly enough two days before Halloween. Spooky costumed characters flitted through the nearly completed station house while Davis and Bush spoke to the press.

Park engineers had discovered several problems with *The Bat's* design before testing even began. "We ran some calculations on that ride, and we thought it was too fast," said Jeff Gramke. "We told their [Arrow] engineers that we thought it was too fast and their engineers said, 'You guys don't know anything about steel roller coasters. You guys are wood roller coaster guys.'"

The park mocked-up temporary cars to hang weights in for the beginning of the testing phase. "When we did, it swung out so far coming into the station that it went over the guide rail coming into the brakes and hit the abutment, actually did a lot of damage to those temporary cars," Gramke continued. "So it was kind of funny, Al [Collins] was over by the [present-day *Vortex*] loop, kind of the boomerang area, and I was in the station at one end of it and John Rood, the engineer from Arrow, was down at the other end. I saw it coming. I thought 'Oh no,' and luckily nobody got hurt, it wasn't any problem. I looked over at John and John looked over at me and he crossed his arms and he said, 'I guess you guys were right!'"

"The first hill was high enough that it got through the curves and everything okay, but we had to slow it down coming into the second lift because it had excess energy and then the same thing off the second lift," explained Davis. "It really had too much energy and the cars were swinging too much, in fact they were hitting against the stops [located below the cars]."

With the opening date looming, management had to figure out a temporary solution to *The Bat's* obvious issues. "We tried using hydraulic cylinders to slow it down, we tried leaf springs, so I made the suggestion, 'What do you think about putting some shock absorbers on them?'" Gramke recalled. "John [Rood] said, 'Yeah, that might be worth a try.'

"So I went over to Van Luenen's Department Store in Mason that had an automotive shop. I walked in the front door, I went up to the counter, there was a young lady at the counter, and I said, 'I need to look at your Monroe shock book.' She said, 'Well, what kind of vehicle is it for?' I said, 'No, I'm not looking for a specific vehicle, I need to look at your specification book for Monroe shocks.' She said, 'We don't have one.' I said, 'Yeah you do. I know you do. Just like oil filters. You've got a major book back there on filters and oil filters and shocks and you've got one, I'm sure.' She said, 'Well, you're welcome to come back.' So I went back and looked and again, they had no computers either, so they had a microfiche system with all their inventory in it, so I was in the back and I went to the back of the book, the biggest shock, and I started calling off numbers. She'd look, 'Nope, we don't have that,' I'd call another number, 'No, we don't have those.' We finally found ones that they had in stock.

"I bought two of them, came over here, the guys welded up a bracket with John Rood's supervision, and they put it on one car and ran the train around. That one car noticeably wasn't swinging as fast or as far as the other ones. So we said, 'Let's do more, let's get some more.' So we did! We wound up, they didn't have any more over there [at Van Luenen's], so we wound up getting a bunch more Monroe shocks [from another source]. Wound up with eight. Eight shocks on each car, four on each side, and that really, really worked. Now, if you go out and look at our *Bat* now, it still has those same shock absorbers on it. So even though they redesigned the track, they made the gauge a lot narrower, they banked it a lot more, they still kept using those same [types of] shocks that we came up with at Van Luenen's in Mason, Ohio."

The $3.8 million *Bat* opened to much fanfare as the world's first suspended coaster on April 26, with a media preview that was held on the 21st.

The issues that plagued *The Bat* throughout testing did not go away after it opened. The ride was down about 30% of the time, compared to only 5% for other rides. Misalignment of the train with the chain lift, wear and tear on the structure, and frequent shutdowns by a hypersensitive computer detecting paint peeling into cars resulted in a closure on July 26 in order to figure out a temporary solution. A modified chain dog system allowed *The Bat* to reopen on July 28. Despite the issues, the ride proved popular, resulting in a 22% increase in attendance at Kings Island by the time of Taft's 1981 annual meeting. Unfortunately, a large number of those people never even got to ride *The Bat* due to its downtime.

On August 20 "minor mechanical problems" shut *The Bat* down again. "While some downtime is not unusual for a prototype ride of *The Bat's* nature, recently this downtime has accelerated to the point that is unacceptable," F.R. Bush told the press. "No date for reopening the ride will be set until the ride manufacturer can guarantee consistent operation." After Arrow flew out to take a two-week look at the ride, *The Bat* reopened on September 5, the Saturday of Labor Day weekend. The ride continued operating throughout the fall, and Kings Island closed for the 1981 season October 4 with an attendance record of 2.76 million people.

The Bat's station was an iconic building in the park from the time it was built until its demolition in 2020. Courtesy of Dave Focke.

CANADA'S WONDERLAND

Taft Broadcasting's third built-from-scratch park, Canada's Wonderland, opened up in Vaughn, Ontario, near Toronto, on May 23, 1981. "That, compared to Kings Island which we got zoned in like sixty days, that took about a year and a half to two years [to get zoned]," said Dudley Taft, then-president of Taft Broadcasting. "There was substantial opposition, and it went through a whole series of contentious hearings and stuff before we got it done. We built Kings Island for $30 million, we built Kings Dominion for $60 [million] and then Canada was about $120 [million]."

TEN YEARS OF FUN

or Kings Island's 10th anniversary, it was decided to completely overhaul the Happy Land of Hanna-Barbera into Hanna-Barbera Land. *Gulliver's Rub-a-Dub* was removed and three new rides were added: *Rawhide Railway* hand-powered cars, an electric railroad called *Scooby Choo*, and the *Hanna-Barbera Carousel*. *Shaggy's Silly Sticks* climbing area, the *Fool House* funhouse, the *MacScrappy's Farm* playground, and the *Jelly Bean Bowl* ball pit added interactive elements to the section. *Squiddly Diddly* was renamed *Jabber Jaw's Tubs*. A puppet show was presented in the *Woodland Theater* inside a fiberglass tree. Two new fountains were added—an elephant fountain and an interactive one featuring the Hanna-Barbera characters. Built-in seats were constructed, shade trees were added, and the blacktop pavement was torn out and replaced with brick-paved walkways.

"We knew we had a lock on the thrill rides, so we looked around for a way to vary the experience, and we decided the participatory route was the way to go," said F.R. Bush.

"I had to go out to the studio and meet with the Hanna-Barbera people, Bill [Hanna] and Joe [Barbera] and all their artists and what-not," said Mike Foley, director of planning, design and development at

Kings Productions. "I spent a lot of time back and forth over there and how to bring their characters to life for real. Like the carousel, having all the animals on the carousel like Yogi Bear and all that...The carousel was the one that I think people really, really [remember], because it had a lot of the characters, it wasn't just one or two. The kids loved it and the characters came to life." The park flew out Bill Hanna and Joe Barbera to officially open up Hanna-Barbera Land.

TimberWolf under construction. Courtesy of Richard Fussner.

TIMBERWOLF

Another major addition for 1982 was the *TimberWolf* amphitheater for big-name talent. "We put those in every park because that was a huge impetus for people," Mike Foley said. "They'd want to go to the amphitheater, but they would come spend the day at the park and then just be there at night for the concert. It's a double hit. They had entertained a lot of folks, that was huge. [We built] *TimberWolf* and the *Paladium* at Carowinds. Then we had *Kingswood* at Canada's Wonderland. Every single [park] had a different [amphitheater]."

"Over the years we have been lacking name talent to go along with our live acts," park spokesman Bill Mefford told the press. "So, presenting concerts is in keeping with the total entertainment package that we offer." The 10,000 seat amphitheater opened July 9 with a concert featuring the band Air Supply.

While extremely popular initially, attracting such acts as Jimmy Buffet, The Beach Boys, and The Moody Blues, the amphitheater fell out of favor by the 1990s with the rise of newer, larger amphitheaters, such as *Riverbend* at Coney Island. Today *TimberWolf* sits mostly vacant except for the popular SpiritSong Christian rock concert series in late June.

RECAR EHT

After installing a major roller coaster, it's not unusual for the next season to have a tighter budget. Such was the case in 1982. Most of that season's budget was set aside for improvements to Hanna-Barbera Land and building the *TimberWolf* amphitheater.

"Usually, we'd have six, seven, eight million bucks a year to rein-vest and build restaurants and rides and everything, and that year corporate didn't want to give us hardly anything for a new attraction," said Walt Davis, by then the director of park operations for Kings Island. "We were sitting around, this park staff worrying about what can we market next year? And somebody [marketing director Tom Nowlin] said, 'Let's just do something crazy like maybe run a coaster backwards!' Everybody laughed. I didn't laugh. I sat there, I thought, knowing how they're designed and how they work on the tracks and how the mechanisms and brakes and how they all work, I pictured in my own mind if we took a train and just reversed the chain dog and the anti-rollbacks and turned them around. Provided it was a comfortable ride, mechanically, no problem."

Davis next approached F.R. Bush. "I said, 'I'm going to do a test.' He said, 'On what?' I said, 'Running a coaster backwards.' He laughed, he said, 'Don't tell me about it, just go ahead and do your test!'" Davis and his crew went out to *The Racer* and it "took a day to just get under the trains and turn those things around." Davis decided that the backwards *Racer* would be a fun, new, marketable change that wouldn't cost a penny. "At first, we were going to turn them both around. Then we decided it was more fun to give them a choice and let people decide. It worked out really well. It basically didn't cost anything, and we had a major attraction come out on that."

The backwards *Racer* opened May 28, the Friday of Memorial Day weekend. Davis refutes the commonly told story that the unreliable *Bat* was the motive for *The Racer* going backwards. "Lack of capital investment cash forced us to think out of the box, and that's what came out of the box."

VIKING FURY AND OTHER ADDITIONS

A last-minute addition for the 1982 season ended up being a park mainstay in *Viking Fury*. "The Intamin rep came into my office one day and he said, 'We have a prototype Giant Swinging Ship,'" said Walt Davis. "Up until then, the swinging ships were a lot smaller, about half that size. He said, 'We have a prototype that runs. We'd like to sell it to somebody, put it in a park and make a deal. I'll offer you a good deal on it.'" The ride would only cost $650,000, far below the $2.1 million for Hanna-Barbera Land or the $3.8 million for *The Bat*. "We had the money and so I went to [F.R. Bush] and told him about it, and he said, 'Let's try it, get some guarantees on it.' So I told the guy, I said, 'Do you have an agreement or proposal?' He said, 'No, I don't have anything. I didn't expect to make a deal today.' I said, 'Well, we're ready to go. We trust you guys, you're a big name.' I'm not a lawyer. I wrote the contract at my desk while he was there. Two-page contract, best contract I ever wrote, best contract I've ever been in! I've been in court fights on contracts and other stuff, that one was perfect and no lawyers were involved!"

The ride, named *Viking Fury*, would be installed at the edge of the pond in Oktoberfest and opened on July 18. "It was a prototype, there were things about it that were unfinished like the control panels and stuff," Davis continued. "A lot of wiring that wasn't circuit boarded. It was patched and stuff. There were some complications, but they made it work. They stood behind it and it went well."

Viking Fury under construction, 1982. Courtesy of Richard Fussner.

A significant change for the 1982 season was a renovation of the International Street streetscape. "When I first came there [to Kings Productions in 1978], the street was literally a street," said Mike Foley. "It was an asphalt street that went from the front gate to the *Eiffel Tower* and it went straight as an arrow; and it was an asphalt street with a curb, and that curb could have been a wall in terms of guests being able to get into the shops and things psychologically. You went from one end of the street to the other, and I had come from a background where I was doing renovations of main streets all over these little towns for my other company all over New York and down in Virginia and all over the East Coast, and the main street became a pedestrian environment, not a road. That background that I had doing all that I brought to the park, and I said, 'The people are just going from the entrance to the *Eiffel Tower*. They're never getting in your buildings until later.'

"We flipped it, and I said, 'Let's get rid of the curb, let's flip it, let's fill it in.' We came up with this product called Unistone, which is not asphalt, because the asphalt got wet and slippery, but the Unistone is porous and it's gritty and the water goes through it, so it doesn't puddle. So you didn't have guests with wet feet and all that all the time or slipping on the asphalt, which was slicker than ice when it got wet. We flipped the street, put the patios on the fountain side [instead of the building side] so that you could actually see the water and all that, and then put the pedestrian [walkway] next to the buildings, which meant they could meander in and out of the buildings while they're walking down the street, and what that did was to increase the per caps enough to pay for probably the renovation of what we did!...If you looked at the street and you saw a trash can and then a bench, the street may have been twenty-five feet wide in asphalt, but it was only about fifteen feet in terms of walkability because you wouldn't walk next to the trash can or the bench with somebody on it.

"We did these in the park in Canada and then we did them in all the parks. We did seat walls, which are basically walls that you could sit on, but they also become a barrier for washdowns so they [park services] don't destroy what they're doing, and they also create raised planters for trees, for shade...So you ended up with a seat wall, Unistone, and then the patios were switched to be on the fountain side, which people loved because they could see the fountains and that beautiful, blue mist and what-not. And you could walk into the shops a whole lot easier, meander in and out...[and it created a] friendly pedestrian environment for basically spending a little more money, which is the goal."

Other 1982 changes included the *Screamin' Demon's* name being shortened to *The Demon*, to go along better with the other coaster names—the park would now have *The Beast*, *The Bat*, *The Demon*, *The Racer* and *The Beastie*. The new live show in the *American Heritage Music Hall* was titled "Celebration," themed to Kings Island's 10th anniversary, and "Belly Up to the Bar Belles" was added to the renovated *Columbia Palace*. Also in the works for a 1983 grand opening was the *Festhaus*, a food and entertainment centerpiece in the Oktoberfest section.

The park opened for the 1982 season on April 25 and wrapped up October 3.

THE BAT'S ISSUES CONTINUE

The Bat opened with the park for the 1982 season. But on May 21, the failure of a weld shut the ride down. The park announced the closure would extend through Memorial Day weekend—and then made the decision to close the ride indefinitely. "It was not operating up to the standards guaranteed by the manufacturer, and we decided to close it rather than inconvenience park patrons," Walt Davis told *The Cincinnati Enquirer*. When would the ride reopen? "That's open to question and that's why we are saying reopening is indefinite," Davis told *The Cincinnati Post*. "We're not sure if they [Arrow] can get it fixed."

"We told them we could have it repaired and ready to go in about a month," retorted Ron Toomer, director of engineering for Arrow. "They have not told us what to do at this point."

"They [Arrow] tried, but they were going through severe financial difficulty at the time, and their ability to do much about it was very limited," Davis said. "They recovered after that, but right during that time it was pretty bad."

"We had these billboards all over the city, and then we'd have them [say], 'The Bat's Back!'" said Dennis Speigel, vice president of operations in the amusement park group. "Then we'd start up and break down, 'It's Closed!' Then, 'The Bat's Back!' 'The Bat's Closed!' 'The Bat's Back!'"

The Bat would remain closed for the rest of the 1982 season.

WALKING IN A WINTER WONDERLAND

Walt Davis had traveled around the world while being a war plans officer in the Air Force. Coming back to the Cincinnati area, Davis began looking for local things to do with his children during the Christmas season. "So you look around for stuff going on and everybody's desperate to do family stuff during Christmas time, and the only thing going on at that time was the model train display down at the bank building downtown," said Davis. "It was front page, big pictures, everything. 'Train display, train display,' that was *it*! I thought, 'Is that it?' I thought, here we're set with this magnificent asset and it just happened that...we had this magnificent *Festhaus* opening up, and it was not only an eating place, but it was a show place. I thought, 'Jeepers, we have that, and if we open up the [*American Heritage Music Hall*] for another show that's another indoor thing, and we have all the shops and we can have crafts and stuff in them. Suddenly, we got quite a bit of indoor stuff and ways to get out of the cold.

"Then I kept looking at the *Royal Fountain*," Davis continued. "I kept looking at it and looking at it, I thought, 'Man, if we could just freeze that sucker and make an ice-skating rink!' And everybody said, 'You're crazy, you're crazy, you can't do it.' I put a guy on it who ran our HVAC department and he was really good. We figured out how to do it." Davis and his team were able to figure out how to use cutting-edge technology to efficiently make ice from the water pumped up from the Little Miami River.

"Then I thought, 'Well, okay,' looked at the *Eiffel Tower*, tried to figure out how to string lights on the frame of the *Eiffel Tower*, and it was all difficult and dangerous. Finally I said to the electrical guys, 'Can't we just tie strings of lights to the ground and run clear to the top?' They had to work on it because you don't get strings of lights that long that will support themselves, with wind and everything. They figured out they could tie those lights to cables, anchor the cables, and then winch them up one at a time and tie them off at the top." With a gigantic star Davis designed, Kings Island could claim the title of having the 'world's tallest Christmas tree.'

"Suddenly we had all the elements, but we didn't have a green light from corporate to go ahead," explained Davis. "They thought, everybody's telling me 'Walt, you're crazy, you're new in this business, you're a soldier, what do you know about entertainment, nobody goes anywhere like that in the wintertime,' just all the reasons in the world not to do it. I kept working and working and working on it...Finally,

he [general manager F.R. Bush] said 'Okay. Put together a presentation.' He figured we'd go downtown, make a presentation, and then
they would shut me down. Well, they started buying it piece by piece.
The *Festhaus*, the fountain, the tower, and finally they said, 'Give us
your worst case and best case scenario.' I said, 'Worst case scenario
would be an attendance of 65,000 people.' That would break even
with a decorating budget of $100,000, $150,000, something like that.
What they did was I gave them the worst case attendance, they gave
me a budget that we would break even in the worst case. It was basically a pilot project, a test. Best case was double that number, 130,000
people, in which we'd make a couple hundred thousand dollars,
quarter of a million, or something."

"I was one of the people that advocated very strongly for Winterfest because it just broke my heart to see all that real estate and the
facility just sit idle during the Christmas season," said Taft Broadcasting CEO Charlie Mechem.

Poster advertising the Festhaus. Courtesy of Paul Bonifield.

Taft Broadcasting president Dudley Taft concurred, "One [reason behind greenlighting] was just to get more use out of this facility that we had sunk a lot of money into and continued to reinvest heavily. So why not pick a period when people are available and families are available to go out there, which is pre-Christmas?"

"We wanted something that would bring in money because after Labor Day and the weekends, there really wasn't any business," agreed Dennis Speigel. "We wanted something that would keep our employees engaged, and they would be back home at Christmas, high school and college, and they could work. And we wanted something that would keep our name out there to people longer in the season."

With a green light from corporate and after the park's closure October 3, Kings Island went ahead with their potentially risky idea. No seasonal park had ever done a Christmas event before! "We spent a lot of time, a lot of energy, effort by the staff, they put their hearts into it," said Davis. "Everybody caught the spirit."

Of course, the signature attraction that needed to be created was the ice skating rink on the *Royal Fountain*. Dave Focke, Kings Island's director of maintenance and construction, recalled, "You needed a level surface for the water to freeze, well, the floor of the *[Royal] Fountain* is not level. It all pitches towards the drains. So we had to bring in loads of sand and level it off, then put down plastic, then put down the refrigerant hoses that would freeze the ice, and then bring in a condenser to cool the refrigerant to freeze the ice. Of course, if the weather was too warm, we couldn't make ice! So you had to have just the right temperature to have the right ice-skating surface." The *Royal Fountain* ended up being filled with 800 tons of gravel to support the 20-ton deck and 1.5 inches of ice.

Discussions were also being held over what exactly the rideless Winterfest would cost. "We had a meeting about what we should charge," said Charlie Mechem. "One of the people said, 'No, no, we just don't charge anything. It's free!' Somebody else said, 'Wait a minute, if it's free, people won't think it amounts to much. If you charge something, however small, people will believe it's worth something.' And that's exactly right, and that's a lesson that I learned and relearned over the years. If you give something away free, people are going to assume it's not worth a whole lot." Admission would be charged—but it would only be $2.50 and free for season passholders.

Opening night was the Friday after Thanksgiving on November 26. "It came the opening night and Butch [Bush] was just nervous as a cat," continued Davis. "He was just sure that we would fall on our butts, and he was going to get fired, and I'd probably go out the door with him." Opening turned out to be "a miserable night. Cold, rainy, windy, just unpleasant as could be. We had a budgeted attendance of about 5,000 that night and we got a little over 2,000 people. And Butch, I thought he was going to jump off the roof of the *International Restaurant*. He was losing his mind. I said, 'Hang on, let's get through this weekend and see how it goes.' Turned out the next night, because it was so lousy Friday night, was clear and crisp and pretty cold, just nice and clear and calm. Perfect conditions. We opened it up and people started streaming in, and I looked out one of the back windows, where we could see the parking lot...And not only was the parking lot filling up, but the line was backed up clear down onto 71! The state patrol was calling us saying, 'Get these people in, we got to get them off the road!' So we opened up another gate and we started getting them in...On a budget, Saturday night, of 5,000 people we got 20,000 people. Sunday night was very similar. All of a sudden, everybody woke up and said 'Holy cow, we got something!' And the reviews were fantastic, the reports from people were fantastic, the money was coming in, we were doing well. And it went very well through the whole season; our optimistic projection was 130,000. We wound up with 272,000 people. That clinched it. I mean, even Taft Broadcasting stock went way up. Not that we earned that much money, but it showed investors that we were thinking out of the box." The park had to scramble to accommodate the crowds, including opening *Smurf's Enchanted Voyage* with a modest holiday overlay. Winterfest proved so popular that it stayed open for ice-skating for several weeks after the event officially ended.

"We made a half a million dollars, which was a lot of money then, that had never been coming in before," Speigel said. "Plus, we created this great experience. The families loved it, and what we didn't antici-pate was that mom and dad brought grandma and grandpa. And grandma and grandpa really hadn't been to Kings Island; they were Coney Island people and they thought, 'We're not going to Kings Island, we're too old for that!' Well, they came out to see this, then they came back because they loved the park! So it was a win-win-win all the way around."

"We worked very hard on that, and it was a strain on everybody there at Kings Island, but they did a terrific job and introduced it well and it was a big success," commented Nelson Schwab III, executive vice president of Taft's theme park group.

Winterfest led to a proliferation of events nationwide, including Six Flags' Holiday in the Park. "When I left [Taft Broadcasting], I took the original plan with me and I went to Six Flags and I said, 'Look guys. You're missing out on something,'" Speigel said. "They said, 'What?' I said, 'You need to do this Christmas plan.' They hired ITPS [International Theme Park Services], I had started the company, and we put it in Texas, Six Flags Over Texas, where it's thirty-four years old this year, I think it is, and it's a huge success. Now they've expanded it throughout their parks."

1983

The biggest change advertised for 1983 actually debuted for Winter-fest 1982. The $2.5 million *Festhaus* opened for 1983 with the show "World Cabaret" and featured international dishes, a glockenspiel above the entrance, and a stained-glass window salvaged from the rubble of Cincinnati's Albee Theatre. Oktoberfest was also overhauled with the addition of a bridge over the pond, new shade structures over the *Bier Garten* patio, more seating, and brick-paved walkways.

"They needed a large, indoor dining facility and they also needed another big stage show," explained Jack Rouse. "The stage shows in those day probably had a cast of twenty to twenty-five and an orchestra of eight to ten, and the *Festhaus* was exactly the same...So the *Festhaus* was just we saw a niche for, frankly, people who wanted to do something other than ride rides."

"Celebration" returned to the *American Heritage Music Hall*, and two new shows debuted in the *International Showplace*: "In Concert '83" and "Play Me That Country Music."

The Wild Animal Safari themed area was renamed Adventure Village, with the animal preserve given the more scientific name of Wild Animal Habitat. Dissatisfied with the lion shelters, the lions were shipped out in 1983.

Tragedy struck May 13 when 17-year-old high school senior John Harter was killed during a Grad Night event. Harter, whose blood alcohol level was found to be over twice the legal limit, had climbed over a fence on the *Eiffel Tower's* fifty foot level and onto the interior emergency staircase. In the interior of the tower's 275-foot platform, Harter climbed out onto a structural beam for reasons that were never discovered. "He was about halfway across, here comes the [ascending] counterweight, and apparently he saw it at the last instant and to brace himself or whatever, it looked like he stuck a knee out like that, and the pulley and the cables caught him across the leg and dragged him up to the top where he was trapped, because he was being held by those cables," said Walt Davis. The operator felt the elevator do a "funny hop" and she decided to take the elevator back up empty, standard procedure for a suspected mechanical malfunction. The cables for the counterweight unwound, releasing Harter. He plunged over 200 feet down the elevator shaft to his death on the elevator's roof. It was the first time in park history a guest was killed. "We expected to be sued, but apparently because of the intoxication, the embarrassment, they decided not to do that," Davis said. In response to Harter's death, Kings Island installed higher fencing inside the fifty-foot level.

1983's Winterfest ran from November 25 through New Year's Eve. The ice skating rink was redesigned from a gravel and sand base into one made with steel and wood. The *Columbia Palace* and *Trading Post* were also opened, expanding the acreage of Winterfest. Two rides were opened for the event—the *Grand Carousel* and *Enchanted Voyage*.

MORE BAT PROBLEMS

"The Bat is Back!" proclaimed the billboards advertising the ride, which reopened for the 1983 season on May 21. Rainy weather hampered the installation of additional bracings for the coaster.

It still wasn't enough. On July 15, park technicians noticed a hairline crack in one of the ride's wheels and shut the coaster down. *The Bat* reopened July 25.

Don Helbig was one train away in August 1983 when *The Bat* went down yet again. "There were these four girls and two of them wanted to know, 'Can we go in front of you so we can ride with our friends?' 'No problem.' You know where this is going! I said, 'No problem, you can ride with your friends.' They get in, the train goes out, the next one comes in, they unload, they send it out empty. The train I would have been on comes back in, they send it out empty. It never ran again with guests riding. You'd be in the park and hear or see a test cycle, but never again did it run with guests. I could have been on that last train."

"They were riding it, testing it, and one of the maintenance team saw this crack," said Dennis Speigel. "Had this crack gone off, the car would have gone off the track and hit a pylon. It would have been catastrophic."

Kings Island officials had had enough. They decided they needed to find a permanent solution to *The Bat's* litany of issues.

The Bat would never open to the public again.

THE FIRST SALE

In 1983 Taft Broadcasting made a definitive decision to sell their theme parks. "By that time, a lot of the restrictions that had been placed on expanding television and radio ownership had been relaxed by the Federal Communications Commission," explained Charlie

Mechem. "Television and radio were still our most profitable businesses from a margin point of view. We wanted to enhance our ability to increase our cash so that we could make those moves."

"Taft was needing to acquire more television and radio stations, so they needed some liquidity on their balance sheet to do that," explained Nelson Schwab III. At the same time, "There was a group of us within the theme park group that wanted to do something on our own." The management of the theme park group formed a new entity called Kings Entertainment Company (KECO).

On December 21, 1983 Taft Broadcasting announced that they would be selling Kings Island, Kings Dominion, Carowinds, and Hanna-Barbera Land, which was under construction in Houston, in a leveraged buyout to Kings Entertainment Company, which would be headquartered at Kings Island. Canada's Wonderland would still be owned by Taft, but would have a management contract with Kings Entertainment.

Schwab became the CEO of the new company, and Taft Broadcasting retained a 1/3 stake in the company. "We basically sold it to the management, so we were comfortable that it would be well run and Heaven knows it was," said Mechem.

"That decision, to do that, do the LBO [begun in 1980 and finalized in 1984], it was one of the worst decisions they [Taft Broadcasting] ever made," according to Dennis Speigel, who left Taft Broadcasting shortly before the sale was finalized to start his own company, International Theme Park Services. "Those parks that they built—let's see here, Kings Island was thirty-one [million dollars], Kings Dominion was sixty [million dollars], Canada's Wonderland was ninety, I think, one hundred [million dollars], we bought Carowinds for seventeen million, but a couple hundred million [altogether]. When it sold to Cedar Fair [in 2006], it sold for [$1.24] billion. So they got off the horse too soon and the business took off, broadcasting went down. It was just crazy."

The sale was also a dramatic change internally with the parks. "Now, for the guys here in the LBO, it was great," Speigel continued. "Because they got on this horse, a rocket really, that was taking off. I was part of that team. I left and started ITPS because I wanted to do something else. But the timing was such that all of the old guys who built Kings Island—blood, sweat, toil, and tears—they were all left in the bus station, and this new group of guys with Nelson Schwab and Lew Hooper and Ron Miller and Dean Nahrup and all these guys, they weren't any of the guys who built the business! Or laid the foundation, or poured the concrete. All they did was get on the rocket at the right time! You don't begrudge them anything, it was just where it was."

The sale of the parks to Kings Entertainment Company was completed on April 9, 1984, with a sale price of $167.5 million.

PART II
KINGS ENTERTAINMENT

EVERYTHING'S CHANGED— NOTHING'S CHANGED

*A*fter the sale, F.R. "Butch" Bush was promoted to chief financial officer for Kings Entertainment Company. He held that position until 1993 when the company was sold to Paramount, after which he retired. Francis R. Bush died of a heart attack in 1997.

Management at Kings Island enjoyed working for Bush while he was at the park, but he was more hands-off than other general managers in the park's history. Walt Davis recalled Bush as "Kind of a quiet guy, not real bold about anything. I'd be out in the park running the park, and he would be sitting in his office looking at the numbers coming in."

"He was a bright guy and he really worked hard," remembered Mike Meadows, Kings Island's director of finance. "He made a lot of great decisions about capital investments and where we allocated our resources. He built for the future, he put money against the *Festhaus* when he knew it wasn't going to drive attendance. When you look at Winterfest and all the other components of it, you needed that *Festhaus* to make it work. It was a very strategic approach, and Butch was really effective at that."

The new general manager was T. Lewis "Lew" Hooper, who was promoted to the position on January 9, 1984. Hooper, a bank teller by trade, began in the amusement industry as the group sales manager of Carowinds. Hooper worked his way through the marketing department up to the position of general manager of Carowinds, then became general manager of Kings Dominion in 1980 before being promoted to general manager of Kings Island.

KINGS ENTERTAINMENT COMPANY DIFFERENCES

The main question on everyone's mind before, during, and after the sale from Taft to Kings Entertainment Company was what would change for the parks? Nelson Schwab said not much did. "We ran them [the parks] in a little more decentralized manner, but they were virtually the same people in a lot of respects. We made a few changes, but they were the same people. I think the difference was folks now felt they had the opportunity to earn what they could where they worked. It wasn't like in a big public company where you're a step removed from that ownership. This was direct ownership, so it was a great incentive for everyone to do well."

Schwab pointed toward the company's data processing department as an example of the new decentralization. "Prior to '83 we had a big mainframe computer that everybody had to link back into...and it wasn't very flexible and it was a pain," Schwab continued. "It was a contingent for every problem that came up! Very quickly, that world spread to your desktop, and so we were able to take advantage of that. We closed that central location and moved everything out to the individual parks so they could get better information quicker and hopefully make better decisions by doing that."

To the officials that built and shaped that group of parks in their early years, KECO, filled with people who joined the company in the early 80s, just wasn't the same. Dennis Speigel lamented, "I was sitting there in the middle of them watching it all, and the shame was the original team that Gary Wachs had put together was all gone and left in the station and these new guys, who really had no experience in the parks—Dean Nahrup was a merchandise guy, Lew Hooper was a marketing guy. I'll never forget, he [Hooper] came in crying in my office when the change was made, 'I'm going to get fired, I'm going to get fired.' Well, he eventually became the president of the new company, of KECO! He didn't have any experience, really. He was a good guy in marketing, but he wasn't there. He was a bank teller!...They were doing the same things we had done ten years earlier, this new team. They thought it was all new, and all that they were doing was doing what we had done, and you'd sit there and go, 'Oh my God, I can't listen to this anymore.'"

KING OF THRILLS

The big new addition that opened for 1984 was actually a product of Taft Broadcasting and not Kings Entertainment, as the concept and construction for the ride took place before the KECO sale was finalized.

The innovative King Cobra was a popular coaster at Kings Island. Courtesy of Dave Focke.

"I was reading *Amusement Business*, and a picture caught my eye in that newspaper," remembered Walt Davis. "It was a coaster loop with people standing up on the train! In the loop, they were upside down. I looked at that and thought, 'That's crazy! Where is that?' We found out it was in Japan, and we talked about it." Davis, F.R. Bush, and Dave Focke flew to Japan to investigate this innovative ride further.

"We met with the TOGO [coaster manufacturer] people, and one of the first things we did was go to one of their parks and ride it," said Davis. "We all looked at each other and said, 'People have done this? Really?' 'Oh yeah, no problem.' We always had to work through an interpreter. We got on it, and I must have been a little nervous, but once you roll out of the station, you kiss your butt goodbye. Whatever happens is going to happen; your fate is determined. Going up that first hill, looking around, just felt so incredibly exposed. Man, there's nothing, no sides around you, I could jump off this thing!..Going down that first hill, looking down over, was much scarier than looking out the seat of a coaster train. Went through the ride, went through the loop, the loop was fine, the ride was very smooth. We got back to the station and said, 'Let's do that again.' We rode it, I think, three or four times in a row and loved it. We were convinced right away that we needed that."

Taft then sent Dennis Speigel over, by then the vice president of international operations for the amusement park group, to meet with Kazuo Yamada, the head of TOGO, and ride the coaster himself. "I went to Tokyo. They had sold one in this little amusement park, and I'll never forget, they put me in like a white painter's suit, and it was raining, and we got on the ride, and every time I would ride a roller coaster for the first time I'd ride it with my hands up. So I get on the ride, we go down the dip, we go through the thing. And Mr. Yamada, when he got off the thing and we come in, he rode it with me, he goes, 'Look, look, look!' And there was an apartment building...or an office building. Every window in the office building had three or four people in the window applauding! Because they saw me riding it with my hands up for the first time." Speigel bought two of the stand-up coasters from TOGO, one for Kings Island to open in 1984 and one for Canada's Wonderland for the following year. The one at Kings Island would be America's first stand-up coaster built from the ground-up.

Working with a foreign company resulted in moments that were lost in translation. Walt Davis recalled one particularly humorous incident during contract negotiations for the Kings Island coaster. "Butch Bush was a Southern boy. He used a lot of slang in his normal conversation. We say something's a 'home run' or 'he hit the ball out of the park,' or 'the sky is the limit.' We all know what they mean. But the Chinese and Japanese people, they hear something like somebody says if something's a big failure, they say, 'That's the ballgame,' they're going, 'How are those connected? How does 'That's the ballgame' relate to this big failure over here?'...Almost 90% of his [Butch's] articulation was slang. We were working through a translator over tea...Finally, we had agreed on all the terms and the delivery dates and everything, and we were all drinking tea, toasting each other, and Butch said, 'Okay, let's wrap it up.' My translator looked at me, looked at Butch, and said something to his Japanese guys, the executives who were sitting there. Then they started, it sounded like a henhouse, all the chattering and jabbering, and finally he came back and said, 'We can't do it for that price.' I said, 'Well, what changed?' The Japanese are big at gift-wrapping stuff. If you've ever watched a Japanese person wrap a gift, it's almost a ceremony, and then it comes out perfectly every time from the size of the paper, the folds and everything. They said, 'We can't wrap it for that price.' I laughed, I said, 'We didn't mean that! Let's finish the deal!' I told Butch, he said, 'Oh God.' Those funny things were always happening."

The decision was made to place the $3 million stand-up roller coaster in the Adventure Village section of the park. The *Maxi Taxi* elephant rides and the *Bayern Kurve* were removed before 1983 to allow for construction of the new attraction. The coaster was announced on February 22, 1983.

The entire roller coaster was assembled and tested at TOGO's Japan plant. After an inspection, the entire ride was dismantled, every piece was numbered, and the pieces were shipped over to Long Beach, California. From Long Beach, fifty-seven trucks carried the ninety-seven crates weighing a combined one million pounds to Kings Island. The pieces arrived between November 9 and November 21, 1983. Assembly began December 5. "I knew we were building it in a very difficult spot because of the lake that was there, for the foundations and the ground was all unstable and stuff," said Walt Davis. "It was very expensive to get the foundations right, get them deep enough and big enough for the ride."

Construction on King Cobra moved throughout the winter.
Courtesy of Dave Focke.

The three designers of the coaster came to Cincinnati for the construction process. "They had an interpreter that came with them. His name was Mieta, and we called him Mickey," said Jeff Gramke. "Mickey was a great guy, but he wasn't an engineer, and I found out pretty quick that the Japanese language is very similar to German language. Not in the language, but engineering German is totally different from conversational German. When we used to get engineering documents [from Germany], we had somebody that used to work here whose father was from Germany. We would send them to him for translations because we didn't have any way to translate them, and he didn't know what the words meant. It wasn't something that Germans are normally taught unless you're an engineer! So apparently, Japanese must be a little bit like that because they would say something to Mickey, and Mickey would get a smile on his face and look at me like, 'I don't know what they said. I'm not sure what they want me to say.' Conversely, the same way with me. I'd tell him something and he didn't know how to put it into their language. So we were in the back room [of the Kings Island maintenance building], all the way in the back where our copy machine is, back there one day, and Sonno, the head engineer, was really getting animated, trying to get something through to me, and he took his Casio calculator and punched in some numbers and showed me the answer. I went into my office, grabbed my Texas Instruments, did this back to him, and we were actually communicating with our calculators because Mickey couldn't tell each other what they were doing! So that was kind of funny."

On January 14, 1984 Kings Island announced at an American Coaster Enthusiast convention in Chicago that the new ride would be named *King Cobra*, although that name almost didn't happen. "[Butch Bush] wanted to name it Anaconda in the worst way. Everybody fought him, they thought, 'Anaconda's an ugly snake, Cobra is a cool name.'"

A model of King Cobra's layout. Courtesy of Dave Focke.

King Cobra opened to the public on April 22, which was Kings Island's opening day for the 1984 season.

Unfortunately, *King Cobra's* inaugural year did not go as smoothly as hoped. On August 8 a manufacturing defect in the last car's axle caused the wheel assembly to fall off, which then caused the car to derail while coming out of the helix. "I was walking through the park one day...I just had cleared the walkway and turned into [Adventure Village] and I heard this 'Kaboom!' and I looked over there and the wheel assembly came off of the front car!" said Richard Fussner. "The whole bogey had come off, and as I turned my head and looked back I could see the bogey falling down through the train like that and hit the ground...And that first car, the whole train, when that bogey fell loose on there, there was nothing to keep control on the train anymore and it started turning like this. The people were standing up. So now you've got people that are standing up and suddenly they're going sideways and it's still going and they come out and they go down like this, and then down a dip behind the station. That dip behind the station is almost on the ground and here's this thing turning upside down with these people in there, and luckily it stopped on the beginning of that dip."

Twenty-four people onboard were injured. Sixteen were treated at Kings Island first aid for minor injuries, while eight people were transported to Bethesda North Hospital. The worst injury was a concussion. *King Cobra* reopened three weeks later.

The ride contributed to the park's main season attendance of 2.8 million people. It was the second-highest summer attendance up to that point, only slightly behind the 1981 numbers.

King Cobra operated for 17 years. Courtesy of Dave Focke.

SMURF INVASION AND OTHER 1984 CHANGES

In 1983 Taft Broadcasting had purchased a ten-year agreement to use the Smurfs in their parks. Now 1984 would be the first season for non-Hanna-Barbera characters at Kings Island. "That was kind-of interesting because Peyo, who created them, a couple of us spent a fair amount of time, me probably more than anybody, working with him over there to try to figure out exactly [what to do]," said Jack Rouse. "He wasn't exactly sure what a theme park was either, obviously he knows what one is now...It was just an integration of characters."

Naturally, they decided that one of the first places to feature the Smurfs would be in the *Enchanted Voyage*, which hadn't had a major update since it opened in 1972. The decision was made to transform it into the *Smurf's Enchanted Voyage*. After 1983's Winterfest wrapped up, the attraction was closed and the transformation began. Park scenic designer Brad Kain designed all-new sets and figures for the ride; the old Hanna-Barbera scenes were torn out and replaced with the four seasons—with a Smurf twist. *Smurf's Enchanted Voyage* opened for the 1984 season along with wandering Smurf-costumed characters and a new show titled "Smurfs Are Here" in the *International Showplace*. To tie in with the new blue additions, one of Kings Island's most beloved treats was introduced—blue ice cream.

New entertainment offerings were created. "Gotta Dance" was the new musical in the *American Heritage Music Hall*, "The Good Old Days Are Back Again" played the *Festhaus*, and "Country Music Showdown" and "In Concert '84" rocked the *International Showplace*. "Rockin' Scooby" appeared on the Hanna-Barbera Land stage, and "The Bar Belles Are Back" was scheduled at the *Columbia Palace*.

THE BAT: A DECISION IS REACHED

On March 15, 1984 Kings Island announced that *The Bat* would not operate for the entirety of that season. "We'll have it under review the entire year and we probably won't be running it," said T. Lewis Hooper.

"This does not mean we're closing down *The Bat* for good. If there's a way we can open it, we will," said spokesman Bill Mefford.

"What Arrow did is they took their regular, three-foot more or less gauge track and just turned it upside-down," said Jeff Gramke. "They didn't really redesign their track much, they just hung the cars the other way and then made bogies to hang on it. Well, they didn't have enough bank angle in it. When it came to a curve, because it was just a free-swinging pendulum, the cars just went wherever gravity and momentum was going to take them!"

"Over time, we could see that it was basically hammering itself apart," said Walt Davis, who left Kings Island in February of 1984. "The hills were too high and all that energy had to get someplace, and it was all self-destructing. Maintenance was very high; it wasn't easy to fix. We would have had to completely replace the track. My solution was to make one hill and make the whole ride just like a normal coaster. [There'd] be that one hill, and then come back into the station nice and easy, and that's how they [Arrow] built them after that. They built them in different places, that's how they made them after. They learned on us! But it was basically irreparable without a major reinvestment, so it became financially unfeasible. I recommended that [we] either spend a million and a half to replace the track or replace the whole ride and get a new ride."

The park opted for the latter. "I used to call it a great weekend ride. If we had all week to work on it, it'd run great for the weekend, but once we opened full-time, it was just difficult to maintain it and it was an inconvenience for the guests," said Dave Focke, director of park operations. "The downtime was too high, and the guests were displeased. It was a tough decision to make, but we finally made the decision it needed to go."

On November 6, 1984 Kings Island officially announced that *The Bat* would be scrapped. Demolition, which ultimately cost $70,000, began the same day. "Modifications on the ride to improve its operating consistency would be very costly," T. Lewis Hooper said in a statement. "Also, they [the modifications] may not guarantee the ride would perform to the satisfaction of our patrons." *The Bat* remains the shortest-lived roller coaster in Kings Island history, only operating for portions of three seasons.

"I gave the company a lot of credit for that," said loss prevention director Richard Fussner. "There're not too many companies that would take a $3 million investment and cut it up with a torch."

Because of its brief lifespan and problematic history, rumors have swirled for years that the ride killed people or completely derailed, the latter of which does have a kernel of truth. "The front cars came off the track going into the second lift," said Fussner. "The anti-roll-backs, something caught in the dogs on the anti-rollbacks, and the chain was still trying to pull it, and the dogs were holding it or jammed, and luckily we had built a chain link floor underneath the ride in that area just to catch anything that fell from the cars. Well, it dropped down, those first two cars, still connected to the train, dropped down on the screen. Nobody got hurt, it didn't go anywhere else, everybody got helped out and that was the end of that!"

Ruth Voss, park spokeswoman, said that park officials were "looking at a lot of possibilities for the area, but nothing certain at all" had been decided by that time.

WINTERFEST 1984

Kings Island closed on October 4 to begin preparations for Winter-fest. A new puppet show played in the *American Heritage Music Hall* and "Christmas Belles" debuted in the *Columbia Palace*. A new nativity scene was added.

On December 16, 1984 the season's three millionth guest entered the park. It was the first time in Kings Island's history that annual attendance surpassed the three million mark.

A

1985

Kings Island's big new addition for 1985 was *White Water Canyon*, an Intamin river rapids ride located in Rivertown.

"That was a time when white water rides were being built all over the country, and we had one at our park Kings Dominion in Richmond, Virginia, and we had one at our park in Toronto," said Dave Focke. "We were a little bit late getting ours!"

Constructing White Water Canyon included building the trough and rotating loading platform. Courtesy of Dave Focke.

Construction began in March of 1984, and the ride was officially announced on August 13. The *Kings Island and Miami Valley Railroad* closed for a few weeks in June to accommodate construction of the ride.

"Each ride our visitors take will be a unique experience because as the water churns, it creates foaming white water-like river rapids, and each raft will seek its own course," Focke told the press. "They will spin, float, bounce from side to side and rock up and down, at different times along the course."

A natural ravine was used to make the reservoir for the attraction. The 1,680-foot long channel was lined with 5,000 tons of rock from a Wilmington, Ohio quarry. Two hundred different pumps circulated

100,000 gallons of water per minute. Although the "river" appeared deep, its depth only ranged from eighteen inches to two feet.

While advertised as the most expensive addition in Kings Island history at $4 million, it really wasn't, as Wild Animal Habitat cost almost $7 million when it was built in 1974.

"It's one of those rides that keeps its popularity year in and year out, and it's not a ride-it-once and forget it type of attraction," Focke added.

White Water Canyon has been a popular family attraction since its opening. Courtesy of Dave Focke.

Kings Island opened for the 1985 season on April 13. Other new additions included the "New Waves" recording studio in Coney Island, which now occupied the old *Cuddle Up* space, and the "Wunderbar" and "Woodchoppers Ball Revue" shows in the *Festhaus*. The *Wheel of Fortune* Trabant ride was sold to Fantasy Farm park in Middletown, Ohio following the 1984 season. It still operates at DelGrosso's Park in Pennsylvania as *Casino*.

WINTERFEST 1985

Kings Island closed October 6 to begin preparations for Winterfest, which opened November 23. New this year was the "Winter Wonderland" puppet show in the *American Heritage Music Hall* and "Home For the Holidays" in the *Festhaus.*

For the main season, the park set yet another attendance record. 2.98 million people attended Kings Island, beating the previous record from 1984. For the entire year, including Winterfest, more than 3.2 million guests passed through the turnstiles, setting a new attendance record.

TWO NEW PARKS ARE ADDED TO THE CHAIN

Great America in Santa Clara, California opened under hotelier Marriott on March 21, 1976. The park fell into a legal tug-of-war between Marriott, the city of Santa Clara, and Caz Development Company. On April 24, 1985 the city of Santa Clara, who owned the park, decided to ask KECO to manage it for them, clearing the way for Marriott to bow out. KECO would later purchase Great America in 1989.

On December 7, 1985, as part of a local joint venture, Kings Entertainment opened Australia's Wonderland in Sydney, a park that had started development under Taft Broadcasting. Its design was largely based off the other international park in the chain, Canada's Wonderland. Australia's Wonderland featured three themed areas and a signature wooden coaster, *The Bush Beast.*

1986

1986 was Kings Island's 15th season of operation, and so it was cause for celebration. The park underwent a $2 million renovation to the Coney Island section, renamed Coney Mall. The vintage 1925 *Tumble Bug* was removed and sent to the scrapyard, replaced with *Skylab,* a HUSS Giant Enterprise ride with a ninety-foot diameter. The *Flying Eagles* were moved down to the end of Coney Mall along the path from the Mall to Rivertown, with their original spot occupied by an expanded *Dodgem* with forty bumper cars. The original *Dodgem* space was filled with *Putter's Place*, a golf putting arena. The *Flying Carpets* slide was moved to Hanna-Barbera Land, renamed to *Scrappy's Slides*, and replaced on Coney Mall with *Zephyr*, a Zierer Wave Swinger.

The whirling Skylab added a visual highlight to the new Coney Mall. Courtesy of Dave Focke.

A brand new movie theater, *Cinema 180*, was built next to *Zodiac* at the end of Coney Mall. The theater featured a thirty-foot high, 180-degree screen that immersed guests in the film. The mall itself also got a general sprucing-up—a new fountain was added in the midway, and the games buildings got fresh coats of paint.

The Wild Animal Habitat area was expanded to include the entire Adventure Village themed area.

Also featured was the new show "Fascinating Rhythm" in the *American Heritage Music Hall*. Kings Island opened for the 1986 season on April 12 and saw its 40 millionth visitor on August 25.

WINTERFEST 1986

Winterfest preparations began October 5, the end of the regular operating season. Opening November 22, it now included the *Kings Island and Miami Valley Railroad* in addition to the *Carousel*, the *Hanna-Barbera Carousel*, and *Smurf's Enchanted Voyage*.

HEADQUARTERS MOVE

In the summer of 1986, KECO's headquarters moved from Kings Island to Charlotte, North Carolina, where Carowinds was located. Charlotte and Carowinds were centrally located to the other KECO parks and was deemed to have a strong transportation network, making it a good spot for corporate headquarters. The main reason behind the move, however, was that four of the seven KECO corporate executives were from North Carolina. Carowinds would remain the flagship park of the chain until Cedar Fair's acquisition twenty years later in 2006.

1987—VORTEX

Before Kings Island had decided to demolish *The Bat*, Arrow had come up with one final proposal for the ride. "Arrow finally said, 'We'll make you a new track. We'll redesign the ride for you, make it smoother,' and nobody wanted to spend a bunch of money on a ride that we've already got, that we already had, so the company [KECO] negotiated with them [Arrow] to come up with the replacement ride," Jeff Gramke said. "Arrow said, 'We'll build you a replacement ride for that site,' so because *The Bat* was more-or-less kind of a failure on their part, [KECO] was able to negotiate a really good deal to build the *Vortex*."

The park settled on the looping coaster model for *The Bat's* replacement. "We felt with *The Bat* being gone, and at that time we had no continuous track [sit-down] looping coasters," said Dave Focke, director of park operations. "All we had was the *Screamin' Demon*, which was a looper that was a shuttle loop. So we felt we needed a continuous-track looping coaster, and we were able to get one that at that time had more inversions than any other coaster in the world. So we had a first to allow marketing to go out and talk about."

Vortex's trains cut an iconic sight at Kings Island for 32 years. Courtesy of Dave Focke.

"That was a big investment but by then, once you got into the mid-80s, we were on a rotation program where we were in an arms race with Cedar Point," added Mike Meadows, director of finance. "Our season passholders kept asking for bigger and faster, and that's what the *Vortex* was; it was a breakthrough kind of concept."

The $4 million coaster would be record breaking with six inversions, more than any other roller coaster, and a 148-foot tall lift hill, making it the tallest continuous circuit roller coaster in the world.

"The designer that they had on the *Vortex* was a gentleman named Steve Okamoto who had worked for other roller coaster companies out in California, and we knew his work and he did a really, really good job on the *Vortex*," said Gramke. "It's a great design."

"We wanted something that could use the terrain that existed for *The Bat*," Focke added. "We thought initially we might be able to use some of the foundations, but that didn't end up being practical. We just wanted something that had a lot of length, a lot of height, and nonstop action, and we really had that with just one lift and all those inversions; it was just nonstop action once you got off the lift."

The Bat's site proved to be a great location for the coaster. "It was an area of the park that was a high-profile area, very visible from the mall area," said Bill Ossim, assistant rides manager at the time. "It was some[where] we knew we wanted to have...a teen thrill type of attraction. It was what you would consider prime real estate visually for the guests. It was a good area of the park to put such a ride."

Coney Mall was a beehive of activity in the 1986-1987 winter.
Courtesy of Dave Focke.

The unnamed coaster was announced the morning of May 30, 1986. Reggie Whitehead, Kings Island's marketing director, met with general manager T. Lewis Hooper to discuss a possible name for the coaster. "Everybody was going through a whole bunch of names, different types of names," Whitehead said. "I was telling him what names [it should] be, because that comes out of marketing. I told him basically it doesn't matter, the name. It has to have some sort of relationship. But once you come up with a name, once people hear it they have to think, 'That's the name. That's a great name for a ride.' And actually, Lew Hooper named that. I was in his office, and he started thumbing through a dictionary and he said, 'Vortex.' And I said, 'Yeah, that's just fine!'"

"When you are caught in a vortex, or whirlpool, you are completely under its control," Whitehead told the press. "Our new coaster will be like that."

Vertical construction for *Vortex* began in October of 1986, but work on more than 300 concrete footings had begun even earlier. Southern Ohio Fabricating Company of Batavia, Ohio manufactured the supports for *Vortex*, while the track, braking system, and trains were manufactured by Arrow. Fortunately for Kings Island, an extremely mild winter meant the ride was able to be built ahead of schedule. Overall, the coaster would use 1,000 tons of steel.

A welder works to build Vortex. Courtesy of Dave Focke.

Vortex opened on April 11, Kings Island's first day for the 1987 season. On *Vortex's* opening day, 12,350 people waited in line to ride! The next day 11,400 people queued up to wait their turn. To this day,

Vortex's opening weekend is the most heavily attended opening weekend in Kings Island's history.

Dave Focke [left] and Lew Hooper introduce the media to Vortex. From the 1987 Kings Island employee yearbook. Courtesy of Richard Fussner.

Also new for 1987 was "Hot Ice," an ice skating show in the *Festhaus* and "Fantasy," a "musical salute to make-believe" in the *American Heritage Music Hall*. Three new shows were created for the *International Showplace*: "In Concert '87," "Sweet Country Music," and "Yogi's Funtastic Machine" for children. The *Zodiac* double Ferris wheel was removed after the 1986 season and shipped down to Australia's Wonderland, leaving its old pad vacant.

The 1987 main season was the first in Kings Island history to surpass three million guests. Final attendance was 3,137,117, topping 1985's previous best of 2,981,861.

THE DEMON FLIES AWAY

1987 was the first season for *Vortex*, but it would end up being the last for the ten year old *Demon*. Kings Island management felt that the ride was rendered obsolete by the additions of both *King Cobra* and *Vortex* and put the coaster on the market.

Berkely Roberts, the owner of Fun Spot amusement park in Angola, Indiana negotiated with Kings Island to buy *The Demon* and relocate it to his park. But even before the coaster was moved, Roberts did his own transaction and sold the coaster to Camden Park in West Virginia.

The Demon was removed from Kings Island following the 1987 season. It continued to operate as *Thunderbolt Express* at Camden Park until 1999. After standing but not operating for four seasons, the former *Demon* was finally demolished in 2004.

Å

THE SECOND SALE

Taft Broadcasting owned 30% of Kings Entertainment. When Cincinnati-based American Financial Corporation, under Carl H. Lindner Jr., bought Taft in 1987 and began restructuring the company, they particularly liked Taft's stake in the highly-profitable KECO. "We [KECO] didn't think we needed a partner at that time, so we were in conflict with them [American Financial Corporation] and the way to resolve that conflict was to sell them Kings Island, and then we retained a management contract on that," Nelson Schwab explained. As part of the sales deal, KECO had a ten year contract to manage the park, and they retained ownership of their other properties, including Carowinds and Kings Dominion.

The sale of Kings Island to American Financial Corporation for about $150 million was announced on August 19, 1987 and finalized on October 31. "We [KECO] moved forward a separate company without the ownership of Kings Island but with the management of it, so we kept all the employees the same and they remained employees of Kings Entertainment Company, so we just moved forward in that way," said Schwab.

PART III
AMERICAN FINANCIAL

NEW OWNER, SAME PARENTS

*W*interfest opened under the new ownership of American Financial Corporation on November 21, 1987, but with the same management team as before. The only major new addition was an ice rink designed for toddlers in Hanna-Barbera Land.

One notable event for Winterfest '87 was not a ride or a restaurant at all, but rather the filming of a movie. *Fresh Horses*, starring Molly Ringwald, was the first, and so far only, movie to be filmed at the park. Kings Island officials pushed hard for the park's name to be incorporated into the script, but producer Alan Marcil rejected it. "[T]he film is not a commercial for Kings Island," he told *The Cincinnati Enquirer*. "We're not going to accommodate the screenplay for that sort of thing. We won't even do that for Coca-Cola [owner of distributor Columbia Pictures]." *Fresh Horses* was released on November 18, 1988, to generally mixed reviews and a poor box office performance. Critics and locals agreed that its strongest points were the shots of Kings Island's Winterfest and other segments filmed around Cincinnati.

Winterfest ran until January 3, 1988, the first time since 1982 that it operated past New Year's. 1987's attendance soared to new heights, totaling 3,463,586 guests.

GENERAL MANAGER #6: DEAN NAHRUP

T. Lewis Hooper was promoted to president of KECO in March of 1988. Hooper stayed in that position until the company was acquired by Paramount in 1992, after which he retired; sadly, Hooper passed away on May 21, 2006.

Contrasting with Dennis Speigel's sentiments, operations director Dave Focke enjoyed working with Hooper. "If I had to list three men in my life that had the biggest impact, Lew would be right up there at the top," Focke said. "He had a wonderful management style. He really believed that everything is accomplished through his people. He believed the customer was always right and we should treat the customer properly. As we used to say, 'The customer may not always be right, but they are always the customer.'"

Kings Island's finance director, Mike Meadows, also thought very highly of Hooper. "Everywhere he went, he was just such a beloved guy because he understood the business. He took such good care of his people and he was a true gentleman. You would give your all for that man. There was just no question about it. He was the kind of person who knew every employee's name, he knew something unique about them, he worked really hard at his job in every detail and he was incredible. He came through the marketing side, so he really understood how to sell. He really understood product selection. Lew had great instincts about what was going to drive attendance."

With Hooper promoted to KECO president, Kings Island would now have a new leader. Dean Nahrup, who had started at the park in merchandise and worked in a variety of positions throughout the company's properties, including as general manager at both Carowinds and Canada's Wonderland, was promoted to general manager of Kings Island in early 1988.

AMERICAN FINANCIAL CORPORATION CHANGES

KECO CEO Nelson Schwab recalls that not much changed after Kings Entertainment sold the park to American Financial, since the same management team remained in place. "It [employees and management remained] pretty much the same. We tried to run it as if it were our own. We felt an obligation to American Financial to do the best job we could."

"I think that's one of the things I liked about American Financial, and when Nelson came over [from Taft's corporate development division] to run the [KECO] parks…it was a very smooth transition," said marketing director Reggie Whitehead.

"Reggie Whitehead and I basically had reporting relationships with the AFC [American Financial] management team," said finance director Mike Meadows. "He and I, along with Lew [Hooper], we'd go down [to AFC headquarters] and do an annual review of the marketing plan and the budget, and Carl Lindner was just an amazing person. He was so sharp. He'd put you through a three or four hour meeting, very detailed review, and his retention and analytical skills were amazing."

By all accounts, Lindner was a hands-off person when it came to Kings Island. "The only time we saw Carl was on the annual reviews, the budgets," said Meadows, adding that KECO president Lew Hooper was the primary contact with both American Financial Corporation board member Bob Lintz and its CEO, Carl Lindner.

Even though Lindner was hands-off for Kings Island, he still commanded a level of respect. Jeff Gramke, former manager of engineering and construction, recalled one memory of Lindner's Christmas party. "It was kind of funny. We were invited to a Christmas party, all the management that worked here, and I had a family event. I had another family thing, a big family get-together for the same night, so I RSVP'd and declined. Well, I got called into the [Kings Island] general manager's office after the party and [he] said 'You said no to Carl.' I said, 'No, I had another family thing and I couldn't go.' He said, 'That's not good. If Carl invites you to a special event, you go!'"

Even with his hands-off approach, Lindner used his influence to promote certain changes at the park. One area he and American Financial addressed soon after taking over was the park police. "He [Lindner] felt that the park police may be giving a little bit more of a rougher appearance than he wished, so they were not to wear their sidearms, which they did not think was such a great idea!" said Perry Denehy, an employee in the park's Fire and Safety Department at the time. "The sergeant was allowed to have a sidearm, but none of the others were allowed to have an open carry weapon, including, we had a Hanna-Barbera character named Quick-Draw McGraw. His gun was taken out of his holster!"

Kings Island management spoke highly of working with American Financial. "They kept an eye on things. They were very supportive of our plans to maintain the facility and our capital needs, so they were a good owner to have," said Dave Focke. Bill Ossim, assistant rides manager at the time of the sale and who was promoted to rides manager in early 1988, added, "Because it was American Financial, it gave us a hometown pride kind of thing a little bit. It was kind of nice to be owned by a local company. But day-to-day, [there were] not a lot of differences there."

"They loved Kings Island and they were very, very supportive," Mike Meadows added. "Culturally, it didn't have much impact at all on the folks that were working there. They did a really nice job of saying, 'Look, we know you guys are a great management team, we really respect what you're doing, we just want to go through this, we want to participate in the decisions about how much capital you get.' They did a very disciplined job of reviewing our budget assumptions and all of our strategic initiatives...American Financial Corporation, from everything I could see, was just an organization that really understood that if you were at the top of the food chain as far as best practices, the way you operate, you're going to do the best. Carl Lindner had an absolute commitment to being the best."

The separate ownership and management teams resulted in a

unique relationship when it came to adding rides. "There would be a capital expenditure plan that was normally at minimum a three-year plan, but could be as much as five years, which would be a little less detailed," explained Kings Island rides manager Ossim. "We would always have what we were looking for, what new ride we were looking for, what we could put in and what that ride wanted to hit. There was usually...a three to four year rotation on what market we wanted to hit, and that was usually decided between talking internally with the KECO group and our people—operations, maintenance— and we would talk about that, and then the [Kings Island] general manager would put together our capital expenditure plan and present it to the AFC [American Financial] people."

American Financial Corporation gave the park lots of capital for continued growth. As finance director Meadows explained, "Actually, I think it was...a little easier to get money '87 to '92, simply because we had tremendous margins, and it was the kind of business where they rewarded success, and we hit our numbers virtually every one of those years. We made our bonus every year, so you had to hit your targets. We were getting rewarded and they basically rewarded us."

Å

FALLING INTO 1988

The first significant addition during American Financial Corporation's ownership had already been planned earlier by Kings Entertainment.

The Demon was replaced with an Intamin Spillwater ride called *Amazon Falls*. KECO had seen large success with an identical attraction, *Diamond Falls*, at Kings Dominion, so the company decided it would be perfect to install at Kings Island. The $1.8 million *Amazon Falls* would feature an 815-foot long trough with a fifty-foot incline and a thirty-four foot drop in the Wild Animal Habitat section.

While manufacturing of parts was already taking place by the time of the announcement, actual on-site construction at Kings Island didn't start until after the park closed for the 1987 main season on October 4. Media previews for *Amazon Falls* took place on April 8, 1988, and the ride premiered on April 9, opening day for the new season.

Kings Island also spent $3 million on live shows for 1988, which included two new offerings in the *American Heritage Music Hall*: "Live at the Palace," the park's new premier musical, and "Sea Dreams," a new 3D movie.

WINTERFEST 1988

Kings Island closed for the main season on October 2. Winterfest opened November 19, with the biggest new addition being a tent on International Street set up for Ozark craftspeople selling their home-made wares. A new show opened in the *Festhaus* entitled "A Hometown Holiday."

Å

1989—KINGS ISLAND MAKES A BIG SPLASH

"I went out to Kings Island in 1982 [from Taft Broadcasting corporate] and I was reading in the IAAPA [International Association of Amusement Parks and Attractions] paper they issued on a weekly basis, and [there was] a lot of talk around waterparks," said Kings Island finance director Mike Meadows. "I managed to get [then-general manager] Butch [Bush] to send Tom Nowlin, the marketing director, and myself to this waterpark convention, and in those years all the waterparks were basically independent, stand-alone attractions and units. I had pitched Butch about the idea, when we were getting slammed on a Saturday or a Sunday...we just had huge lines at all of our rides. We had serious capacity issues about where do you put the people? I said to Butch, I said, 'Man, if we could throw a waterpark into the mix, people going to and from the waterpark as well as all the people that might be tied up in a lazy river and all the slides, we could probably absorb 10,000 people, and actually they'd be happy as opposed to being angry about standing in a long line to ride a flat ride.'"

"At the time, they [Taft Broadcasting corporate] didn't want to hear it," added Walt Davis, director of park operations at the time. "We had a site picked and feasibility done and everything, but corporate said, 'Why should we spend ten to fifteen million on a waterpark when we could spend that on another broadcast property or another radio station and make a profit margin of 65% instead of a profit margin on a waterpark of 35%?' I tried for a couple of years to get them; they just wouldn't come off it." In February of 1984, Davis left Kings Island to start his own waterpark, The Beach, which opened in 1985 across the highway from Kings Island.

Aerial concept of WaterWorks. Courtesy of Dave Focke.

Even before American Financial took over ownership, Kings Island management moved quickly, deciding they just could not abdicate that segment of business to The Beach. "We had been looking at a possible waterpark product when The Beach opened, and then once they opened and they were successful in that, we felt that it would be strategic for us to get in the game at that point," said rides manager Bill Ossim. "The idea just morphed from, we were already looking at it when The Beach opened, and then we did some more research and looked at what the possibilities were. And we just felt that strategically it would be a big product that would encourage multi-day visits from tourists [and] also really increase the season pass sales as well, because that park had a lot of season passholders who would come out and enjoy the park some days and go to the water park on other days. It encouraged longer visits as well; people would ride some rides and then go to the waterpark in the afternoon or evening. It did encourage longer visits as well as multiple visits."

"We had done this elsewhere. We had waterparks, at Carowinds I know for sure, and we had found that it had really become very attractive, particularly to season passholders," said Kings Entertainment Company CEO Nelson Schwab. "It became almost a swim club to them and they could go in the park too."

Planning for the waterpark began in 1987, before the American Financial purchase. The decision was made to place the waterpark in a section of park property that played host to a portion of the *Kings Island and Miami Valley Railroad*. The twelve-acre WaterWorks was announced September 8, 1988 and was advertised as the first themed area added to Kings Island since Lion Country Safari in 1974. It would also be the most expensive addition since the $7 million safari, costing $4.2 million. Its main attractions were:

- *The Plunge*: 70-foot body slide
- *White Lightning*: 55-foot body slide
- *The Streak* and *Thunder Run*: Two "multi-bump" body slides featured on the same complex as *The Plunge* and *White Lightning*
- *Ultra Twister*: Intertwined body slides
- *Bonzai Pipeline*: Three enclosed body slides
- *Sidewinder*: Twin inner tube slides
- *The Helix*: A complex of four body slides
- *Kings Mills Run*: A ¼ mile long lazy river
- *Splash Island*: Children's area with pint-sized slides
- *Snack Stop*: Food stand serving hot dogs and pretzels
- *On Shore*: Gift shop selling swimwear and WaterWorks branded items

"They did not have a lot of sunbathing. They had the attractions that you would change into your swimming suit, go there, ride them, and then get your clothes back on and come into the main park and spend money on games and buying things and eating. [There was a] sort of apprehension that if all of our guests end up just laying around the swimming pool all day, they're really not spending the money, the per cap that we'd like," said Perry Denehy, who was with the park's Fire and Safety Department at the time.

WaterWorks would be included in the cost of park admission and treated as another section of the park—not as a separate gated park. The only way to access WaterWorks was via the train or a pathway from Rivertown. "That was the other thing that I had to really fight for was the concept of it not being an additional pay tier," Meadows said. "I kept insisting that one of the things that would really benefit us the most is if we could include it in the same price so that we could spread out all of this attendance throughout everything. It really did work to our benefit. We were the first ones to do it and everybody followed. Everybody. Kings Island led that and we did it."

As soon as Kings Island closed for the main season on October 2, 1988, work on the waterpark began immediately. The *Kings Island and Miami Valley Railroad* would have to be rerouted to accommodate WaterWorks while adding a second station for the waterpark. More than 1,300 feet of track was rerouted in time for Winterfest's opening on November 19, and the train was able to operate for the entirety of Winterfest.

Kings Island opened for the 1989 season on April 8. WaterWorks, which was scheduled to open the same day, did not. Rainy weather resulted in the grand opening being postponed until April 22. "Since February, it's been a couple days of rain, a couple days of dry, but not enough long stretches when we could make real progress," Dave Focke told the press.

With the weather finally cooperating, WaterWorks opened in stages. Nine of the fifteen slides opened April 22 along with the *King Mills Run* lazy river attraction; the remaining six slides debuted the following weekend. The *Splash Island* children's area opened in May.

Even with the delay, the opening date still proved to be a problem. "We were trying to figure out when do we open it," Focke said. "Do we open it like your neighborhood swimming pool on Memorial Day weekend? Or because you're really not getting submerged in water, can we open it earlier? We had planned to open it when the park opened in mid-April. The weather was cool, and we didn't really have much success for that. But we learned on that year and started opening it later."

Other challenges of operating a waterpark had to be addressed. Initially, Kings Island's ride department covered all rides in the dry park as well as every position in the waterpark. It proved to be an onerous undertaking for that team. "...Expanding our department [Rides] to take on all the lifeguards and operations and facilities, and for a few years we did everything including the food service and merchandise areas," said Ossim. "That fell under ride operations for a few years and then I also took on admissions, and then I think that's when we gave those departments back!"

Kings Island's waterpark is still a cool relief on hot summer days. Courtesy of Dave Focke.

In addition to the new WaterWorks area, five new stage shows debuted for the 1989 season including "Dancing in the City" in the *American Heritage Music Hall* and "Surf's Up" in *International Showplace*.

1989 ended up being the best main season in park history up to that time. 3.17 million people turned out (exclusive of Winterfest), besting 1987's 3.14 million people. This year was also the final season for the *Der Spinnen Keggers* attraction, which was removed and scrapped.

WINTERFEST 1989

Kings Island closed for Winterfest preparations on October 8 and reopened November 18. The major new addition to Winterfest was a new stage show, "Santa's Toy Factory," presented in the *American Heritage Music Hall.*

Å

1990

The 1990 season kicked off on April 14. The success of WaterWorks led to the decision to install another water slide just a year after the waterpark had been introduced. The 700-foot long *Rushing River* opened at a cost of $1 million.

Over on the dry side of the park, the $2 million *Flight Commander*, an Intamin Flight Trainer, opened on the spot of the old *Zodiac*, which had been vacant since 1987. "We were looking for a thrill ride, but not a fully teen thrill ride, but kind of a family thrill ride that had some excitement to it but wasn't a *Vortex*," said Bill Ossim. "It probably didn't really fit the teen thrill, but was kind of a family thrill, which would be a softer type of ride. It was a ride that we felt had a good appeal also from the people watching it with the pods turning back over itself, going in and out."

"It gave an interesting ride experience, something we didn't have before," added Dave Focke.

KECO had also previously installed Flight Trainers at Kings Dominion and Great America in 1989.

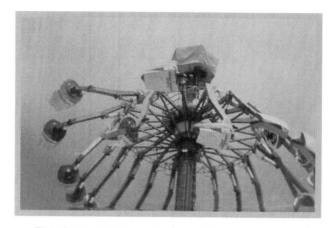

Flight Commander delivered a unique ride experience when it opened in 1990. Courtesy of Lelia Andrews.

The major new show for 1990 was "It's Magic!" featuring the award-winning magician Mark Wilson and dancer Tara Patrick, using the stage name of Carmen Electra, in the *American Heritage Music Hall.*

On July 15 Mary Burns of Columbia, Kentucky became the park's 50-millionth visitor and received a free trip to Great America, spending money, and season passes for the 1991 season.

The main 1990 season was a record breaking one: 3,209,777 guests, the highest in park history up to that time.

WINTERFEST 1990

Kings Island closed to begin setting up Winterfest October 14 and reopened November 17. The newest addition was "Laser Night," a laser light show over the *Royal Fountain* skating rink.

1991—ADVENTURE EXPRESS

Kings Island announced their 1991 coaster, *Adventure Express*, in September of 1990. "There had been a couple other ones built similar to that around the country. They had one at Disney, they had a little mine train ride at Disney, so I think it made sense to do something that we could do in-house with building the wood structures and then have somebody just make the track...It was just another way to get a coaster in for not spending a ton of money," said Jeff Gramke, Kings Island's manager of engineering and construction.

Adventure Express has thrilled families since opening in 1991.
Courtesy of Rick Bastrup.

After a slew of record-breaking coasters, the family-oriented *Adventure Express* was a change of pace from the park's previous additions. "It was just a way to balance out our offerings," Dave Focke explained. "Every year we'd decide, do we want to do a family attraction? Do we want to do a children's attraction? Or do we want to do an extreme thrill, teen attraction? You had to balance it because the popularity life of a teen attraction was limited. That market segment could be very fickle. It's the hot ride this year, but now somebody built one that's a little bigger, a little longer, a little faster, they'll forget about it. Where a family attraction like *Adventure Express* or *White Water Canyon* keeps its legs year after year."

A hilly location was chosen for the ride with a footprint in Wild Animal Habitat. "I think [the location was chosen] partly because of the terrain over there so that the ride could take advantage of some of that terrain," said Bill Ossim. "On one hand, it helped a little bit on construction costs because you didn't have to build much structure and that sort of thing, but at the same time we were working on hillsides and foundations were a little tough."

The park partnered with California-based R&R Creative Amusement Designs to complete a theming package for *Adventure Express* that naturally fit the Wild Animal Habitat section. "We kind of had the idea of the Lost Kingdom," Focke said. "The initial concept when you left the station was to go down and have a dead-end track to the side that you thought you were going to go on, but all of a sudden you duck to the right and go down into the first tunnel. We hired R&R to come up with a presentation, and they did storyboards and animation and everything and we liked it so we went with it."

"Indiana Jones was very popular, so they [Kings Island] had an idea that they wanted to do something like that with a coaster," added Rick Bastrup, president of R&R Creative Amusement Designs. "And of course the coaster went all along the side of the hill and all that, so that's where we came up with the concept for the various tunnels, the themed tunnels and so forth that it went through." Bastrup even ended up naming the coaster. "I usually name everything that we do, that's part of what I do, so I called it *Adventure Express* for a working name and they [Kings Island] went out to a couple of ad agencies and said, 'What's the name of the coaster? What could we do?'" Bastrup said. "And they had all these people work on it and contests and two ad agencies and when they came back, they said, 'We're going to call it *Adventure Express!*'"

One design choice that has left countless guests scratching their heads over the years is the finale—a lift hill...*up into* the station. "It had to be [a lift hill at the end] because we wanted the station up where people could get to it, so we had to build the station up on top and most of the ride goes down into the valley...so we just had to put another lift in to get them back up to the station," Gramke explained. "And then that became a huge theming thing. They decided to do the big theming tunnel as part of the ride so instead of just having it be anticlimactic, riding a lift back up into the station, it had stuff going on."

A custom musical score brought the final tunnel to life. "We do all the music tracks and all of that, so I went into the studio when we got the music from that and got a big kettle drum, and I played the kettle drum through our reverb and stuff to add the big booming sound to it!" Bastrup said. "It was a lot of fun to work on, something real different." In addition to the tunnels, the "jungle" floor would be covered in fog. "They [Kings Island] left it [the fog machines] on, the first time they turned it on," Bastrup laughed. "We came back in the morning, it was [a] real cool [temperature], and the entire ride had disappeared because the fog was sitting over the entire ride because it wasn't windy! It was like, 'Where's the ride?'"

To accommodate the entrance and queue for the ride, the *Flying Dutchman* was removed and sold to Kentucky Kingdom in Louisville. The Oktoberfest *Ferris Wheel* was also removed and sold to Liberty-land in Memphis, Tennessee.

They were the last two flat rides removed under the ownership and management period of Kings Entertainment Company, a "purge" that ultimately resulted in the removal of six family-friendly attractions over five years. Focke explained, "It's really a combination of two things. One is reaching the end of their service life, maintenance cost getting too high. Then the guest acceptance, the guest interest in a ride. As you kept adding more attractions, you had to balance it out or you would have too much. So it was a combination. We'd analyze ridership on rides and make decisions based on maintenance cost and ridership."

Adventure Express had a press preview on April 12 and opened for the 1991 season, along with the rest of Kings Island, on April 13. "It was the [night before] opening day and we were up all night and Sally [Corporation, who fabricated the animatronic drummers] was working on all the animatronics and they just weren't quite getting the drummers right," Bastrup said. "Those are big pieces to be moving, you know, pneumatically and so forth. Anyway, we're still up there trying to get it to work and then they did the opening.

"Well, in the opening they had [business partner Richard Ferrin] and me standing there, and they introduce us and they said, 'Okay, now these are the guys who designed it and we're going to put them in the front car and they're going to take the first ride!' We had never ridden it before because it was being worked on. So all the press and everybody got in the train behind us, we're going 'Oh no, I sure hope everything's working!' So we went through, the fog was working, that was great, the red lights and that, it was spooky and all the things were working. So we get into that last lift, as it started going up we're going, 'Please work!' All of a sudden, all the drummers came on there, 'Poom, poom, poom,' they're pounding on the drums and all of that. It got to the top, it came in and we thought, 'Wow.' We really would have been embarrassed if it didn't work! Well, later on, we found out that all the people from Sally were behind the drummers pushing them manually. Their whole crew was there working them manually...They saved us! So that was the opening of *Adventure Express*."

"BLACK SUNDAY"

On June 9, 1991, three people were killed at the park in two unrelated accidents within an hour.

Tim Binning, 22, was electrically shocked in the Oktoberfest pond at 8:48 p.m. when he touched a fountain spraying up from an aerator pump. His friend William Haithcoat, 21, jumped into the pond to pull Binning out but was also electrically shocked. Park security guard Darrell Robertson, 20, saw both men go into the water, jumped in himself to attempt a rescue, and was shocked as well. Robertson and Haithcoat were pronounced dead at 10 p.m. at the University of Cincinnati Medical Center. Binning was taken to Bethesda North Hospital in Montgomery and released June 12.

An investigation traced the source of the electricity to a faulty aerator pump that had been installed without a federally-mandated ground fault circuit interrupter. Kings Island was fined $23,500 over the pond accident by OSHA; within a month following the incident, the park installed GFCIs on all of their electrical outlets.

Less than an hour after the pond incident, Candy Taylor, 32, tragi-cally plunged to her death from *Flight Commander* at 9:45 pm. Taylor, who had been visiting the park with two friends, had been drinking heavily throughout the day. Taylor boarded *Flight Commander* after her friends and sat alone in capsule four. After boarding, she passed out and slid from her inside seat to the outside seat, which was empty and unrestrained. As Taylor slid, her leg caught on the joystick, rotating the capsule. Halfway through the second rotation, Taylor fell sixty feet from the ride and landed on the landscaped hillside in front of *Flight Commander*. Taylor was pronounced dead at 10:34 p.m. at Miami Valley Hospital in Dayton.

An investigation by the Ohio Department of Agriculture laid the blame on Intamin for a design flaw. Limp passengers could slide from beneath their restraint and into the seat next to theirs. "The restraints should have been designed...to keep her in her seat no matter what condition she was in," said Department of Agriculture director Fred Dailey.

"We went through a lot of interviews with the state inspectors and trying to determine what happened and whether there was any mechanical failure or anything like that, and then again it was determined that there wasn't," said Bill Ossim. "It was just a real tough two weeks there going through all that. The one thing that I just continued to lean on was the training and the safety procedures and our safety systems, and that our folks performed and did everything they were supposed to and they really did. Still, at the end of the day, it was a very difficult time."

A poor economy and news of the deaths negatively affected park attendance that year. Turnstile clicks for the 1991 main season dropped 10% from 1990 to 2.85 million. *Flight Commander* would remain closed for the rest of the 1991 season, but reopened for 1992 with extensive safety modifications.

WINTERFEST 1991

Kings Island closed October 13 to get ready for Winterfest, opening back up November 23. *Smurf's Enchanted Voyage* was closed for the transformation into *Phantom Theater*, so in its place the park opened

Dodgem and *Les Taxis*. The two carousels and the *Kings Island and Miami Valley Railroad* remained open for the event. 1991 had the highest ride count of any Winterfest up to that time with five rides open.

A new show ran in the *Festhaus*, "Snowdrift Inn." A new *Fun Station* activity tent for children was located beneath the *Eiffel Tower* and featured cookie decorating, crafts, and a marionette show.

$$\textstyle\unicode{x1F5FC}$$

20TH ANNIVERSARY—PHANTOM THEATER

For Kings Island's 20th season, the park refreshed Hanna-Barbera Land, the first renovation to that section since 1982.

The biggest change would be the removal of *Smurf's Enchanted Voyage*. "We liked the indoor attraction, it was air-conditioned, folks liked it in the summertime, but we thought that the story was getting a little stale and needed some freshening," explained Dave Focke.

For its replacement, the park turned to the many comments guests had left in park surveys. "We would look at those and review those during the season, at the end of the season, and look at our marketing department, what they were looking for, and we would always, every year, get comments, 'You guys need a haunted house! You need a haunted house!'" recalled Bill Ossim. "So we delivered a haunted house!"

Phantom Theater was a $3.5 million effort intended to take the dark ride in that building to the next level. "We were trying to do the regional park version of the *Haunted Mansion* at Disney, on a regional park budget instead of a Disney budget!" Focke laughed.

The park once again brought on R&R Creative Amusement Designs to design the ride. "We were working on *Adventure Express*, so they showed us the old dark ride, essentially the building, and said they wanted to do something different in there, and that's how we did it because we were already doing *Adventure Express*, we already had that relationship with the park people there," explained the firm's president, Rick Bastrup.

Phantom Theater featured a host of colorful characters. Courtesy of Rick Bastrup.

Bastrup and his team got to work writing the story for the eerie new ride, which would be based around a haunted theater. "They [Kings Island] wanted to do something in the vein of the *Haunted Mansion* at Disney," Bastrup continued. "Not copy it, but they wanted that kind of a level and we ratcheted it up a little bit with the music and all that. It was meant to be a little scary, but more funny and fun with all the characters—the Great Garbanzo and all these kind of goofy characters that lurked around the theater. So basically I came up with the story that these aren't ghosts necessarily, they're phantoms. Once the theater closed, they refused to leave the vaudevillian era and so they all hang out in the old theater."

The boat flume was removed and replaced with an Omnimover-type system, nearly identical to the Doombuggies used on the *Haunted Mansion*. "The capacity [of the Omnimover] is tremendous compared to a boat because it's just continuously moving," Bastrup explains. "You just get onto it with a rotating walkway and capacity was one thing. It just moves whereas a boat is one individual boat at a time going through. Plus...dealing with water is always tough. You've got rust and leaks and filters and all of those things. So I think the [dry dark] ride is the easier way to go, particularly indoors it's tougher working with water."

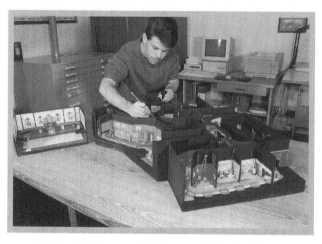

R&R Creative Amusement Designs created a detailed scale model while designing Phantom Theater. Courtesy of Rick Bastrup.

Thirty-eight animatronics would be added to the ride, along with many other clever special effects and illusions, some of which were first popularized in the Victorian era. "When you go back through it, we had two places where we had projected images," Bastrup describes. "As you walked in through the lobby and that, we had Maestro, of course, playing away on the organ, then turning around and talking to the crowd to entertain them while they were in the queue line. Then we had some reverse-image statue carvings as you walked farther up in the queue line. So some of the effects from *Haunted Mansion* we used, Pepper's Ghost, those things have been around for a hundred years."

Most impressive of all was the ride's climax: a spectacular Pepper's Ghost illusion a la the *Haunted Mansion* ballroom. "They [Kings Island] did want one effect which was a copy from the *Haunted Mansion*, and that was the theater scene," said Bastrup. "They wanted to do a thing with the reflected images on the glass, so that's where we came up with the theater scene where all these various things are happening and people are sitting out in the audience, and that was the same kind of effect that *Haunted Mansion* has in their dining room scene because you go by and you see the characters in the reflection. Actually, you're looking at glass and the characters are below and above you and are being lit and are reflecting on the glass, but they look like a ghost."

Thirty-eight animatronics were built by AVG Technologies for Phantom Theater. Courtesy of Rick Bastrup.

Bastrup also tried creating a more visceral experience for the riders, such as in the lighting panel scene, rather than simply riding past sets. "As you came through, the character would talk and say, 'Hey, what are you doing here,' or whatever, and then he would turn the lights off and he had a flashlight in his hand, and then he would play the flashlight across your eyes and across your face, then [he] would switch it [the main lights] back on again," Bastrup said. "All of a sudden you became part of it [the attraction]. The light was shining in your eyes, the lights were off, and it was like you were being touched by the characters there."

The installation and construction of the ride presented some challenges. Bastrup commented, "That piece of glass [for the theater scene] was so huge, it had to be custom-made and they had to bring it into the building before anything else was done so they could build the ride around it because you wouldn't be able to get that glass in once the ride was built around it."

Dave Focke recalled that the building's transformation "wasn't too bad other than we had to get in and build a lot of wood platforms to hold the show elements. Because...the drive system is underneath the tracks...everything has to be raised up. Doing that Pepper's Ghost experience near the end, those were huge sheets of glass that had to be brought in there so we could get that ghost appearance in that scene. Our HVAC engineer, Everett Bond, had a great time creating; near the end in front of the furnace, he put a heater straight above it so you'd blast the riders with heat to simulate the furnace!"

Real antiques from the vaudevillian era helped make the environment come to life. "When we were dressing the place out, once we got the characters and stuff in, we went to antique shops in Cincinnati and we're going down into some dingy, dungy-type things and stuff and we picked up a lot of props that we used throughout the ride," Bastrup said. "Like the hanging pictures that are around and that kind of thing. And actually, when we bought the hanging pictures, they had round glass...We put those in because they really looked cool, and once we put the lights on, we had to take glass off because they were picking up all the show lighting and it was reflecting it all over! So you learn something new all the time when you're working on this stuff. But we got a lot of the props like in the prop room from local shops and antique stores."

Phantom Theater's installation ended up being a little bit of a race against time. "The night before we opened, [business partner] Richard [Ferrin] and I spent the entire night in the ride finishing focusing the lights and putting some of the gels in and that. We finished at like eight in the morning, ran to the hotel, changed, came for the grand opening! But we've done many, many themed rides, so that's typical. It always takes longer because there's so many moving parts, getting the music right, adjusting everything."

Phantom Theater opened on April 11, 1992. "People loved it,"

Bastrup said. "We rode it a number of times. I actually flew my mom and dad in, they're both gone now, but I flew them in to ride it and they just loved it."

For Focke, *Phantom Theater* was one of the most memorable projects that he worked on. "When you do animation like that, you start out by an artist doing a clay maquette, a figure being about that big," Focke said. "When I left Kings Island, they gave me...all the maquettes! I've got all the maquettes of the Maestro, the Great Garbanzo, my favorite was the Usher, beckoning, 'Right this way!'"

"We had a great time," Bastrup concluded. "We loved working from Kings Island, [they had] really good people and [it was an] enjoyable experience. Even though we were still hanging lights ten minutes before the first ride, but that's all part of the fun! Part of the adventure."

Kings Island opened for the 1992 season on April 11. A small children's coaster, *Scooby Zoom*, was added to the space formerly occupied by a portion of the *Smurf's Enchanted Voyage* queue. Part of the building was renovated to become the *Enchanted Theater*, featuring new live shows. Added to Hanna-Barbera Land were *Red Baron's Biplanes* and *Flintstone's Flyers* (replacing *Winnie Witch's Cauldrons*). *Jetson's Spaceport* was the new name for *Flintstones Flyboys*.

A new 20th anniversary parade was also added, starting at Hanna-Barbera Land, going out to the International Street bandstand for a production number, then heading back to Hanna-Barbera Land.

Two major new shows were added: "Escapade" at the *American Heritage Music Hall* and "Reflections on Ice" at the *Festhaus*. Kings Island also debuted its television 20th Anniversary Special on May 28, which was hosted by Beverly Hills 90210 star Jason Priestly. "I remember we operated a lot of rides during that and he [Jason Priestly] seemed like a good guy to work with and all of that, but as with all of those things there's like three hours of sitting around for two minutes of action, and then three hours of sitting around," Ossim recalled. "It made for some long days."

Å

THE THIRD SALE

The late '80s and early '90s signaled a massive change in the amusement world—the rise of the big corporations. Kings Entertainment CEO Nelson Schwab III began looking for opportunities to help keep the KECO-owned parks current in the dramatically-changing industry. "We had gotten to a point where the major players in the industry were all corporations like Disney or Anheuser-Busch and Time-Warner," Schwab explained. "We [KECO] were the odd man out as far as size, and so we were concerned that somebody would try to do something that would really hurt us competitively."

Kings Island finance director Mike Meadows shed another light on the state of the company. "Nelson, Lew [Hooper], and Butch [Bush] very generously reconfigured the original LBO [leveraged buy-out] to include all the direct reports to the general managers in what they called a phantom stock deal. This had the desired effect of retention of key management talent. Eventually, some of the guys were approaching retirement age, and they were tired of working the nights and the weekends and the holidays and kept asking about potential buyers."

When KECO began looking around at potential partners, they found that New York City-based Paramount Communications Inc. was also looking at new ways to leverage their brands. "I think Nelson and Lew and Butch felt pressure to try to get a deal put together [due to the phantom stock deal and certain management wanting to retire] and were really happy when Paramount said they wanted to do a deal," Meadows added. "We were out shopping for buyers for probably three years."

"We just started talking, and the more we talked the more it just made sense to do that," Schwab continued. "They saw value in taking all the brands they had from Paramount Studios primarily and using those in the parks."

While initially just planning on having Paramount as a corporate partner, as negotiations continued it became a 100% sale. The deal would include complete ownership of Carowinds, Kings Dominion, Great America, and KECO's 20% stake in Canada's Wonderland.

That left KECO's unique situation at Kings Island. KECO had a ten-year management contract on the park, but as talks between KECO and Paramount intensified, Carl Lindner felt that it would be pointless to retain the contract for a management company that wouldn't technically exist following the Paramount sale. Feeling he had no other choice, Lindner decided to end the contract and take over management of the park himself following the sale of the rest of the parks to Paramount. In January 1992, Lindner created a new division of American Financial Corporation, Kings Island Company, and appointed Richard Belmont, a bank executive with no theme park experience, as president of the division with the intent that they would manage the park following the termination of KECO's contract on December 31, 1992.

Mike Meadows explained, "In our annual [KECO] management meeting in January or February of '92, all the Kings Island guys were saying goodbye to all the other guys because we thought, 'This is it, we're going to end up going with Carl Lindner and you guys are all going to go with Paramount...We had been told that we'd still have a job, [but] we'd be working [directly] for Carl."

But as things turned out, American Financial and Kings Island would get involved in the transaction after all. "During our negotiations we recommended to them [Paramount] that if they were serious about this business that they should approach American Financial about Kings Island ownership to coincide with that," Schwab explained.

Paramount approached Lindner, who ironically at one time was Paramount's largest single shareholder. Lindner was reluctant to part with the park. But Paramount "approached us with an offer we couldn't refuse," said American Financial spokeswoman Sandra Heimann. After much negotiating, Lindner eventually agreed to sell Kings Island to Paramount.

With details of the two sales ironed out, the announcement was made July 31, 1992; both transactions closed on the same day,

October 1. The entire deal would cost over $400 million—with more than $200 million going to the Kings Island sale alone. The KECO parks were now reunited and back under one ownership umbrella, with KECO's minority stake in Australia's Wonderland sold to a group of Australian investors. Paramount created a new subsidiary, Paramount Parks, whose headquarters would remain in Charlotte. Nelson Schwab would remain in charge as the CEO of Paramount Parks.

The reaction of Kings Island management was "kind of mixed," said Bill Ossim. "Knowing that we would become part of this big company and just the unknown of what exactly that meant...The opportunities seemed pretty good. We now had all these intellectual properties that we would be able to leverage a little bit to give a ride recognition. The Paramount brand was a good, strong brand, the library was huge that we could tap into, plus the things that they had coming up in the future. It was a little bit mixed, but knowing that these opportunities would then be there felt like there were going to be very positive things in the future."

"I think they knew about movies, we knew about theme parks, so they pretty much left us alone," said Kings Island marketing director Reggie Whitehead. "That worked out well because we'd had a span there of having record years. Year after year in attendance. They just wanted to put their characters and stuff inside to give them more exposure. We were fine with that and thought it would be something people enjoy. That was not a very difficult transition."

Other officials were just relieved that Kings Island would not end up being a standalone property under Lindner. "I think if he'd have just kept it as a one-alone park, it would have been a negative, especially now" said Jeff Gramke. "Part of the advantage of being a part of a huge amusement park group is you have a lot of leverage with ride manufacturers. If we had been a stand-alone park, it would have been very difficult to build, for instance, B&M [Bolliger & Mabillard] rides. Because B&M only builds four or five rides a year worldwide and you have to buy B&M rides several years in advance, you have to get into their queue to buy something. It would have been tough as a stand-alone company to do that."

"We benefited so much by being able to work collaboratively with one another," Meadows said. "We had really good groups in the finance, the HR, all of those areas, we really worked well together and I think that was a big benefit for us to have one another. One, we'd go visit each other and see what we had changed and what was working at one park. Being a standalone park, I think the resources would have been there, but I think it would have been difficult for us to stay as current as when you're in a larger organization. That would have been my primary concern, had we gone forward just with AFC [American Financial Corporation]. I know we would have gotten great support. I know they would have been willing to pay for us to continue professional development on certain initiatives. There was never a question about their commitment to trying to be the best."

PART IV
PARAMOUNT PARKS

BECOMING A MOVIE PARK

*T*he sale to Paramount was finalized October 1, 1992. That same day Kings Island named a new general manager, Alexander "Al" Weber Jr. Weber was a long-timer in the amusement industry, getting his start at Coney Island as a seasonal employee. When Kings Island opened, he became the park's first director of park operations. In 1980 Taft Broadcasting moved him to Carowinds, then later to Hanna-Barbera Land in Houston. In 1985 he was appointed general manager of Great America; several years later, on October 1, 1992, he was promoted to general manager of Kings Island, the park's first general manager under Paramount ownership.

Dean Nahrup, the park's previous general manager, left the amusement industry completely following the Paramount sale.

WINTERFEST 1992

Kings Island closed on October 11 to begin preparing for Winterfest's 10th anniversary season. "Winterfest was on the one hand a very successful thing for our guests," explained Nelson Schwab, CEO of Paramount Parks. "On the other hand, it was a huge imposition on the staff. It became a second season. You had to close the park down and then open a good part of the park again for Winterfest. Then close Winterfest down, and get ready to open the park in April. It was a big deal there and so we thought, with the introduction of the Paramount product, it would be an even bigger job to open the park with all the re-theming and everything."

So on November 20 came the announcement that 1992 would be the last season for Winterfest. For years, the blame for ending the beloved event has been cast toward Paramount. However, the decision to end Winterfest had been made before Paramount purchased the park. "We were looking at a season that ran probably about forty-five days, maybe, at the most, probably even less than that, and the bulk of that business was on Friday [and] Saturday," said rides manager Bill Ossim. "You get one Friday-Saturday that's cold and rainy, which we do in Cincinnati, [and] you don't have any time to make up for that loss in income. From a business point of view, it was a difficult venture to really make any money. Plus, it felt like we were distracted by having to do Winterfest and delayed having to work on next year's stuff."

"It was a decision after years of trying to make it work, trying to balance the maintenance needs of the park with the set-up for Winterfest. It would really take our eye off the ball as far as...a lot of people think that the amusement park people live in Florida during the winter time when that's actually our busiest time of year," added Dave Focke, who became Kings Island's vice president of maintenance and construction following the Paramount sale. "And it was so weather-dependent; as I said, if it got too warm, the ice would not make on the fountain...they just decided that we'd be concentrated on the summer season and not split our time with winter and summer."

Mike Meadows, vice president of finance added, "When you got cold weather, everybody wanted to be inside and you've got a finite amount of inside capacity; completely different from the model of a summer day...Once we let the season passholders in, then we couldn't sell enough general admission tickets to make it profitable! Passholders just flooded the place. And there was no incremental revenue with the season pass. The in-park spending was dramatically lower than the summer per caps due to a shorter length of stay and limited retail capacity."

"I don't think that was a Paramount-driven decision—that was a business decision," Ossim concluded.

Winterfest 1992 opened on November 21 with two new shows: "Santa's Christmas Wish" in the *American Heritage Music Hall* and "Yogi's Showstoppers" in the *Enchanted Theater*. Available rides included *Phantom Theater*, the two carousels, the train, and *Scooby Zoom*, which was the first roller coaster to ever operate during Winterfest.

After the lights were switched off, the strands were donated to the Greater Cincinnati and Lebanon Chambers of Commerce, ending the ten-year run of what had become a beloved Cincinnati tradition.

♑

1993—TOP GUN (THE RIDE)

The biggest addition for 1993 was already designed and under construction at the time of the sale to Paramount. A second Arrow suspended coaster might seem at first to be an odd choice for a park that just ten years earlier had suffered through the failure of *The Bat*. However, Bill Ossim explained, "It was probably third generation, I would guess by then, and it was more of a proven ride as opposed to a prototype, first-off-the-shelf kind of ride. The reliability we felt was something we could count on." The park's marketing department tossed around potential names such as *Thunder Road*, *Thunder Run*, and the bird-themed *Swoop*.

Once Paramount acquired the parks, they decided to rebrand the ride as a Paramount tie-in. *Top Gun* was announced by Al Weber on November 10, 1992; the media preview was on April 8, 1993, and it opened with the rest of the park on the 9th. The coaster, with "Danger Zone" blasting over the speakers and a queue designed by John DeCuir Jr., the film's production designer, was a drastic and obvious departure from the previous owners' additions.

Top Gun was not the only immediate sign of the new Hollywood style. The park's name was changed to Paramount's Kings Island and the park got a new logo, the first since 1972. The *American Heritage Music Hall* was renamed *The Paramount Theatre* and got a new show, "The Lazer Zone: Mission Impossible." The *Festhaus* featured "Paramount on Ice," and the *Enchanted Theater* became home to "Flintstones Go Hollyrock." Walk-around Star Trek and Top Gun characters were added to the classic Hanna-Barbera characters. *Tower Gardens* was converted to *The Paramount Story*, a Paramount Pictures walk of fame with real motion picture props. *Quick Draw's Cafe* in Hanna-Barbera Land became *Busytown Grill*, based on the Richard Scarry books; Paramount controlled the rights as part of their ownership of the publisher Simon and Schuster. Even the *Columbia Palace*, a staple since 1972, was renovated to *The WINGS Diner*, based on Paramount's 1927 movie *Wings*.

"That [the conversion of *Tower Gardens* to *The Paramount Story*] was one of the more fun things I've ever done in my life...The studio is just these huge warehouses full of stuff from all the pictures they've done," said Mike Foley, director of master planning and landscape architecture at Paramount Parks. "They never throw anything away! I mean, they had just huge amounts of stuff, so I got to go out and tag stuff to bring back to Kings Island and use and put together a program, and then we also developed the kiosks to put a lot of the stuff in around the park, where you'd put the little memorabilia stuff in Paramount kiosks."

"The motto when they bought us was 'The Magic of the Movies Meets the Thrills of a Lifetime,'" Dave Focke said. "That was a great line; we loved it...it [the changes] was all exciting."

Ed Dangler, who became Kings Island's manager of rides maintenance in December of 1992, traveled back and forth from Ohio to the Paramount Studios in California to help coordinate the transition during the 1992 to 1993 off-season. "Paramount is a well-run studio, it was really impressive," Dangler said. "Very clean. I've been to Warner Brothers Studio and other places out there, and they're just not the same. The level of professionalism with the set designers, the builders and all was just phenomenal. So everything was movie things, you had to have that kind of quality and understand the movies."

The Paramount Story, formerly Tower Gardens, featured a variety of movie props and replicas. Courtesy of Monique Gubser Strucke.

"Switching over to Paramount Parks was a tremendous task because we had to change all the signage, we had to change uniforms, we had to change virtually everything," said Nelson Schwab. "Characters, all kinds of stuff. Plus introduce new rides that were themed in the Paramount way. It was a big deal and it took a lot of work."

The sale to Paramount also resulted in a major change to the design philosophy of the park. "The scenic, the decor, all that kind of stuff was held pretty true to the early '70s vision [before the Paramount sale]," explained Mark Schoelwer, who grew up in Cincinnati and is currently the senior corporate designer for Cedar Fair. "But when Paramount took over, they pushed it a little bit. They were all about themed environments and that experience, but it was more exaggerated. So the colors were no longer natural, muted tones, they were screaming fuchsias and super poppy purples and yellows and reds."

In addition to morphing the design philosophy, the rides mainte-

nance division was tightened with the hiring of a new manager, Ed
Dangler, who believed that "'We can't let these rides, these rebuilds, go
out unless absolutely perfect for one reason and one reason only—my
children are riding these rides.' And I've managed that way my whole
career...We X-rayed a lot of stuff, we got into more of nondestructive
testing in-house, just better everything. The morale was just building
like an avalanche falls, the morale was just pushing right back up fast.
I took that as a life lesson that you can't necessarily manage people,
you have to lead them and you can't lead them by example all the
time, you've got to lead them by connection. Who are these folks and
are they respectful of the job and are they proud of it? One example
I've used several times was, it was such an uplifting thing for me when
someone would ask my son, for example, 'What does your father do?'
And he would say, 'He works at Kings Island, he fixes roller coasters.'
And the other kids go, 'Wow, that's great!' So we saw that kind of
enthusiasm grow through the years there, that, you know, it's not just
a job, it's a vocation. It's a purpose. There's a purpose in life and that
was my purpose, was working with people to make people happy and
have fun."

In addition to all the aesthetic changes, Paramount management
instituted a park-wide ban on alcohol sales. Beer would only be available in the *International Restaurant* and at private parties in the *Picnic
Grove*. To reflect this change, *Der Bier Garten* was renamed *Oktoberfest
Gardens*. "We were told that they wanted us to be more like the [Dis-
ney] Magic Kingdom than a themed amusement park," explained
Kings Island finance director Mike Meadows. "The Magic Kingdom
did not serve alcohol, and that became a very big issue. They [Para-
mount] agreed to permit us to serve beer in the *Picnic Grove*, but not in
the park proper. That decision took between $500,000 and $600,000
off the bottom line. Fortunately for us, Canada's Wonderland took an
extra year to convert to Paramount. We had a financial counterparts
meeting in June of that year at Canada's Wonderland. When their
CFO took us into the park, we enjoyed a Labatt's draft at their beer
garden. Once we returned to the offices, I immediately called [new
Kings Island general manager] Al Weber and told him they were

selling beer at Canada's Wonderland. He called Nelson [Schwab], and we were back in the beer business in a matter of days!"

The new logo for Paramount's Kings Island. The park received new logos in 1972, 1992, 2003, and 2007. Courtesy of Dave Focke.

CHANGES FOR THE ENTIRE PARK CHAIN

While there were many outward changes in the park that reflected the new Paramount ownership, numerous developments were also taking place internally within the chain of parks. "There was much more uniformity after the Paramount sale," said Nelson Schwab. "Anything that we applied, like a *Top Gun*, we did that at Carowinds, that had to be done almost exactly the same. The look and feel of the parks with the wardrobe and things and how we applied the intellectual property, we had to spend an awful lot of time together coordinating that to make sure that was done right. It took a fair measure of autonomy away from the parks. There were some growing pains as it morphed into a different type of operation. But everybody stepped up and did a really nice job."

At Kings Island, some employees did not view the sale with such positivity. "The entire Kings Island Police was basically eliminated," said Perry Denehy of the Fire and Safety Department. "I think they saved two officers just to save money, reduce the number of full-time employees, reduce the overhead. A lot of departments experienced that. I don't know the specifics, but at one point we had a lot of painters, electricians, plumbers, carpenters, landscaping, and all the departments—merchandise, food service—slashed 10%, 15%, so they had to terminate a lot of employees that had probably worked there from the beginning."

"There were some real serious cultural adjustments, and I think eventually Nelson saw the need to bring everybody together from the Paramount side and the Kings Entertainment side, and we had a big 'Come to Jesus' meeting where we had to turn around and redo the mission statement. Basically we needed to wipe the slate clean and get everybody on the same page!" Mike Meadows recalled. "We thought we were selling it [to Paramount], [and] we were going to get a bunch of money, and we could go to the next level of attractions, and I think a lot of people at the parks were really concerned about how much money the Paramount people wanted to put into things we didn't think would drive any attendance. They wanted to do a lot of theming around the Paramount name that didn't really have any thrill to it...There were a lot of cultural issues that really had to be hammered out."

The sale brought about hopes of improvement that never materialized. "The first thing that came to my mind was the entertainment," said Don Helbig. "I'm thinking the movies and stuff, the shows and everything, but that's the thing that got cut, was the shows! The thing that I was most excited about ended up being the most disappointing thing for me. You went from having eight, ten different shows and the *Clown Band* and all those kinds of things, to being real scaled back with what they were doing. But it brought a different kind of thing to it, where there would be more theming with the rides, like when you had *Top Gun* and things like that. I mean, we were excited about that too, but for me I really was disappointed because the entertainment point of it wasn't there. As a guest, and then at that time I had just got married and everything too, if you're just there to ride rides, great. I started thinking about the guests—the grandparents that come with their grandkids, they're not going to ride rides or some of the parents aren't going to ride rides. They wanted to have something to do during the day, and then you would see, like, *International Showplace* would be dark for the summer, something like that. So for me, it went from every time no matter where you went in the park, there was some kind of entertainment going on with the mimes and you had *Rufus the Rainmaker*, you had the *Clown Band*, then you had two shows going on in the *International Showplace* with a pop show and a country show. You had a Broadway show in the [*American Heritage Music Hall*] and you had other shows going on in the *Festhaus*. To go from that to what it was in the '90s, as a guest who enjoyed the entertainment as much as I did the roller coasters, that wasn't what I was expecting."

Another loss was a planned wooden coaster in Swan Lake. "The only bad thing for me, personally, is when Paramount first bought us, I had designed a wood roller coaster that we were going to build," said Jeff Gramke. "It was my total design; I did it all. We had hired a structural engineer to do a lot of the structural design, we had pre-ordered the trains from PTC for it, we...did a lot of clearing for the ride, and then as soon as Paramount bought us, they froze all the capital spending...I would have liked to have built that coaster, because I think that would've been a good coaster. But what we put in wound up being great too [*Diamondback* under Cedar Fair in 2009]."

WILD ANIMAL HABITAT: PERMANENTLY CLOSED

Paramount's Kings Island closed for the 1993 season on October 31, later than in previous years. The cancellation of Winterfest allowed the park to extend its operating season since they didn't have to prepare for the seasonal event.

The end of the 1993 season also meant the end of a classic park attraction. Three days after closing, the park announced the retirement of the Wild Animal Habitat monorail. Similar to Winterfest, the monorail was already on its way out before the sale. "I know that one of the reasons for its closure, and also for the Winterfest at the time, is the existing management was telling the Paramount folks that the monorail and the animals aren't profitable," explained Ed Dangler, manager of rides maintenance at the time. "It [was] getting harder and harder to get exotic animals in the United States and the Winterfest was inconvenient and not necessarily profitable because it was so weather-dependent. So basically, from the Paramount view, is 'Why are we operating something that's losing money?'"

The attraction had seen years of sagging attendance, was extremely costly to operate, and took up a massive amount of space—over 100 acres. Park spokeswoman Carolyn Boos told the press that the space could be better used for "attractions that bring Paramount movie, television, and publishing intellectual properties to life." More than 300 animals were shipped off to zoos and other organizations approved by the American Association of Zoological Parks and Aquariums.

With the animals now gone, the park initially toyed with keeping the monorail and converting it into an attraction called the *Movierail*. "We did have a creative group come in to look at doing the *Movierail* attraction where we'd have vignettes set back in the Wild Animal Habitat animal section, maybe a set from a movie back there," said Dave Focke, vice president of maintenance and construction. "It just never got enough support. A lot of those decisions are a combination of doing what marketing thinks they can do, [and] we would do the cost estimates, operations would do the estimates to operate the attraction, so it was kind of a team decision in what you do."

VIACOM ENTERS THE PICTURE

On September 12, 1993 cable television giant Viacom Inc. announced they were acquiring Paramount Communications for $8.3 billion. The new company became Paramount Viacom International. Despite speculation that the merger would result in yet another sale of the parks as a way to pay off Viacom's debt from the sale, it was ultimately unfounded. "We love the theme parks," said Viacom spokesman Elliot Sloan. "We think they're a great business...The parks are a complementary asset to everything Viacom owns."

The parks would not be sold off for the time being. But Paramount

Parks was now folded into a much larger organization that, as a group, had significantly less focus on running a few seasonal theme parks.

Å

1994—DAYS OF THUNDER

The major new addition for 1994 was *Days of Thunder*, a 4-D motion simulator movie based off the 1990 Tom Cruise movie of the same name. The attraction had debuted the previous season at Paramount's Carowinds and Paramount's Kings Dominion and had been a very popular addition at those parks. A brand new building housing two seventy-four seat theaters with 26-foot tall and 59-foot wide screens was built between the tracks where *The Racer* splits to go into its turn-around. "This attraction is very symbolic of what our marriage to Paramount really means," Al Weber said at the ride's announcement on September 8, 1993. Just like *Top Gun*, *Days of Thunder's* theming elements were designed by Hollywood production designer John DeCuir Jr. The ride also opened in 1994 at Paramount's Great America and Paramount Canada's Wonderland.

"I think really the only thing Paramount said was, 'Come up with something we can put a brand to,'" said Bill Ossim. "They'd say, 'We want you to do this' or 'We want you to do that,'...[and] they said, 'Here's what we got, see what you can do,' and we looked at different things and *Days of Thunder*, the motion theater really kind of fits that, we can put in a good ride. That was a neat attraction."

The major new show for 1994 was "Paramount on Ice: Lights! Camera! Action!" in *The Paramount Theatre*. The classic *Kings of Komedy* clown band was modified to become the *Marx Brothers' Monkey Business Band*. The *Saltwater Friends* show became *Friends of a Feather*, starring birds instead of sea lions. "Game On!" was an audience participation game show featured in the *Festhaus*.

Coney Cafe became *Preston T. Tucker's Roadside Cafe*, based on the 1988 movie "Tucker: The Man and His Dream." Wild Animal Habitat's name was also changed to the more generic Adventure Village, the same name the area had from 1983-1986, as a result of the habitat's closure. The area still contained the other attractions, including *Top Gun*, *Amazon Falls*, and *Kafe Kilimanjaro*.

Paramount's Kings Island's 1994 season ran from April 9 to October 23.

$$\unicode{x2434}$$

1995

The biggest addition for the 1995 season was a new three-acre children's area, Nickelodeon Splat City, built on the former location of the *Sunshine Turnpike*. Based on shows from Viacom's Nickelodeon channel, Nickelodeon Splat City sprayed 6,700 green-tinted gallons of water a minute from all kinds of devices. *Green Slime Zone* was an interactive water maze, the thirty-five foot tall *Slime Derrick* shot "slime" fifty feet into the air, and the *Crystal Slime Aerobic Mining Maze* was an interactive jungle gym for kids and adults. Guests could now test their skills at a new *Legends of the Hidden Temple* game and *Double Dare Slime Shot Challenge*. Other interactive elements included the *Green Slime Transfer Truck* and the *Emergency Green Slime Shower* and *Green Slime Pit*. A 725-seat amphitheater was built featuring the audience participation show "Mega Mess-a-Mania." A *Snack Bar* and *GAK Kitchen* were added as well. Similar Nickelodeon-themed areas were added to Paramount's Kings Dominion and Paramount's Great America.

Other changes throughout the park included "Cheers: The Show" in the *Festhaus* and "Paramount on Ice: Legends" in *The Paramount Theatre*. The theater that housed "Friends of a Feather," and "Saltwater Circus" before that, was demolished. Paramount's Kings Island opened for the 1995 season on April 15.

A new ride opened June 1, several weeks into the new season. *Drop Zone* was a Skycoaster named after the 1994 movie starring Wesley Snipes. The upcharge attraction was added in Adventure

Village in the old location of the Wild Animal Habitat monorail station.

"Betty Rehbock was the games manager at the time and I was the rides manager, and we were charged with evaluating something that the park would do, would work for us," said Bill Ossim. "I flew down to Orlando and looked at it [the original Skycoaster] and rode it and came back and was like, 'This is pretty cool!' Then Betty said, 'I think we could sell tickets to this thing.' I don't remember exactly what it made in the first year, but it more than paid for itself, I'll tell you that! That was a neat project because Betty was in charge of selling the tickets for it, scheduling and all that, and ride operations operated it."

Paramount's Kings Island closed for the season October 22.

A NEW CEO FOR PARAMOUNT PARKS

Nelson Schwab left Paramount Parks in 1995 to start up Carousel Capital, a private equity investment firm. It would be the first time in fifteen years someone other than Schwab would be heading the park chain. "We always felt Kings Island was a tremendous asset with a tremendous market to serve," Schwab reflected on his time with the park. "It was just how to take advantage of that opportunity. On the one hand, take advantage, on the other hand not lose that market-place, not lose the market share in that. We were constantly looking for ways to innovate and bring the next new thing to Kings Island. It was a big enough park that it could perhaps take more risk in that you had dollars to spend that you might not have at a smaller park. You could build a bigger coaster or have marketing dollars that were a little larger so you could advertise in more markets...I think that Kings Island was in many ways an innovator through all [the owner-ship/management changes]."

He was replaced on June 1 by Jane G. Cooper. Cooper began as a seasonal merchandise associate at Kings Island in 1972 and worked her way up to supervisor of merchandise operations. In 1977 she became a full-time employee of Kings Island as a buyer for the merchandise department. By 1979 she had become merchandise manager for the park, and in 1982 was promoted to director of merchandise and games. Cooper transferred to Great America in California in 1985 to become that park's resale director, a job she held until 1992 when she was promoted to vice president and general manager of Great America when Al Weber was sent to Kings Island. Cooper was in that position for only eighteen months before being promoted to president of Paramount Parks, and then CEO after that.

Å

1996—TAKING COASTERS TO THE OUTER LIMITS

"The company originally was basically five individual theme parks," Jane Cooper explains. "When the company was sold to Paramount initially, their objective was to take their brands and do more with them. They wanted to bring the movies, Hollywood, to the parks and take them to the next level a la Universal Studios or Disney. We were looking for attractions that not only we knew our consumers really wanted, obviously coasters were very popular with our customers, but then something we could also put one of the Paramount brands on that we could get access to. As a company, we [also] tried to do unique, a little bit prototypical-type attractions."

"We knew we wanted to do an indoor coaster," said manager of engineering and construction Jeff Gramke. "We didn't know we wanted to build a linear induction motor coaster, we didn't know *what* we wanted to build! So the company said, 'Okay, we want to build a coaster in this size of a building, here's how big of a building we can afford and we want to build, you tell us what you can put in here.' Several different coaster companies bid on that...It was all pretty much spaghetti in a drum. Pretty much all of them were the same...Most of them had a regular lift [hill]. Most of them had a sloping part of the building to get up into the drum with a standard coaster."

As the concept evolved, park management wanted to not only introduce an indoor coaster, but a cutting-edge one as well. "Al Weber was our general manager at the time and he was really visionary. He was really pushing us to do more, more, more," said Dave Focke, vice president of maintenance and construction. "'Let's not only do it indoors, let's make it have inversions! Let's do a launch system!' So our original intent was to do a flywheel launch system, like the [Schwarzkopf] shuttle loop coasters were using. We went to Europe and met with Anton Schwarzkopf, who was still alive at that time. So he was going to be a partner in the project, and Werner Stengel, he was going to do the dynamic design. So we actually did the contract based on a flywheel launch. When they started doing the engineering, we wanted it to be high-capacity; we wanted to run four trains [with] five cars; we wanted to crank people through. But they found out that the flywheel couldn't dissipate the heat of the launch enough. You couldn't get a launch in every, let's say, forty seconds. You couldn't get the flywheel to do a forty second launch. So Premier [Rides] proposed to us a concept of linear induction motors, which we knew nothing about at the time, and [we] sent Ed Dangler over to Germany to one of the companies that made them, to see if he thought it was practical. And it did, and we actually had a little scale model of the launch for a press introduction! Just shoot a little part down the track. It [the LIM launch] came about kind of as a second decision."

"That was a really, really good idea to be able to get enough energy into the train to not have to take all the time to lift somebody up a lift," said Gramke. "That's the beauty of linear induction motors; you're able to get the same amount of potential energy into the train in the same three seconds that normally takes twenty seconds to go up a lift."

The otherworldly "Outer Limits" television show proved to be the perfect tie-in to the ride, which would also be cloned for Paramount's Kings Dominion. "I'm a big believer of following your passions and ideas and stories, and I was a big Sci-Fi nut and I loved the topic of UFOs," said Anthony Esparza, the senior vice president of design and entertainment for Paramount Parks. "The Outer Limits [show] was an umbrella that allowed us to tell a whole bunch of interesting stories, so I zeroed in on the UFO angle." Esparza and his team began developing an immersive, out-of-this-world story for the coaster. "We were trying to figure out a concept that could be executed at a relatively affordable price, and we struck upon this idea of creating this warehouse, and of course this is that place the government always denied ever having, harboring a UFO, and then of course you as a guest discover your way in and cross the borders of security into the place where, sure enough, there's a UFO in here! Then we let you do what you dreamed to do, which is board it."

The Outer Limits: Flight of Fear, the world's first linear induction motor-launched coaster, was announced for Kings Island on August 17, 1995. The ride was to be built in a one-acre building beyond *The Racer* in a former parcel of Wild Animal Habitat. "It's the most ambitious undertaking at Paramount's Kings Island in the history of the park," Focke told the press.

The LIM launch technology would catapult riders from zero to fifty-four miles per hour in four seconds, the fastest acceleration of any coaster in the world up to that time. The Premier Rides coaster was also the park's most expensive. While exact figures were not released, Focke told the press it cost "over $10 million."

Laying out and designing the infamous Hangar 18 led to several ingenious moments for the design team. "We built half a UFO with a big mirror so it appeared it was twice as big as it was, and the warehouse was twice as big, and then, of course, you could go into the UFO, and because of that you could actually have all the space you needed behind that wall to fulfill the interior of that UFO and, of course, all the launch mechanisms and everything we needed to 'get abducted,'" said Esparza.

The park wanted the coaster built first, and then the building built around it. But difficulties with the manufacturing of parts in Europe required creative solutions. "We weren't getting really good answers on schedules, delivery dates, things seemed to be slipping," said rides maintenance manager Ed Dangler. "So a few of us went over to Italy, and I went over several times, and after a while you realize that there's a money issue and these folks wanted to get paid. One thing I learned over there is that if I'm manufacturing something for you and you're supposed to come pay me on 3:00 on a Friday and you don't show up, I move your stuff outside. I start someone else's work. So that was happening. We didn't know exactly why, so the job was straightening out the finances, get back in the manufacturing, so I went to a lot of plants, a couple meetings, and it was definitely unusual...The finances got straightened out, we had to ask the subcontractors to reduce their cost by like 15%, and that was not a really productive meeting because there was a lot of resistance from the manufacturers. The deal was that Paramount's going to guarantee this contract now and if you don't take this deal, what are you going to do with all that raw material and bent pipe? The columns that you're making, what are you going to do with it all?"

These issues resulted in the construction of the building before the coaster! "While this was all going on, we have to build something," Dangler continued. "We only have the winter to do it! November 1 to May 1 or April 1, so working with Jeff Gramke, who always was a good friend and an excellent construction manager, they started building the building, and then we had some structural engineers design heavy, large beams to span the building, so we could put winches so that when we got there, we could winch the pieces up into the track. It was a very difficult thing, so we had to build something and that building was almost complete when the first track started showing up. We worked with an ironworker, Kevin Jones who now works for B&M, and we would measure track, 40 feet lengths of track, and consider the shapes and all that, and we'd go, 'We've got four inches of clearance, let's go! Let's put it in place.' That's how close and tight it was in that building."

Paramount's Kings Island opened for the 1996 season on April 13. *The Outer Limits: Flight of Fear* did not. "That was the most challenging [ride opening] I ever worked on," recalled Paramount Parks CEO Jane Cooper. "Partially because they were prototypical, we had two of them, and trying to get them open and testing them and going, 'Okay, well here's our date we want to open' and you test them and it's like, 'Oh, we've got to adjust this, we have to adjust that.' It was the first time a [LIM] launched coaster had ever been done, so it was incredibly stressful."

"Initially, the plates that stick out the side of the wings, they go into the linear induction motors, we learned those are made out of aluminum, and we learned that the grade of aluminum that we used was very important to how much thrust we got out of the linear induction motors," Focke added. "We had done a lot of experimentation and finally connected with a professor down at University of Kentucky who was experienced in this technology who helped us find the right aluminum. Once we found that, then it became easier."

Rides manager Bill Ossim elaborated on the process. "We were already on a tight schedule, and then once we got it installed we were working around the clock. We had day shifts, night shifts, overnight shifts. For a good part of that, I was working the overnight shift. We'd work during the day, go sleep for awhile, then go overnight. That got to be a pretty tough project because we just couldn't get the speed out of the trains that we were looking for, and it was all in the timing of firing those LIMs. We couldn't get the LIMs to get enough power, so we had to start sequencing when they were turning off and turning on in order to get the power we needed to launch it. It was only by turning off the ones it had just gone through and turning the other ones on and firing them up and doing that all the way down the line to get that thing around. That was a tough time too! Kings Dominion opened that one the same year. Neither one of them was working, so we made the decision to focus on getting ours working, then get theirs going. The rides manager from Kings Dominion came over, and [he] and I were working on it with our maintenance folks to get things going at the same time."

"The power consumption was so critical that we couldn't have all the LIMs on at one time," Dangler explained. "We'd brown-out the cities! So we had to turn them on just before the train got there and turn the one off that the train just left, and that was a really difficult thing. We had a hard time really dialing that in. We had a lot of experts come and help us, and then one night we just said, 'No more experts for a couple days. Leave us alone!' And some electricians there came up with a great method. They would put lightbulbs on the series of the LIMs so we could watch what we call the 'wave' of the lights going on and off. Then we could say, 'Oh, that LIM is turning on way too soon,' that kind of thing. Then the other relative success that made the ride more reliable, more accurate, was we hired Kevin Russell who was a former Arrow engineer...[and] he came up with a system with a laser that measured that train leaving the station, all the way down that track every couple millimeters. So he knew when the train hit a switch, what was the distance. So with that, we could calculate the acceleration rates and velocity at these different points, and really turn the LIMs on and off exactly."

Once the ride was actually testing, another issue arose with the pitch-dark building—a rider couldn't see what was coming in order to physically brace themselves, which was pretty important considering the uncomfortable over-the-shoulder restraints. Fortunately, this one had a pretty easy solution. "It was important to be able to have a little bit of light so you could get reference points while you're riding so that you could prepare for it," Ossim continued. "That's the reason why it wasn't pitch-black in there. Some of us rode it in the pitch-black and it was like 'Oh, this isn't going to work this way.' Just getting those reference points of a little bit of light here and there. Once we got it launching, then we had to figure out how to safely operate it, and that was one of the things we had to do was introduce some strategic light."

The Outer Limits: Flight of Fear finally opened to the public on June 18, with a media preview held the day before. "When that ride first opened, it was so energy-hungry. It took so much energy, that when they'd launch a train, my lights would flicker here in my office at the other end of the park!" Gramke chuckled. "It took a lot of energy."

The coaster was a major technological advancement in the amusement park industry. "It had never been done before; we had a lot of interest from outside companies—elevator companies, the United States Navy, on and on it went once we got it up and running...So that was a real big breakthrough to have that ride open at that time. It was a lot of new stuff and I've got to tell you, it was really something," Dangler concluded.

To provide guest access to *The Outer Limits: Flight of Fear*, the park opened up a former maintenance pathway underneath *The Racer*. It was also decided to remove the final bunny hill on each track of *The Racer*, ostensibly to increase the path's height clearance for guest traffic (some park historians believe this was for other reasons, perhaps to increase the final train braking distance). With the work being completed in-house by park staff, resources and time only allowed the forward side's hill to be removed prior to the 1996 season. The hill on the backwards side was removed following the 1996 season.

Other additions for 1996 included *XS Raceway*, an upcharge go-kart ride in Adventure Village, and *Q-TV*, an in-park television network with park-specific content. The *Festhaus* did not feature any live shows for the first time in the building's history, merely showing *Q-TV* content on screens. *Drop Zone* was renamed *Xtreme Skyflyer*. "Paramount on Ice: BLOCKBUSTERS!" was the new featured show in *The Paramount Theatre*.

The *International Restaurant* had closed after 1995, although it would see more seasonal event use over time. With a checkered history and decline in guest interest, *Flight Commander* also did not return for the 1996 season.

Paramount's Kings Island closed for the 1996 season on October 27.

CELEBRATING A QUARTER-CENTURY

*P*aramount's Kings Island opened for its 25th anniversary season on April 19, 1997. A new signature show, "Entertainment Tonight: Special Edition Live," debuted in *The Paramount Theatre*. A *Back Porch Stage* was built in Rivertown to host "Hot Country Trax," and a new "International Street Spectacular" fireworks show was the centerpiece of the celebration.

The biggest transformation for 1997 was the doubling in size of WaterWorks. The expansion included the additions of *Surfside Bay*, a 600,000 gallon wave pool, and the *Buccaneer Island* play area for children. The *Snack Shop* was reworked into *Caribbean Cones*, and the *Oasis* drink stand was changed to *Island Coolers*. A full-sized food stand was added in *Sharkey's Eats,* and a new gift shop, *Trader Jake's,* was added as well. WaterWorks even received a new logo.

The most significant piece of the expansion was the wave pool, featuring an innovative new design. "We were on a flight, on a plane from Cincinnati to go to the people in Canada who did waterpark construction and did all the slides and that kind of stuff," said Mike Foley, director of master planning and landscape architecture for Paramount Parks. "We actually were on the plane and we came up with the idea of, you know how a wave pool is really long and thin, and it's very narrow in the back, and you've got a little neck that has the end where the waves come out and they dissipate? Well, I'd say 80 to 90% of people stay in the first two or three feet, just in terms of depth, and that's only about a 10th or less of the area of water...We came up with the idea that basically, if you took the same amount of concrete, same amount of everything, if you turned it sideways...[it creates] more of a splayed [design]. The waterfront area, where the beach is, so to speak, is triple the amount on the [traditional wave pool].

"We turned the same amount of money spent building it, basically, we turned the whole thing sideways and that increased the capacity by 300% of people being able to entertain themselves in the first two or three feet, especially kids and the moms and dads. Just by doing a little twist of the design. We were scratching a drawing on the plane and we got to the guy who builds the wave pools in Canada, and we showed it to him and he said, 'Sure, just turn it this way and do this, we can put the motors here and do this here.' So that was the beginning of that new type of wave pool, which we've done everywhere since."

It was the first time under Paramount's ownership that a major new addition was not tied to a brand. The expanded WaterWorks opened May 22.

The season ran through October 26. During the final few weekends in October, the park rolled out Kids' Howl-o-Fest '97, a family-oriented Halloween event in the *Festhaus* and Hanna-Barbera Land with a straw maze, a magician, and face-painting.

GENERAL MANAGER #8: TIM V. FISHER

In October 1997 Al Weber was promoted from Kings Island general manager to executive vice president and chief operating officer of Paramount Parks.

He was replaced at Paramount's Kings Island by Tim Fisher. Fisher had started as a ride operator at Carowinds in 1976 and worked his way up through the rides department, eventually transferring to

Australia's Wonderland in Sydney as the rides director there, where he was soon promoted to general manager of that park. Fisher stayed in Sydney for several years before he became the executive producer and general manager of the new Paramount Parks attraction *Star Trek: The Experience* in Las Vegas. In 1997 Fisher became the general manager of Kings Island.

Å

1998

The new year saw a major refurbishment to Hanna-Barbera Land. Three new rides were added: *Scooby's Ghoster Coaster*, *Yogi's Sky Tours*, and *Atom Ant's Airways*. Existing attractions were renamed and repainted—*Scooby Zoom* became *Top Cat's Taxi Jam*, *Jabber Jaw's Tubs* became *Boo-Boo's Baggage Claim*, *Rawhide Railway* became *Baba Looey's Buggies*, and *Red Baron's Bi-Planes* became *Dick Dastardly's Biplanes*. Even *The Beastie* got a new purple paint scheme. Part of the *Animation Station* gift shop became home to a Hanna-Barbera character meet-and-greet. "The only thing [we left] intact is the area's paving and some of the seating walls," Jeff Gramke told the *Cincinnati Post*. In the other children's area, Nickelodeon SPLAT CITY, the "Mega Mess-a-Mania" show was replaced with "Nicktoons Block Party," featuring the Rugrats characters.

Days of Thunder was replaced in the *Paramount Action FX Theater* with a new 4-D movie, "James Bond 007: A License to Thrill." Over in WaterWorks, a new *WipeOut Beach*, a Wave Loch Inc. FlowRider, was added. *Skylab*, plagued with maintenance issues since it opened, was removed and replaced by *The Edge*, an upcharge climbing wall. The signature new show for the 1998 season was "RetroACTIVE!" in *The Paramount Theatre*. Paramount's Kings Island closed on October 25, and Howl-o-Fest returned for another season.

Å

AN ACTION-PACKED CHANGE FOR 1999

Adventure Village had been a pathetic shell since its signature attraction, Wild Animal Habitat, closed at the end of the 1993 season. While *Xtreme Skyflyer* and *XS Raceway* added some foot traffic and increased revenue to the area, Paramount Parks executives knew it needed a complete overhaul.

"It was one thing to remove the monorail, but then what did you do with all that space, and how could you re-theme it so that it was credible in the consumer's eyes?" said Jane Cooper, CEO of Paramount Parks. "It was a little bit of an underutilized footprint, so we wanted to put in an attraction over there that would draw people [over there]."

Park officials saw the opportunity in that space to create something that would grow their attendance base. "Going back to '98, when I arrived, we were talking about how much we could push the envelope in terms of growth," said general manager Tim Fisher. "We had just done a children's area redevelopment. We thought there might be the opportunity to move the needle from an attendance perspective by pursuing the teen demographic a bit more. We wanted to do something that would be attractive to them, that age group. That's what made us decide to develop the Action Zone."

Eager to continue to capitalize on the Paramount and Viacom brands, plans were made to reimagine Adventure Village into the Paramount Action Zone, designed to emulate the Paramount backlot. "The Action Zone was taking what I would call the coolest and most fun properties of Paramount and being able to present a basket of them together," said Anthony Esparza, senior vice president of design and entertainment for Paramount Parks. "The Action Zone was the idea that it was the umbrella that could be flexible, thus not tied to one specific name of a movie, but it was this platform to launch multiple different movie themes under that umbrella."

The popular explanation given online by various articles and supposed "insiders" is that this massive overhaul was done to compete with ambitious expansion plans by Six Flags Kentucky Kingdom.

There's no truth to that explanation, according to the management in charge of the change. "I think it would be safe to say that decisions in terms of capital expansion were made on the basis of what we felt the park needed at the time; what we felt the market opportunities might be," Fisher said. "We were doing things that we thought were in the best interest of Kings Island...I think there was an opportunity to grow that particular segment of the marketplace [teenagers] and that was the reason why we decided to do those attractions."

"When the animals went away, it didn't make sense to have an animal safari that doesn't have anything in it...It was pretty much just an evolution of when [Wild Animal Habitat] went away, we had to do something else," added Jeff Gramke.

Two rides would be added to the new Paramount Action Zone: *FACE/OFF*, advertised as the only face-to-face inverted roller coaster in the Midwest, would be a Vekoma Inverted Boomerang clone based on the 1997 film *Face/Off*. The second ride, *DROP ZONE*, was based on the 1994 film of the same name and was scheduled to open in mid-May of 1999. It would be the world's tallest Intamin gyro drop tower at 315 feet tall, even higher than Kings Island's *Eiffel Tower*. It is, to this day, the tallest structure at Kings Island.

The Paramount Action Zone makeover included the addition of two new rides: Drop Zone and Face/Off. Courtesy of Josh Kellerman.

"We didn't have an inverted coaster that did inversions, so [FACE/OFF] took care of that," said Dave Focke. "It was a giant Invertigo, so it was larger than your typical boomerang coaster, so it gave us some marketing appeal. Same with the drop tower—300 feet high and the spinning. So we had two very unique attractions at one time. In fact, that was one of our biggest capital years, putting both of those in at the same time."

"Those rides were already in existence, but they were still somewhat new to the marketplace and the consumer in that particular part of the country had not had that type of experience, so we thought we could be impactful," Fisher added.

DROP ZONE's tower was built in a Hungarian manufacturing plant. "They [Hungary] were a democracy and the employees [of the plant] owned 53%, I think the state still had 8% and there were various banks and investors," said Kings Island rides maintenance manager Ed Dangler. "These people are working hard, things are buzzing, and you wonder, 'Are they doing this for show for the Americans?' So we went to the paint shop, we went around, it was a huge facility, and I just...looked inside and everybody's still working hard and I realized—they figured out capitalism! They owned the company and the more they worked, the more they got paid, you know? It was just incredible. That place was picked by Intamin because the bottom section of that tower is so thick. It's almost four inches thick and it had to be rolled in a perfect circle and welded at the seam and that was one of the few places that could do that in the world, so that's how they got that place."

Kafe Kilimanjaro was renovated into Stunt Crew Grill and the Outback Discounters gift shop was demolished and replaced with the Ice Scream Zone stand. A brand new gift shop, On Location, was added to the previously barren central plaza. A miniature replica of the Paramount Studios water tower was built as the central focal piece, with a Paramount Action Zone Stunt Show designed around it. King Cobra and Top Gun received new paint jobs, Amazon Falls was renamed Congo Falls after the 1995 movie Congo, and the XS Raceway was renamed

Days of Thunder. The renovation would be the most expensive investment in the park's history up to that time.

Paramount's Kings Island opened with its new Paramount Action Zone area, minus *DROP ZONE*, on April 17, 1999, with a media preview held on April 14. *DROP ZONE* opened as scheduled on May 22. The park closed for the 1999 season on October 31.

KINGS ISLAND ANNEXED TO MASON

In addition to Paramount Action Zone, 1999 also brought an address change to the park. It had been officially located in Deerfield Township. However, since 1995 Kings Island had been working to be annexed to the City of Mason. In July of 1995, Kings Island formally filed a petition in Warren County asking to be annexed to the city of Mason. "We thought it was in the best interest of the park," then-Kings Island spokeswoman Karen Hunt told the press. "We've had a great long-term relationship with the county. The city of Mason [had] the ability to provide key services for our park."

The Warren County Commissioners agreed on January 23, 1996 to annex the park from Kings Mills, a census-designated place in Deerfield Township, into Mason.

However, when Mason decided to withdraw from Deerfield Township completely, thereby completely removing Kings Island from Deerfield Township, Kings Island officials reversed their position. "When annexation began, we thought Mason would be part of Deerfield Township. Now we are in the position of having to choose between the communities in what has been an adversarial climate," said Lauren Green-Caldwell, the park's spokeswoman at the time. A compromise was reached in 1997 that allowed Deerfield Township to temporarily retain a share in the taxes it collected from the park and keep a part of the park temporarily in the township.

On September 13, 1999, Mason City Council voted 6–1 to completely annex Paramount's Kings Island to Mason. Because of this, Kings Island can uniquely claim to be one of America's only amusement parks to have changed locations without moving an inch.

Ⱥ

2000—SON OF BEAST

In 1997 a company called Roller Coaster Corporation of America ("RCCA") came calling to Paramount's Kings Island to make a pitch to Al Weber and his management team. The group had recently built *The Rattler*, a record-breaking but problematic wooden coaster, at Fiesta Texas. They were trying to persuade Paramount to buy a new wooden coaster concept they had designed—one that RCCA felt would redefine the genre.

"*Son of Beast* was a situation where a company came to us with a proprietary idea to build the biggest, fastest, longest wood roller coaster in the world," said Kings Island's manager of engineering and construction Jeff Gramke. "They had gone to who knows who else to try to sell that coaster. They came in and they made the pitch. They were using Premier Rides [for the trains], who had done our *Flight of Fear* ride. They were using Werner Stengel, who was one of the best roller coaster designers in the world, as the ride designer...They were a company out of Atlanta, Roller Coaster Corporation of America, and they came to us as a group of three to sell us that ride. They made their pitch. It was going to have a wood loop, they wanted a wood loop in it, it was going to break the record of *The Beast*. It was going to be longer than *The Beast*, so we said, 'Wait a minute. We've already got the longest wooden roller coaster in the world, we don't want to beat our own record!' One thing led to another and the company decided to buy what became the *Son of Beast*."

RCCA's pitch particularly appealed to Jane Cooper, who had been a seasonal supervisor in Kings Island's merchandise department when *The Beast* first opened in 1979. "It was so popular and it had such an incredible reputation, when you think about, okay, what next at Kings Island? What can we do that would out-Beast *The Beast*? That's how we ended up doing the wooden roller coaster, and the hook was the fact that it was going to be the [only] wooden roller coaster with a loop."

The wooden coaster would not only be the only wooden coaster with a loop, but also the tallest, at 218 feet, and fastest, at 78 miles per hour, wooden coaster ever built. The project, set to open in 2000, would be the second stage of the Paramount Action Zone renovation. Unlike the park's other projects during the Paramount years, the corporate Design and Entertainment team was not involved with the coaster at all—the project was led entirely by the park.

The name, *Son of Beast*, was a natural fit. "I think the more we dug into it, and I think we even did some consumer research, and basically the obvious answer came back is, 'It should be *Son of Beast*,'" said Cooper. "Nothing else resonated quite like that did."

Son of Beast's massive structure loomed over the park.
Courtesy of Paul Bonifield.

The coaster layout was already designed when RCCA made the pitch to Kings Island, so "We really didn't have much to say about it [the layout]," Gramke said. "We told them where we wanted the station, but they pretty much did the design themselves. We pretty much bought that ride from them. Some of the things I wish we'd done over, because they didn't take advantage of the topography like we did for *The Beast*. They had some of the highest structure in some of the lowest valleys! They didn't take advantage of the topography;

they didn't really have time to, I guess, but they didn't want to do a whole bunch of redesigning on that ride." One aspect Gramke and his engineering and construction crew did get a say in was the loop. "The people we bought it from wanted to do a totally wood structure loop, and we decided not to do that. We wanted to do steel structure with a wood track...we just didn't feel comfortable long-term about the viability of keeping wood for 30-40 years without having some sort of insect or termite damage or rot. So we wanted to do the steel loop."

Son of Beast became the world's only looping wooden coaster when it opened. Courtesy of Josh Kellerman.

In late 1997 Tim Fisher became Paramount's Kings Island's general manager, and he inherited the *Son of Beast* project from his predecessor, Al Weber. "I thought it was a great approach and concept," Fisher said. "Unfortunately, it didn't turn out to be as successful as we would have hoped."

Son of Beast was announced on May 11, 1999 by TV star Montel Williams, who was still recovering from health issues at the time. "[*Son of Beast*] will be the millennium coaster; it will stand as a monumental symbol of Paramount's Kings Island's commitment to quality in world-class rides and entertainment," Fisher told the press.

"I thought [the name] *Son of Beast* gave the ride an expectation that it couldn't possibly live up to; that it would be compared with *The*

Beast instead of standing on its own with no tie-in to a legendary attraction," Don Helbig commented on his first reaction.

Son of Beast would have an innovative construction process. "When you build a wood coaster, like most rides, it would be designed and engineered, but you would actually build the coaster on-site," said Fisher. "The wood would be delivered, you'd cut it to fit basically. That ride was prefabbed in terms of, the whole idea was that the ride would go together almost like an erector set. That was the intent behind the development of that ride; it would be put together much faster; that was the approach. So it was pre-drilled...The idea was it would be the type of ride that would go together quickly, but in the end, it still took quite a bit of time. It was just such a massive attraction. It was so significant in terms of scale that it still took quite a bit of time to actually put that ride together and actually get it open."

"We went down to Norcross, Georgia, where their factory was, and saw how they were building it," Gramke added. "They were pre-drilling everything, making up all the pieces; it was like a big tinker toy set. They were making the timbers and drilling the holes and doing the routing in them for all the duplers they were going to hold them together with, and pretty much you just put it together like an erector set. When they started shipping the parts here, they made some design changes. They redesigned how they were doing the connections, and we weren't real happy about that, and it turns out Werner Stengel wasn't real happy about that, because he had designed the structural design. So they [RCCA] went to another structural designer to design the structure, and that's where some of the problems wound up on the ride. They went to a single bolt connection and didn't use any dupler plates or any split rings in that connection, so it was very difficult to keep the wood where it's supposed to be."

"The structure was under-engineered by an engineer from Georgia...After it was built, we realized the mistake he made," added Ed Dangler. "He [the structural engineer] didn't use the right loads. He used wind loads as the majority loads...Because the structure wasn't as perfect as the path, the heartline turns and all, the structure couldn't maintain the track shape...There was something missing on that ride and that [the redesigned bolt connections], with the design flaw of the structure using wind loads as the majority load, was the real issue."

One hundred sixty flatbed trucks brought the 2.5 million board feet of lumber that was used to build the coaster's imposing structure. "The site was tough, and we did a different approach there where we built two large tower cranes, rather than using mobile cranes," said Dave Focke, vice president of maintenance and construction. "We had one down in the helix and one up on the hill near the station to try to reach most of the ride's structure."

The park began running into construction issues soon after. "Everyday, one of the maintenance guys would come to my office every day, and he would say, 'Mike, I need more money because we need to buy more gloves; we need to buy more tools,'" said Mike Koontz, who became the park's vice president of finance in November of 1999. "His name was Sam and I said, 'What's going on with all these tools and gloves?' The wood *Son of Beast* was built out of [was] treated with arsenic [to prevent termite damage]. They needed the gloves because that arsenic was eating the gloves." With the cost beginning to overrun, Paramount executives fired RCCA and decided to finish *Son of Beast* by themselves, thereby hoping to decrease the ride's construction cost.

On January 11, 2000, a 50 by 100 foot section that wasn't properly braced collapsed during high winds. OSHA investigated and fined the park $110,000 for eighteen workplace safety violations, most of which were based around inadequate fall protection. It turned out to be OSHA's second investigation of the *Son of Beast* worksite in five months.

Other employees began feeling something strange was going on with the coaster. "They [nighttime maintenance] would come and get fire hoses from the fire-safety department. They would hook it up, we wouldn't, and they would run these large aerations, like you might see out in a farm field," said fire and safety employee Perry Denehy. "They would be doing that to wet down the wood of the superstructure of the coaster. I never questioned it. I figured somebody knows what they're doing. I'm not saying they knew there was a disaster waiting, but something's odd about that. We don't water down *The Racer* or *The Beast* and here this thing is being watered down, and not from the standpoint of fire prevention."

Despite the issues with the ride's construction, management remained optimistic about the ride. "We think it'll drive ticket sales for a long time," Tim Fisher told the *Cincinnati Enquirer*. "*The Beast* was built with the idea that there would never be anything like it, and that stood for more than twenty years. That's what we hope for from *Son of Beast*."

As Paramount's Kings Island's April 14 opening date neared, it became obvious that the coaster wasn't going to be completed in time. "It was a prototypical project, so every time you turned around it would be 'Yes, but...'" said Jane Cooper. "We are still hoping to have it done as close to opening day as possible," park spokesman Jeff Siebert alerted the press on March 31. The park opened without *Son of Beast* on April 14, 2000.

Testing began soon afterwards. "When we first sent the first train over, we valleyed it in the dip at the very top, because the tempera-tures were a little cool and the train was light so it didn't make it," said Jamie Gaffney, Kings Island's area manager of electrical services at the time. "The next morning we got it over and had to add some kicker wheels, booster wheels to the ride to give it more power to get it out of that first dip."

"I thought it was a great ride," said Mike Koontz. "The first time it was smooth, it lived up to all the hype. It was the fastest, tallest, only looping wooden roller coaster in the world! I remember the loop, going through that the first time was phenomenal. To think that here's a wooden roller coaster with a loop in it; it had never been done [in modern times]."

On April 20, officials notified the press that the ride would open on April 28. "We are truly excited that *Son of Beast* is up and ready to roll," Siebert announced. A media preview was scheduled for April 25, and two additional previews for season passholders and radio contest winners were also scheduled. Unfortunately, a lightning strike on April 20 caused a power surge that affected the ride's computers, causing the media day to be cancelled and the other two previews to go on without *Son of Beast.*

Ironically, *Son of Beast* didn't even open on time on April 28. Scheduled to open at 5 p.m., "minor adjustments" delayed the ride's opening until 7:15 p.m.

The ride ultimately went $9 million over budget. What was planned to be a $15 million project ballooned into a $24 million coaster.

For all the superlatives park representatives were giving it, reviews from the public were mixed. "It was a mystifying paradox each time a trainload of thirty-six riders came into the station, half of them cheering and half of them noticeably not," wrote Tim Baldwin in *RollerCoaster!* magazine. "It was certainly one of the most debated, discussed and puzzling coaster debuts in years." Some loved the ride's intense drop and unrelenting speed, while others critiqued the ride's notable roughness and uninspired layout.

"I didn't mind the ride," said Don Helbig. "At the same time, I thought it was probably a little too intense for the average park guest. I'd see guests getting off the ride, looking at the park map to see what they wanted to ride next instead of getting right back in line to ride again."

Just one day after *Son of Beast* opened, it was closed to retrack a fifteen foot section of track that "wasn't running as smoothly as we would like," according to Jeff Seibert. Three weeks later, the ride reopened May 27.

Designed for three-train operation, *Son of Beast* ran most of the 2000 season with only one train. The second train was added near the end of the season.

On November 22, 2000, Paramount's Kings Island sued RCCA, Wooden Structures Inc., the lead structural engineering firm on the project, and Universal Forest Products, which supplied the coaster's lumber. The lawsuit alleged that the coaster was built with subgrade lumber and was poorly designed and constructed. The park claimed that the three firms engaged in negligence, malpractice, and breach of contract that resulted in the park having to spend money correcting the ride, losing income from the delayed opening, and suffering damage to Kings Island's business reputation.

RCCA fired back on December 14 that it was Paramount's Kings Island's fault and not theirs. RCCA maintained that since Paramount had fired them during construction to save on costs, it was the park's fault for any issues they had. "We believe that by attempting to save money by doing the job themselves, Paramount's officials in charge of the project made ill-advised decisions and errors which have cost their company millions of dollars," RCCA managing partner Michael Black said in a statement.

The lawsuit spent several years working its way through the court systems. The courts ruled in 2005 that RCCA should pay $20 million to Kings Island, but the park ultimately lost the case when a 2008 decision ruled that RCCA's commercial insurance policy excluded coverage for the types of issues Kings Island encountered with *Son of Beast*.

FEARFEST

Paramount wanted to drive repeat visitation at their parks. One of the easiest ways to do that was to create special events. "The whole idea of events was to get our season passholders to continue to fall even more in love with coming to the park, and they would come obviously for the new ride of the year, and that would be maybe a summer visit, but the overlay of events to drive other incremental visits was a strategy...to build around the idea that we should come back, especially in the evening, which allows you to have another meal and certain things like that to enjoy yourself," explained Anthony Esparza, senior vice president of design and entertainment for Paramount Parks.

The popularity of intense and frightening Halloween events at other parks led to the decision to create Paramount's Kings Island's own Halloween event—one decidedly *not* family-friendly. "I think the idea was that we thought there was tons of potential with Halloween. We wanted to be on the front-end, the cutting-edge of that type of event and we had the good fortune of having the opportunity to be able to put something like that together with the planning and design group at Paramount," said Tim Fisher.

"The live entertainment side of theme parks was very lightweight at the time," Esparza continued. "We focused mostly on daytime shows and atmospheric entertainment, and the events became more of a focus with the same money to drive repeat visits versus what I call a satisfier: something you see once you're there—shifting it from something that you discovered after you determined you were ready to go to being something that would drive you to go."

FearFest opened September 29, 2000, with five haunted mazes: *Torture Tower*, atop the *Eiffel Tower*, *The Freezer*, at the *Eiffel Tower's* base, *Pirate Jack and the Legend of Halloween*, in *The Paramount Theatre*, *The Sewer*, in the *Festhaus*, and the *Mummy's Revenge* in the *Enchanted Theater*.

"When you're starting an event like that, you have no inventory," Esparza said. "A big part of this are the different mazes and environments that you need, and of course capital is something you use sparingly. When you start an event, it's a bigger commitment to fund the first round of content. Since there was no attendance history or any of that, we had to do a lot of thinking to determine how much we needed to open with." The solution to this problem was to purchase the mazes from an outside company, Sudden Impact! Entertainment Company, which was a professional haunted house builder located in New York City. Besides the haunted mazes, the rides in Paramount Action Zone would remain open and *Phantom Theater*, temporarily renamed *Museum of Horrors*, was re-themed and filled with live actors. A live show, "Studio Fifty-Gore," was produced in the *Festhaus*.

FearFest was a huge success. "We put something together that over the years has grown into a very successful event," Fisher said. "I'm proud of what we were able to create. The team at Kings Island and Design and Entertainment did a great job."

Paramount's Kings Island closed out the 2000 season on October 31.

A RETURN TO (PARAMOUNT) FORM

*Rugrats Runaway Reptar was one of the new attractions in
Nickelodeon Central. Courtesy of Paul Bonifield.*

*F*or the 2001 season which opened on April 7, the park again turned to their Paramount and Viacom brands, refurbishing Nickelodeon SPLAT CITY into Nickelodeon Central, featuring the Nickelodeon cartoon characters.

"Nickelodeon is a powerful way to express kids' characters," said Anthony Esparza. "They're fun; however to make something like that happen required a very large amount of time behind the scenes in New York, meeting with executives to get them comfortable with the brand jumping off a 2D television screen into a brick-and-mortar environment. In the early days, particularly with MTV, they never wanted to have anything that would lock their brand down because they saw themselves as constantly evolving. So we created a concept for the Nickelodeon brand that allowed the characters to overlay on different rides, but all of the different characters and different brands were designed to unbolt and come off and migrate to something else. No one knew whether Rugrats would stick around forever, or the Wild Thornberrys or Dora the Explorer or Blue's Clues, all these things. We had to keep it very flexible. Interestingly, the brands expressed themselves very well as a collection, again, as a basket of characters and shows under the Nick [Central] moniker. It also opened up a huge merchandise sales revenue that wasn't there before." The expansion included *Rugrats Runaway Reptar*, a Vekoma Family Suspended Coaster, and adding a Nickelodeon Character Studio meet-and-greet area along with the *Krusty Krab Snack Shack*.

The aging *Kings Mills Log Flume* was left standing but not operating for the entire 2000 season while officials completely refurbished it into the *Wild Thornberrys River Adventure*, annexing it into Nickelodeon Central in the process. "The flume was a very popular ride at the park, and we thought it made more sense to refurbish that ride and keep it in the park than to take it out," said Tim Fisher. "I'm glad we did; it played a great role in that themed area refurbishment and was very successful for us." New fiberglass figures and sound effects were added that told the story of the popular Nickelodeon show, and the trough was entirely replaced by manufacturer O.D. Hopkins, which maintained its original dimensions and layout.

Kings Mills Log Flume was completely renovated for the 2001 season. Courtesy of Josh Kellerman.

A new film was also added to the *Paramount Action FX Theater: The 7th Portal*, a superhero adventure designed by Stan Lee Media, Inc.

Paramount Parks lost the licensing for "The Outer Limits" show, and the Outer Limits-themed sections of *Flight of Fear* were dropped, including the name, sections of the preshow, and audio at the unloading platform. The over-the-shoulder restraints were additionally replaced by more comfortable lap bars.

FEARFEST 2001

FearFest returned for 2001 on October 5. More of the park was open, including more rides. *The Beast, Flight of Fear, Vortex, Adventure Express, The Racer, Xtreme Skyflyer,* and *Days of Thunder* made their FearFest debut, along with *Son of Beast* and *Drop Zone.* Seven new mazes debuted, replacing the seven from the year prior, which were moved to Paramount's Kings Dominion.

- *House of Darkness*, located in storage space across from *The Racer*

- *Circus of Horrors 3D*, located in the *Festhaus*
- *Curse of the Crypt*, which was placed behind the Coney Mall arcade
- *Maze of Madness*, located in a storage barn next to *Flight of Fear*
- *Trail of Terror*, an outdoor haunted trail through the woods behind *The Racer*
- "Elvira's Superstition," a motion simulator in the *Paramount Action FX Theater*
- *Sleepy Hollow*, located along the pathway between Coney Mall and Rivertown

For children during the daytime hours, the park debuted the "Trick-or-Treat Spooktacular," which took place on International Street and Hanna-Barbera Land.

Paramount's Kings Island closed for the 2001 season November 4.

⚲

2002—TOMB RAIDER: THE RIDE

"To be honest, during that period of time, Paramount did not generate a high volume of theme park-friendly movies," said Anthony Esparza. "They [the movies] did very well, they were doing Braveheart and Forrest Gump. Those kinds of movies which were wonderful, Academy Award-winning movies, but translating that to a theme park environment in a natural way was difficult. When we finally heard that Tomb Raider was coming, we were all over that. That had Angelina Jolie tied to it; that had flexibility to create a platform for different stories."

"We were looking at the Paramount lineup, and if you were going to use intellectual property, you have to pay for it," said Paramount Parks CEO Jane Cooper. "If you're going to pay for it, we wanted something that we thought the brand we were going to put on it would resonate and that people would want to experience it. When we went through the movie repertoire of the last couple of years, we started with Tomb Raider. We thought, 'This would be a cool one, it would make a good theme park attraction, and what could it be?' We didn't always look at it that way. We didn't always try the IP first. On that particular one, we did. So then it was, what can we do that would be somewhat true to the brand and also interesting to the consumer?"

The construction fence was painted with this enigmatic phrase. Courtesy of Josh Kellerman.

"We had caught wind of the movie coming before it was even made, and so we were able to connect with the studio and go to the movie shoot itself to scope out all the sets and the scenery they were using to film," Esparza said. "You don't usually drive your stories this way, but we did since we knew what the movie was about and we knew what environments they were using. We talked them into giving us the sets and shipping it all in cargo containers from England, where it was being done, and basically supplementing our budget at a very high-quality level. So we created a story around the sets and the scenery we knew we were getting!"

With an initial story being developed, the next step was the ride vehicle to tell the Tomb Raider story. "We wanted to not reinvent hardware from scratch so we took the idea of taking an existing ride type, the [HUSS] Top Spin, and at the time they had just created a giant version of it, which was new," Esparza continued. "We thought,

'Hmm. Could we index this ride and actually program it to spin and turn and twist and do things in certain places,' and we would build a building around it." Initially, *TOMB RAIDER: The Ride* was planned to be outdoors, but Esparza eventually decided to place the ride indoors. "We knew the ride was fun by itself [but] by adding the building, now we could hang you over lava, we could spin you in the dark because you were cursed, ultimately turn the lights back on and reveal you almost crashing into ice shards on the ceiling and stop inches away, and then of course rise above the large tomb icon that we had in there with its laser eyes, scanning you to see if you were a friend or a foe."

The location for the ride would be the site of *Kenton's Cove Keelboat Canal*, which closed at the end of the 2000 season. "That ride was so far up in the air and it was so low-capacity because you just couldn't get so many people in those boats and lift them up that big lift, so it was just a natural place to build a ride," said Jeff Gramke. "It had kind-of seen the end of its life, and we wanted to get out of that and drain that lake and take that out of there. It was just a logical place to build *Tomb Raider* since we had that big site and it was good to drive business into Rivertown again."

The ride's seeming misplacement in the frontier-themed River-town area was also because it was "basically where we could find space big enough to put a big giant building," said Esparza. "Also, to have that building face the periphery of the perimeter of the park so that we didn't have to look at it from multiple sides."

TOMB RAIDER: The Ride was announced on July 2, 2001. Park officials would not reveal exactly *what* the ride was, only claiming it would be "the most ambitious project in the history of our park," and that it would be a "heavily-themed, totally-immersive, dark ride adventure."

Vague concept art and the construction of the unremarkable, boxy show building piqued the interest of the public, one of the reasons that Paramount Parks executives had greenlit the ride to begin with. "At that time, we wanted to explore whether that type of ride would be impactful in the marketplace," said Tim Fisher. "We wanted to do something that was a little bit different from attractions we had done in the past, and that's what spurred that."

Throughout the rest of the season and into the winter, park executives teased at what exactly would be inside the ride's massive 80-foot tall show building. "The actual ride experience is literally a physical adventure ride," Jeff Siebert told the press during an exclusive tour on March 1, 2002. "It's not a video screen; it's not a 3-D projection. This ride literally can catapult you throughout the whole chamber."

Tomb Raider: The Ride's show building under construction.
Courtesy of Josh Kellerman.

Unfortunately, the attraction came with multiple design flaws. "One of the issues with that was that it was just under-powered electrically," said rides maintenance manager Ed Dangler. "It's not that hard to get [the ride] moving, but it's hard during the ride cycle to stop it and get it moving again, plus have the gondola do a spin. It was tough. We worked many, many late nights working on it, trying to figure out how to get it to spin correctly."

TOMB RAIDER: The Ride opened along with the rest of Paramount's Kings Island on April 5.

Missing from the park for 2002 was *King Cobra*. "The *King Cobra* was the first stand-up looping roller coaster and it was at the end of its life," Gramke said. "It wasn't built like how B&M coasters are built! The steel on that ride had a definite, finite life expectancy."

"The maintenance cost kept going up as it got older, the structural cost went up some more...so we were at the point where we had had to put a lot of money into the *King Cobra* to extend its life and looking to ridership again, it was good when it was initially put in but it wasn't the draw that it had been in '84," added Dave Focke.

King Cobra was carefully dismantled in the hopes it could be sold. Courtesy of Josh Kellerman.

"We tried to sell that ride," Gramke continued. "It was built in a parking lot in Tokyo before we bought it on temporary foundations; it was like a carnival ride. We were hoping we could sell it to a state fair or somebody that sold tickets where they'd only run it a month or two a year and then that wouldn't wear it out. We run from 9:00 in the morning until 10:30 at night every day nonstop. So we were hoping to sell it, but we couldn't sell the thing."

The ride was eventually scrapped and the trains sent to Kings Dominion for spare parts for their TOGO stand-up coaster *Shockwave*. Contrary to an often-repeated urban legend, there was never a plan to replace *King Cobra* with a Vekoma flying coaster. The plan was always to replace *King Cobra* with *Delirium*, which opened in 2003.

A NEW CEO FOR PARAMOUNT PARKS AND GENERAL MANAGER FOR KINGS ISLAND

Jane Cooper left Paramount Parks May 31, 2002 to "pursue other interests." However, she stayed on in the amusement industry and is currently the COO of Herschend Family Entertainment, which operates parks and attractions including Silver Dollar City and Dollywood. "I would say the number one thing at Kings Island was for it to continue to be the number one tourist destination within the region," Cooper said on her vision for the park. "I think it had a great reputation; it was a great park. We wanted to continue that and grow it from there. Something unique about Kings Island is the community owns it. Originally, we had a deal with the Bengals there, we did the Cincinnati Reds, we had Winterfest. All of that was changed after Paramount bought the company because it didn't fit with Paramount's vision of we're going to have all these parks and they're going to be based on the Paramount/Viacom brands. It was how to marry those Paramount/Viacom brands with a connection to the community. To me, it was always one of the best parks in the country, and we wanted [it] to continue to be...I just think Kings Island is a really special place. I have lots of fond memories and was very happy to be associated with it for the time that I was."

Replacing her as CEO of Paramount Parks was Al Weber, who had been COO since 1997. One of the first things Weber did in his new position was a reorganization of management, which moved Tim Fisher from his general manager position at Kings Island to general manager of Paramount's Great America in California. Fisher was not at Great America for long, and he was soon moved to the position of general manager of Carowinds. After the 2004 season, he was promoted to chief operating officer of Paramount Parks. Following the sale to Cedar Fair in 2006, Fisher moved to Village Roadshow Theme Parks based out of Australia, where he soon became CEO of that group. In December 2017, Fisher returned to Cedar Fair as chief operating officer of the company, a position that he continues in today.

"I'm pleased when I look back at my time there [as general manager] and the growth we had. We were able to continue a tradition there that had been in place well before me and that was providing an experience that appealed to all age groups. The park was much-loved in the marketplace, and I believe that we were able to continue that tradition in a very successful way, and I'm pleased to have been a part of that. It was an honor and privilege for me to be able to work there."

The reorganization included a new general manager for Paramount's Kings Island: Craig M. Ross. Ross began as a seasonal employee at Kings Dominion in 1975 in the foods department. He worked his way up through the ranks at that park and was hired as the merchandise department manager for Kings Dominion in 1982. Ten years later, when Kings Dominion was purchased by Paramount, he was promoted to Kings Dominion's vice president of resale, a position he held until 1995 when he became the vice president of resale for Kings Island. A few years later, Ross was promoted to corporate vice president of resale for Paramount Parks. In the summer of 2002, Al Weber sent Ross back to Kings Island as the park's ninth vice president and general manager.

The new leadership took Kings Island and Paramount Parks in a different direction. Dave Cobb, who became the senior creative director of Paramount Parks in 2002, said, "Their appetite, for the years that I was there [2002-2006], was much more modest in terms of like, 'Alright, we want to stay with a ride system that we know. How can you improve it to bring this thematic or storytelling or interactive or brand-based work?' So that became the charge of simpler, no 'science projects,' as we like to call it in the industry, and that was an added layer of challenge to match up to the determination of the Paramount Parks' early years of making their own voice and making a stand in the very crowded theme park market of, 'We have this innovative new product, that's who we are.' So it was a very interesting challenge to mold that to a different business plan for the last couple years of the parks chain."

FEARFEST 2002

The third FearFest opened on October 4, 2002. *Trail of Terror* was revamped into the *PsychoPath*. A new show, "Celebrity Slaughter," debuted in the *International Showplace*, featuring both local celebrities and celebrity look-alikes.

Paramount's Kings Island closed for the 2002 season on November 3.

⚲

2003—DELIRIUM AND SCOOBY-DOO AND THE HAUNTED CASTLE

Phantom Theater closed on July 14, 2002 to begin construction on one of the two new rides scheduled for 2003—*Scooby-Doo and the Haunted Castle*, a ride that had already debuted as *Scooby-Doo's Haunted Mansion* at both Paramount Canada's Wonderland and Paramount's Carowinds.

"I think that it was...time to update the ride [*Phantom Theater*], and we felt like adding the Scooby overlay to it in terms of the theming would be well-received in the market, and it was," said Tim Fisher, who was general manager at the time the park decided to replace *Phantom Theater* with *Scooby-Doo*.

The animatronics and set-pieces from *Phantom Theater* were gutted and replaced by an interactive dark ride made by Sally Corporation. Every other Omnimover-type car would be removed to allow for the targets to reset, but the vehicles would be sped up to twice their previous speed so that the capacity would remain the same.

"That was a very successful ride for us," said Fisher. "Very popular with a very broad age group, and that ride has been successful for a number of years."

The closure of *Phantom Theater* was an emotional one for guests and the ride's designer, Rick Bastrup. "The kind of work you put into that—the amount of hours and labor and we recorded all of the soundtracks with actors," Bastrup said. "There's just all those details that you do, so they really become a part of you...I like that we touched a lot of people and it's still alive for a lot of people, those characters," Bastrup said.

Several props and parts from Phantom Theater continued to be used during the Halloween season. Pictured here is a buggy displayed in 2007. Courtesy of Paul Bonifield.

The second 2003 attraction, *Delirium*, would be a HUSS Giant Frisbee located on the former spot of *King Cobra's* helix. It would be part of "Just the overall makeover of that area, Action Zone," said general manager Craig Ross. "It featured *Delirium* but it also featured a makeover, a rebranding of that entire area. We had done *Drop Zone*, and then *Delirium* came in after that."

Delirium was assembled in Budapest and tested there before being shipped over for assembly at Paramount's Kings Island. "That ride, I was in a field one night...[by] the Danube River when we first rode that," said Ed Dangler. "We had to use a stepladder to get out to the seats because of the pit with the collapsing floor and all. The headlights on cars for lighting and stuff, you know, I thought, 'Wow, this is pretty unusual!' But that ride came out pretty good, it was a lot of fun, and it was nice for me to be able to see that ride in Budapest and then build it here, put it up here."

Delirium goes through test cycles for the 2003 season.
Courtesy of Josh Kellerman.

A new film showed in the *Paramount Action FX Theater*, "SpongeBob SquarePants 3-D."

One of Craig Ross's main goals for the park was stepping up the food scene, largely because of his background in the food services department. For 2003, the park debuted *Bubba Gump's Shrimp Shack* in place of the *Oktoberfest Gardens*, *Subway* in place of the *Sweet Tooth* on Coney Mall, and *Mandarin Cuisine* on International Street.

Paramount's Kings Island opened on April 12, and *Bubba Gump's Shrimp Shack* opened on June 13.

An unfortunate, accidental casualty during the 2003 season was the Kings Island entrance sign, which toppled over in 80-100 mph winds on September 27. A brand new marquee sign was built in 2004 by Advance Sign Group from Columbus, designed to resemble the iconic gate to the Paramount Studios in Hollywood.

FEARFEST 2003

FearFest opened for its 2003 run on October 4 with a new attraction, *Route 666* on the *Antique Cars*, and a refurbished *Curse of the Crypt*. *Delirium* was added to the event's ride line-up. Also for 2003, the park dropped the extra admission fee for passholders to the event. For families during the day, the *Kings Island and Miami Valley Railroad* was transformed into the *Pumpkin Patch Express*, with stops at a pumpkin patch and an entertainment area in the Picnic Grove. Paramount's Kings Island closed for the 2003 season on November 2.

Å

CROCODILE DUNDEE'S BOOMERANG BAY

For 2004, the attention would be on WaterWorks, completely transforming it into the Australian-themed Crocodile Dundee's Boomerang Bay. The *FasTracks* slides were removed, but their complex was reused by *Coolangatta Racer*. Another new slide was added, *Tasmanian Typhoon*, along with a new kid's play structure, *Jackaroo Landing*. *Kookaburra Bay*, a relaxing lagoon, was added as well.

All existing attractions in the waterpark were renamed to fit in with the new theme:

- The *Kings Mills Run* lazy river became *Crocodile Run*
- *Ultra Twister* became *Awesome Aussie Twister*
- *Bonzai Pipeline* became *Bondi Pipeline*
- *Sidewinder* became *Sydney Sidewinder*
- *The Helix* became *Down Under Thunder*
- *Rushing River* became *Snowy River Rampage*
- *Surfside Bay* became *Great Barrier Reef*
- *WipeOut Beach* became *Pipeline Paradise*
- The *Trader Jake's* and *On Shore* gift shops became *Aussie Outfitters* and *Matilda's*, respectively
- *Sharkey's Eats* was renamed *Dundee's Outback Shack*, which also now included *Wally's Walkabout Pub* on the side
- A *Subway* shop was added

More amenities, including cabanas next to the new wave pool, new bathrooms, and more landscaping were added. "We've taken the world's ugliest waterpark and turned it into something really special," said Jeff Siebert.

The view of Crocodile Dundee's Boomerang Bay from Coolangatta Racer. Courtesy of Paul Bonifield.

Back in the dry park, a new show with audience interaction, "Paramount's Magic of the Movies Live," debuted in *The Paramount Theatre*, which had its benches replaced with seats and a brand new digital projection system installed. The *Nickelodeon Central* amphitheater was refurbished to house character meet-and-greets.

The park celebrated the 25th anniversary of *The Beast* with new sound effects on the lift hills and a documentary on the ride's history playing in line. Paramount's Kings Island opened for the 2004 season on April 9. Crocodile Dundee's Boomerang Bay debuted on May 29.

"Nickelodeon Celebration Parade," traveling through the Paramount Parks, also ran at Kings Island from July 17 through August 15.

FEARFEST 2004

Sleepy Hollow Horror, a new maze, was built in a temporary tent on the path from International Street to Rivertown. *The Paramount Theatre* became home to *Friday the 13th*, with film clips from the movies and a live actor playing Jason "wreaking havoc and causing mayhem," according to Jeff Siebert. A new experience was added to the *Paramount Action FX Theater*, "Dracula's Haunted Castle," which replaced "Elvira's Superstition."

During the day, a few family-friendly mazes operated out of Nickelodeon Central and Hanna-Barbera Land.

FearFest 2004 ran from October 1 through October 31. On October 9, a small fire started on some rope netting used on the *PsychoPath*. Guests were escorted out and no one was injured, and *PsychoPath* reopened the next day.

⚓

2005—THE ITALIAN JOB: STUNT TRACK

In 2003 park leadership moved forward with one goal in mind for 2005—add a family-oriented coaster to the park. "The company was particularly interested in looking at small-footprint coasters that would be impactful and would bring or deliver an exhilarating experience to the parks and in the right price range from a capital perspective," said Tim Fisher, COO of Paramount Parks. "That was the intent with that type of attraction. Can we deliver an exciting, small-footprint coaster for the right price that would be impactful in the marketplace?"

A push from the Paramount Parks corporate office led to the decision to use the highly-visible and central plot of land occupied by the *Antique Cars* and the 1940 *Flying Eagles*.

"There was a considerable amount of debate around that, recognizing the classic appeal of that attraction [*Antique Cars*], but at the same time I think it was starting to live its useful life and we were faced with the challenge of do we upgrade an existing attraction or do we introduce something new?" Craig Ross said. "I think at the time the sentiment was that something new would be more preferred by our guests, so we made the difficult decision to leverage that real estate...That particular [decision] was not an easy one because a lot of folks had a lot of interest in that ride, myself included."

The finale of THE ITALIAN JOB: Stunt Track. Courtesy of Paul Bonifield.

Despite pushback from Kings Island management, Paramount Parks corporate decided to relocate the *Flying Eagles* to Paramount's Carowinds. "The decision is, do you relocate it somewhere in the park, find a new home for it, or what we ended up doing, which was transferring it to another park, which let that park have something new that year," said Jason McClure, Kings Island's vice president of finance at the time. "They [Carowinds] got a new project. From time to time in the business, that pops up as a trend where we move rides from one park to another park...You need the space in one park, the space is available in another park, it saves you a little bit of money instead of buying something new, and gives new life to an old ride."

With those concepts settled, Paramount Parks executives tasked senior creative director Dave Cobb to further develop that idea into a full-scale attraction. "We looked at a number of different IP [intellectual property] to fill that space," Cobb said. "One [idea]...was to do a

Gerstlauer vertical lift and beyond vertical drop [coaster] themed to the Addams Family. And that drop was going to be inside the bell tower of the house, so we had the house facade and there was this little pre-show and the ride vehicles looked like some sort of torture device, like an iron maiden that you were strapped into."

Ultimately, Cobb and his design team settled on an attraction based on the 2003 film *The Italian Job*. "We knew because of the budget, that it couldn't be a fully enclosed attraction [like the Addams Family concept]," Cobb said. "We wouldn't be able to afford a show building, lots of special effects, and a pre-show, so it really became about what property can we do that can work in a sort of urban look and put most of the emphasis on the vehicles. And instantly, *Italian Job* popped in my head because it had just come out, maybe the year before, and it was a big hit and obviously the Mini-Cooper was on top of the world at that point. The movies are what put it on the map after they got rebooted from the '60s and into this new classic, as it were. We went to find out if the Mini-Cooper was part of the movie license and could we use it, and we could, and so we started talking to BMW Mini because they do all the styling, and they sent us pictures of the then-unreleased Mini-Cooper convertible. That made us very excited because that was exactly what we needed! So that set us off on a first pass, blue sky concept...There's these pages of line illustrations with color showing the layout you know, but a little bit longer. It was kind of a presentation book put together for the executives. I also did a sizzle reel...which was...the very first draft of that [the coaster layout] in NoLimits 1.0, intercut with scenes from the movie to show what the coaster moves are meant to represent and the vibe, and it was all cut to music like a movie trailer. I showed that and showed the plans and they greenlit it."

Park officials felt that the Premier Rides coaster perfectly fit *The Italian Job* theme. "We had worked with Jim Seay and Premier [Rides] for years and we felt like it was a really great combination of the Mini-Cooper car and then the dynamic of the car with a LIM launch coaster and the tight footprint and what-not," Craig Ross continued.

THE ITALIAN JOB: Stunt Track would be added to Paramount's

Kings Island for 2005. After the initial planning was finished, the attraction was duplicated at Paramount Canada's Wonderland for 2005 and Paramount's Kings Dominion for 2006.

The public announcement was made August 12, 2004. *Antique Cars*, an opening day attraction, closed three days later, much to the disappointment of many long-time guests. "I think when you're in that moment when you're saying 'We want to do *ITALIAN JOB*, and that's going to mean taking out the *Antique Cars*,' and I don't think you realize until after you do it what the results or repercussions of that could be," said Mike Koontz, CFO of Paramount Parks. Still, management promised a ride full of special effects that would wow park guests. "It's much more in line with what you see at MGM and Universal Studios instead of your backyard theme park," park spokesman Jeff Siebert said at the announcement.

Construction crews worked through an extremely harsh winter. "We had to make sure all the excavations for the footings for the columns were well-marked and roped off, because with the snow you couldn't tell they were there sometimes," rides maintenance manager Ed Dangler said. "It was just a tough winter...the theming worked out really well because we put the controls in shipping containers and they were just perfect for that industrial feel of the backlot as part of the ride. It was just natural, it was really nice. But I think the toughest thing, the challenge was the weather that year. Just a lot of snow, a lot of wind. It was probably the coldest, snowiest winter that I spent down there."

THE ITALIAN JOB was unique in that it not only combined the brand of the *Italian Job* motion picture, but also the brand of the Mini-Cooper. "We had their [BMW Mini] chief stylist and...Premier had sub-contracted S&S to do the sculpting [of the trains] in Utah," Dave Cobb said. "So S&S sculpted the vehicle and made the fiberglass shells, and so, like you'd sculpt a real car, the full-sized clay model was there and their artists were doing it based on some early 3-D models that we had done...The hard part was, it wasn't just about shrinking down the Mini. You can't just say, '3-D printed Mini at 75%' and have branding for a coaster. It's very, very much harder than that. It was about proportion, it's about scale, not size, and it's about visual cues that embody the Mini brand, down to the exhaust pipes that need to line up with your mental map of what a Mini is. Not what a Mini looks like, what a Mini is, and that's a big difference! And that's hard to do within the confines of a coaster vehicle.

"It has accessibility requirements, human interface requirements of how you're seated and secured with the lap bar, motion envelope. We did the scenery and the station, there's so many restrictions on that that an off-the-shelf coaster doesn't have to think about. So just working with Mini on many, many trips to Utah and literally shaving off, they would take a ruler and shave off like an eighth of an inch of clay off of something and you would go, 'Okay, now I see it.' It was that iterative process of getting this hunk of clay that was supposed to be a roller coaster vehicle down to make you feel like it was correct as a Mini-Cooper. That was a very long process and a lot of fun to do!"

Additional unique features required innovative solutions. "While the big parks like Disney and Universal had done on-board audio, it had never been done to a regional park yet, and Premier hadn't done it yet," Cobb added. "So it was a lot of trial and error, and...the audio floor of a space or attraction is a certain dB level, depending on what it is. A coaster like that has a dB level of about eight [sic], so you have to get above that, which is very loud! And so just getting a system that worked reliably for a regional park on a budget that wasn't as high as the custom systems that Universal and Disney were engineering was a real challenge. I'm very happy they did it...because it helped make it a cinematic experience, from the announcement of the director in the loading instructions to 'Action!' to the music, and the 'And, cut!' at the end with the splashdown. It really helped sell that scene, that theme to everybody, and so I'm very glad we introduced the idea that a regional park could have something like that. And that is a custom score made specifically for that ride, and if you listen to the safety announcements or the welcome back announcement...that is all me! I'm the director and they pitched me down a bunch and I was the helicopter pilot, so all the voices that you hear on the 'crew' were actually just me doing all the lines, and then we just pitched it at different levels. Just because I don't have the money for a VO [voice-over] guy, so I did it."

"...we engineered a sway to the vehicles so that when it went around corners, it would fishtail a little bit," Cobb said. "It's still there...I think, but it's turned off, it's locked in place. What happened was, for weight distribution and engineering reasons, they calculated that it was going to put straining on the track that would be off-the-shelf major...So they reduced the sway to a pretty small amount that, seated in a chair and being shoved back and forth and testing it in a room was like, 'Oh, that feels really cool.' But once we put it on the ride, it was so minimal that nobody really noticed it. It ended up being a bit of an engineering boondoggle that didn't quite work..."

Paramount's Kings Island opened for the 2005 season on April 9, and "technical rehearsals" for gold passholders began for *THE ITALIAN JOB: Stunt Track* on April 29. A media preview was held on May 19, and the coaster officially opened to the general public on May 20, 2005.

"Everybody thinks a blue sky is unfettered design, anything is possible. Well, that's not really true. Most parks have a definite plot of land, a definite demographic, or a definite budget. We, luckily, had all three! Which creates a pretty specific and challenging canvas to create, but we squeezed every penny out of the budget we had to get that coaster that's there. I know it's been de-themed and had all the theming taken off of it, but I'm very proud of that ride for a lot of reasons and thought it was a perfect example of bringing a big movie brand to life in a regional park in a fiscally responsible, but still wide-audience ranging way," Cobb concluded.

Also new for 2005 was a *Graeter's Ice Cream* store and *Starbucks* on International Street, *Chick-fil-A*, and *Happy Days Diner*, a refurbished *Preston T. Tucker's Roadside Cafe*.

FEARFEST 2005

For FearFest 2005, the park transformed Rivertown into the Curse of Sleepy Hollow, a themed area encompassing *Massacre Manor* (a renamed *Sleepy Hollow Horror*), *CornSTALKERS* (along the pathway from the *Eiffel Tower* into Rivertown), and *Headless Hollow* (involving the train and *White Water Canyon* exit line). The *House of Darkness* was replaced by *R.L. Stine Fear Street*, inspired by the stories of Ohio-born R.L. Stine. Two films, "Elvira's Superstition" and "Funhouse Express" played in the two theaters in the *Paramount Action FX Theater*.

FearFest 2005 ran from October 1 through October 29, and the park closed for the main season October 30.

WINTERFEST RETURNS FOR 2005

Even though Winterfest had been cut from the park's lineup in 1992, there had been much thought over the years about bringing the event back and extending the season. By 2005, "I think that we were at a point where we felt like it was time to bring it back," stated Craig Ross. "We had our guests constantly asking us to bring it back, and I think from a business perspective, there was support for it from Paramount to look at the extended season."

"It was such a traditional, well-received experience, event, at Kings Island it just seemed the right thing to do for that marketplace," added Tim Fisher. "The history of it at Kings Island, the way the market had responded to it in years past, it just made good sense to bring it back."

Winterfest (now stylized as WinterFest) was announced on July 25, 2005. That same day, Paramount's Carowinds announced their WinterFest, the first time that park would hold a Christmas event since 1983.

While Kings Island had been working on infrastructure improvements for the event for several years, like the 2004 renovation of *The Paramount Theatre* and the 2005 additions of indoor seating at *Graeter's* and *Starbucks*, the actual details of what the event would contain were planned in a relatively short period of time and on a very tight budget.

On International Street, the classic ice skating experience on the *Royal Fountain* would return, along with the *Eiffel Tower* Christmas tree. Lighting on International Street, and throughout the park, would prove to be an issue, as the park would have to start from scratch since all of the original Winterfest decor had been sold off or donated. "To do that [the original Winterfest lighting package] again was cost-prohibitive so we had to innovate a bit on how to really get the decor and the lighting done affordably, but also at a good level and get it done quickly, because as I recall from the time we made the decision to do it to the time we had to get it up and going, we didn't have a lot of time," Ross said.

Another goal was to eliminate some unnecessarily labor-intensive aspects from the original event. "When I interviewed there [for a job] in 1992, it was in the fall, it was like October or so, and there were people on stepladders around that fountain picking leaves off trees," said Ed Dangler, manager of rides maintenance. "And I'm thinking, 'What are they doing?' And it was all preparing for putting the lights up on the trees, all the lights."

The signature show for the new WinterFest was the return of "Santa's Toy Factory" in *The Paramount Theatre*. "Santa's Toy Factory" was a show that our entertainment people said had played well before and was very appealing to a broad market [of] families and adults," Ross explained. More entertainment came in the way of the "Home For the Holidays Parade." The Paramount Story was transformed into Nickelodeon's Holiday Tree Lot, a character meet-and-greet.

In Oktoberfest, the *Festhaus* became the *Winter Festhaus*, which hadn't played host to a live show since 1996. "I remember trying to think through how best to treat the *Festhaus* because it had more or less evolved into being a major location in the park to go eat, and as Winterfest had been done before, people went there for the show and not so much to eat," Ross said. "So we tried to keep the *Festhaus* offering in-line with the food experience versus a strength from the shows standpoint." Nonetheless, a small stage was built in the middle of the facility for rotating performances from choral groups and other local artists.

Swan Lake in Rivertown was now home to the "Holiday Illuminations Light Show." The *Kings Island and Miami Valley Railroad* became the *White Christmas Express*, with scenes and characters based on the 1954 film.

Hanna-Barbera Land, undergoing a large-scale renovation, was renamed Santa Land for the event with Santa taking up residence in the *Animation Station* gift shop. In addition to the *Grand Carousel* and the train, the other rides that would be operating for WinterFest included the *Hanna-Barbera Carousel, Pixie & Dixie's Swing Set, Scooby-Doo and the Haunted Castle*, and *Top Cat's Taxi Jam*. Guests had to reserve tickets for "Santa's Toy Factory," and, in a drastic departure from the previous Winterfests, season passholders would have to pay the same price as average guests: $24.99 per person, if bought at the gate.

"I think at the time, it was felt like because it was an added event...that season passholders wouldn't have a problem paying for it," said Mike Koontz, the CFO of Paramount Parks. "Their pass was paying for the park, but adding WinterFest in 2005, it was felt like it was an addition to what their normal pass paid for."

Executives expected crushing crowds for the return of the popular event. This didn't happen. "The mistake we made was charging season passholders," admitted Koontz. "The attendance in 2005 was, I don't want to say disastrous, but it was very bad." An extremely cold winter drove whatever crowds would have come away. The issue was not exclusive to Kings Island. The *Charlotte Observer* titled their Carowinds WinterFest feature "Walking in Empty Wonderland."

The guests that did come enjoyed themselves, but it didn't live up to the original, which was done on a significantly larger budget. "It was well done in 2005. I thought the park did a nice job with it, but the experience wasn't what it was in the 1980s," recalled Don Helbig. "The entertainment lineup wasn't on the same level. At the same time, there were things they were able to do better in 2005 because technology had improved."

Despite the disappointing attendance, executives were optimistic about the future of the event. "While we weren't dancing in the streets over the first year's result due to the cold weather, I think we felt like we were off to a good start," Ross said.

What was expected to be the first year of a new WinterFest ran from November 25–December 31.

Å

2006—YOGI BEAR WAVES GOODBYE

The Hanna-Barbera characters, fixtures since Kings Island opened in 1972, were retired after the 2005 season in favor of something far more hip and modern for the time: Nickelodeon. Nickelodeon Central and Hanna-Barbera Land were combined into one section for the 2006 season and was named Nickelodeon Universe. Three new rides were added: *Plankton's Plunge*, a Zamperla Jumpin' Star, *Phantom Flyers*, a Zamperla Kite Flyer, and *Avatar: The Last Airbender*, a Zamperla Skater Coaster.

Timmy's Air Tours, part of the Nickelodeon makeover landing in Hanna-Barbera Land in 2006. Courtesy of Paul Bonifield.

Nearly everything else was re-themed and renamed.

- *Hanna-Barbera Carousel* became the *Nick-O-Round*

- *Pixie & Dixie's Swing Set* was renamed *Backyardigans Swing-Along*
- *Flintstone's Boulder Bumpers* became *Jimmy Neutron's Atom Smashers*
- *Alley Cat 500* became *Swiper's Sweeper*
- *Fender Bender 500* became *Nick Jr. Drivers*
- *Huck's Hot Rods* became *Go Diego Go!*
- *Atom Ant's Airways* became *Timmy's Air Tours*
- *Quick Draw's Railway* became *La Aventura de Azul*
- *Yogi's Sky Tours* became *LazyTown Sportacopters*
- *Top Cat's Taxi Jam* became *Little Bill's Giggle Coaster*
- *GREEN SLIME Zone* became *SpongeBob SquarePants Bikini Bottom Bash*
- *Dick Dastardly's Biplanes* became *Blue's Skidoo*
- *The Beastie* became the *Fairly Odd Coaster*—the first name change the coaster received in 26 years

Pathways were also widened to lessen congestion and allow more strollers. To make way for the expansion, *Scooby's Ghoster Coaster, Baba Looey's Buggies, Boo-Boo's Baggage Claim*, and *Jetson's Jet Orbiters* were all removed.

Paramount's Kings Island opened for the 2006 season on April 14.

FOR SALE: PARAMOUNT PARKS

Frustrated by a languishing stock price, Viacom Inc. announced in March of 2005 that they were considering splitting into two separate companies: one for its cable networks such as MTV and one for its broadcast television properties such as CBS. On October 5 of that year, Viacom announced more details on the split. The new Viacom would include the company's television and movie divisions, including MTV and Paramount Pictures. The other company, CBS Corp., would include CBS Television. The two companies formally split in early January of 2006, with the Paramount Parks division going to CBS. CBS wanted to focus on television and broadcasting and had no interest in running amusement parks. In late January, CBS put the Paramount Parks up for sale. Viacom had been planning on selling off the parks anyway, but the split with CBS only sped up the process.

"We knew internally that we would be for sale as soon as we went under the CBS eye, because every other company under that CBS eye had something to do with broadcasting and studios," said Ed Dangler, manager of rides maintenance at Kings Island. "We were the only outlier there. So we knew that was going to happen, so we were prepared for it."

Kings Island's finance department went into overdrive to make sure that the park was prepared for whatever happened next. "A lot of the original assets would have been fully depreciated, so now we needed to assign them value again," said Jason McClure, vice president of finance. "We had to do a complete new inventory fixed asset list of every building, every ride. Most of them were there, but it was always funny, you'd have to research one of the original Kings Island associates to [ask], 'This building is on the report, and the name of the building doesn't exist anywhere. What is it?' And they'd say, 'Oh, that's the French Building on International Street.' They always knew the original name. So there was a lot of boring finance work that went into getting the balance sheet ready to be ready to move forward with whatever the financial transaction would be."

During the time the parks were for sale, Kings Island was put into a sort of "B-Mode" while awaiting a buyer, to maximize the value of the company. Craig Ross was sent back to corporate headquarters in Charlotte and was temporarily replaced by Tim Fisher as interim general manager. Live entertainment was nearly non-existent and the *International Showplace* simply sat vacant for the year.

Paramount left a mixed legacy at Kings Island. "The Paramount thing was one of the best things that ever happened to Kings Island," believes analyst Dennis Speigel. "It brought that IP. Kings Island was just hovering at this level of attendance, and when Paramount came in it went up here [very high]. Same thing happened with Six Flags. When Time-Warner bought them, it brought in the DC characters,

Superman and all that; schoom, it went up here. So that movie association really is what moved those numbers so much for the parks. So the Paramount thing was a great thing while it was there."

Still, Paramount's ownership left a bad taste in the mouths of many longtime guests and even former management from the Taft Broadcasting days. A complete disregard for the history, design, and thematic principles of the park and the lack of a true standout, high-quality addition after *The Outer Limits: Flight of Fear* in 1996, along with the severe decline of live entertainment and general park upkeep, brought up many criticisms during their ownership period.

Fortunately for Kings Island and the rest of the Paramount Parks, they did not have to wait long for a buyer—one that would ultimately take Kings Island to new heights of quality, both literally and figuratively.

CEDAR FAIR ENTERTAINMENT COMPANY

An entire amusement park chain being put up for sale doesn't happen every day. The parks quickly fell under the eye of many interested parties. "There were several private equity companies that came and visited," said Jason McClure. "One of the interesting things in a sales transaction like that, you have to qualify to move forward because a lot of people would love to come and take a look at your books. The competition would love to come and see what are your financial results and what are your plans for the future. You have to qualify in as an investor...Most of the people that were looking at the acquisition were financial entities. Whether they were venture capital groups like Apollo, I know the Canadian Teachers Pension Fund was very interested in Canada's Wonderland, so they were looking for partners to partner with to make a purchase. There were several [interested parties], but most of them were from outside of the [amusement] industry, that were more just financial entities...The fun part was when folks would show up at the park and you'd be able to give them a tour, brag about the park, tell them what made it great. That was the nice part of the acquisition!"

One potential buyer was someone with actual amusement park experience. Sandusky, Ohio-based Cedar Fair had been founded in 1983 to take ownership of the then 113-year-old Cedar Point amusement park and newer sister park Valleyfair. The company went public as a master limited partnership in 1987. Shortly after becoming CEO, Dick Kinzel decided the best way to grow the company was by acquiring other amusement parks. Under Kinzel, Cedar Fair acquired Pennsylvania's Dorney Park in 1992, Missouri's Worlds of Fun in 1995, Knott's Berry Farm in 1997, Michigan's Adventure in 2001, and Aurora, Ohio's Six Flags Worlds of Adventure in 2004. Throughout these acquisitions, one park remained high on Kinzel's list—Kings Island. "I started at Cedar Point in 1972; Kings Island opened in '72," Kinzel said. "At that time, Cedar Point was the only [large] amusement park in Ohio, and Kings Island was bragging they were the best, so a good rivalry built from that point on." The park's high profitability and great location made Kings Island a target for Cedar Fair almost immediately after Kinzel was named CEO in 1986.

"I first approached American Financial out of Cincinnati way back when, and I told them if they were ever interested in selling Kings Island we would be interested in talking to them," Kinzel explained. "Never heard anything for a long time. Then I got a call from him one day; their CFO called. My CFO and I went to Cincinnati and we talked to him, and nothing really happened about it."

"Then a couple years later, Carl Lindner who owned American Financial, they hadn't announced it, but they called us and said that they were going to sell Kings Island to Paramount. They said that we had really shown an interest in it; seemed like we were good operators. There was a $40 million tax problem because we were a master limited partnership and they were a C Corp. If we solved the tax issue, they would be glad to sell us the property. We called a board meeting on a Saturday. It was decided that $40 million was just a little higher than what we wanted, and so we turned down the offer." Kings Island was sold to Paramount instead.

When the Paramount Parks went up for sale in 2006, Kinzel couldn't resist. The perfect opportunity had arrived. Now, Cedar Fair could finally acquire Kings Island, as well as the four other Paramount Parks, which would double the size of the company. "That was always our strategy, to try to grow the company through expansion; not through outside sources but basically through things that we knew, and that was the amusement park industry," said Kinzel.

On May 22, 2006, Cedar Fair publicly announced that they were purchasing the Paramount Parks for $1.24 billion, which plunged Cedar Fair into debt. "We paid a little higher for the Paramount Parks than what I wanted to pay, or what the board wanted to pay, but we really felt that they were underperforming parks, and that they had a tremendous potential, and it would really double the size of the company," Kinzel said. "We paid a little bit more than what some people thought we should, but as it turned out years later, it ended up being probably the best acquisition that Cedar Fair ever made."

"I actually was part of the executive group of people that walked through a couple of the parks with Cedar Fair to show them the assets and explain how we got to design each one of these things," said Dave Cobb, senior creative director for Paramount Parks. "So that was an interesting process, sort of a week or two trip around the country...Every park chain has its own sort of culture, so it was interesting watching their culture. It wasn't so much that it clashed with us, it was just different. So it was very clear that the parks were going to be a different place."

Rob Decker, Cedar Fair's former senior vice president of planning and design, grew up going to Kings Island and lived in Cincinnati for seventeen years. For him, the sale meant astonishing new opportunities. "I was really excited," Decker said. "I knew some of the people within the system, and I was just ecstatic to be associated with them. But it took a long time to really roll up our sleeves and get down to getting everything executed. The two different philosophies, they weren't too far apart, but the two different philosophies of the company really melded together in the end very well. I think both of the park systems have benefited by the association."

"We worked together to have a 'glass is half full' sort of mindset about it, and anyone that bought us we felt like was going to want to own us and we were excited for the proposition of whatever this new chapter would hold," said Craig Ross on the thoughts of Paramount Parks executives. "It's not like we hadn't been through changes in ownership before. We looked upon it as, 'Hey, here's an opportunity for us.' Of course, it would be unrealistic for me to say there wasn't some uneasiness in it, but as it turned out, I think things have a way of working out for all that are concerned."

The sale to Cedar Fair was finalized on June 30, 2006.

PART V
CEDAR FAIR

NEW OWNER—NEW DIRECTION

On June 30, 2006 Cedar Fair named Greg Scheid general manager of Kings Island. Scheid had a long history with Cedar Fair starting in 1978, when he began working seasonally at Cedar Point—first in the Hotel Breakers and then in the park's games department. After graduating from college in 1988, he began working full time at Cedar Point. In 2000 he was promoted to vice president of the merchandise and games division. He stayed in that position for four years before being promoted in 2005 to vice president and general manager of Dorney Park. Now Scheid was the new vice president and general manager of Kings Island.

Craig Ross became the vice president of marketing for Kings Island immediately following the sale and left the chain shortly afterwards for Herschend Family Entertainment; he is currently serving as the interim general manager for Kentucky Kingdom, which was acquired by Herschend in 2021. "My vision [at Kings Island] was to recognize the brand equity that Kings Island had from its inception in 1972 while keeping it aligned to Paramount and Viacom and the other brands that came by way of our being a part of those companies. From a brand standpoint, I was always balancing out both brands. I took a lot of pride in being responsible for one of the top brands and businesses in all of Greater Cincinnati. To me, it was a personal reflection on me and my family. I took it really, really seriously. It was important to me to be an effective but a respected leader there.

"For all the years that Kings Island's been around, there's been some extraordinary leaders there that cared an awful lot about the community and about the park and all that went into it," Ross concluded. "I'm honored to have had a little bit of time there at the helm, and I have a lot of respect for all the people that have preceded me and that will follow me."

Al Weber, the CEO of Paramount Parks immediately prior to the sale to Cedar Fair, continued his illustrious career as CEO of Palace Entertainment, interim CEO of Six Flags Entertainment Corporation, and as founder and CEO of Apex Parks Group. He passed away suddenly while on vacation in 2016; Weber was posthumously inducted into the Kings Island Hall of Fame in 2019.

"Al was a really good leader," recalls Mike Meadows, who was Kings Island's vice president of finance while Weber was general manager. "He focused on leadership issues. Once he got to Kings Island, he attended Xavier University and got an executive MBA and he eventually pursued and completed his PhD. Al was a dedicated, lifelong learner; he did everything he could to be cutting-edge about management philosophy and how he implemented strategic planning. He was a very supportive boss. He was the one who pushed for my promotion [to general manager at Great America], so I was a huge fan of Al!"

"He was the number two most influential [man]; he was a very team-oriented, team-building kind of guy," fondly remembers Dave Focke. "We did a lot of team building with him. He had a lot of confidence in the crew we had at that time, and he was really great to work for. In fact, after I started my consulting business, I did a lot of work with Al after he moved to start Apex Parks Group."

BAPTISM BY FIRE

Just nine days after Cedar Fair took charge, *Son of Beast* had a serious accident. On July 9, 2006 a train running through the course experienced a "jolt." All twenty-seven passengers on the train were injured. "It certainly was not a horrific scene of gore when we got there," said Perry Denehy, a first responder from the park's Fire and Safety Department. "It was almost like a minor fender-bender. People are going to be a little uncomfortable, but they weren't yelling and screaming in pain." Nearly all aboard suffered minor injuries, such as bumps and bruises, although one woman did suffer a broken chest bone. *Son of Beast* would remain closed for the rest of 2006 while the Ohio Department of Agriculture conducted an investigation and park executives debated what to do with the ride. Multiple lawsuits were filed by the injured riders, resulting in negative publicity for the park and its brand-new owners, who had unknowingly inherited a mess.

Ultimately, the investigation blamed a cracked bent (support structure frame) that caused a dip in the track, resulting in an effect similar to running over a pothole at seventy miles an hour. Over the years the structure had been stiffened by additional supports, with bracing added to the coaster's structure. This allowed the energy from the coaster's heavy trains to travel through the structure, causing the bent made of sub-grade lumber to snap.

WINTERFEST IS CANCELLED (FOR NOW)

Cedar Fair's first major announcement after taking over was not a surprising one: WinterFest had been canceled for the second time in Kings Island's history. "At that point I would say they [Cedar Fair corporate] didn't have all their ducks in a row," said general manager Greg Scheid. "There was a lot of confusion over what WinterFest wanted to really be. I didn't see it in '05, I just saw videos and pictures. It was well done. But we had lost a lot of money, '05 was a rough winter, and we knew it was very weather-dependent. We just said, 'Nah. We need to put it to bed.' When we did make that decision, we always knew it could come back; it just wasn't going to any time soon."

FEARFEST 2006

FearFest, however, continued on for 2006 with new attractions, including *Cowboy Carnage*, a maze located inside the *Rivertown Mining Company* building, The Worksite scare zone in Paramount Action Zone, Holiday Horror scare zone located across from Zephyr, and the "Monster Bash" live show inside *The Paramount Theatre*. The event ran from September 30 through October 28. Paramount's Kings Island closed for the 2006 season on October 29.

Å

2007—CEDAR FAIR'S FIRST ADDITION

Cedar Fair management decided to close their Geauga Lake property at the end of 2007, but the distribution of salvageable parts would begin even before the park closed for good. "Unfortunately, we had to close Geauga Lake, and right before we purchased Geauga Lake, Six Flags had put in five coasters!" said Cedar Fair CEO Dick Kinzel. "Five very expensive, excellent coasters, and we weren't just going to tear them down, so we relocated them. We relocated them to different parks within the Cedar Fair family, and it just so happened that's where we felt Kings Island would benefit most, by having that ride."

The maintenance-heavy Vekoma Flying Dutchman, *X-Flight*, seemed to be an ideal ride to relocate and overhaul. "Sometimes it's hard to justify, if a ride needed major overhauls or if a ride needed to be refreshed or changed in any way, it's hard to just do that on the ground, do it in place, and then remarket it," said Rob Decker, Cedar Fair's former senior vice president of planning and design. "But when you bring new equipment and new experiences into other parks, you get another bite at the apple."

Greg Scheid recalls a time during Halloween 2006 when Kinzel and COO Jack Falfas "called me and said, 'Do you want this ride?' I said, 'I don't know.' They said, 'We'll give it to you but you have to have it in by Memorial Day.' That's unheard of. That's too tight of a timeline, but knowing the only way we could get a ride was saying yes, I said 'Yeah.' That call came in about 4 or 5 p.m. on that day and the next morning we were clearing trees!"

Firehawk swooped above guests in the queue. Courtesy of Paul Bonifield.

Beginning in January of 2007, the bright-green pieces of track from *X-Flight* began "landing" in Kings Island's parking lot. Rumors began *flying*—could Cedar Fair really be installing a full-sized roller coaster at Kings Island so soon after taking over?

The answer was yes, as revealed on February 5, 2007. *X-Flight*, repainted and renamed as *Firehawk*, would call Kings Island home for 2007 next to *Flight of Fear* in an area of Coney Mall that was renamed X-Base.

The project gave deja vu to some staff at Kings Island. "It's funny because I was at Carowinds when we moved the *Borg Assimilator*, we called it then, from Great America to Carowinds, which was the [Vekoma] flying coaster there, then I get to Kings Island and I'm doing it again!" laughed Jason McClure, Kings Island's vice president of finance. "I'm like, 'Why, everywhere I go, does a flying coaster relocation project follow me?'"

It was a similar story for Russell Flatt, Kings Island's new vice president of maintenance and construction, who worked on the previous relocation at Carowinds. Fortunately for Kings Island, this meant that *Firehawk* would be almost like doing the Carowinds project over again. "The biggest challenge was the decision was made late and trying to get that ride taken apart and moved to Cincinnati was in the very bitter part of the winter," recalled Flatt. "I think we really probably didn't start any demolition until probably the end of December. And it's cold out there!...The schedule was tight, but a lot of good contractors in the Cincinnati area helped us out and that was great."

Vertical construction began in March. "The thing about *Firehawk* was we had to rewire the entire ride," Scheid commented. "There were a lot more electronics involved with that ride than the typical ride for that stature."

Another issue that arose was whether the ride's station would be one-sided or two. "It was much easier to install it as a one-side, but we knew we needed capacity because that ride is just so slow [at loading]," Scheid continued. "We decided, whatever we were going to do, we were going to do it right." *Firehawk* would be installed as a two-sided ride, just as it was at Geauga Lake. The coaster utilized three trains at Geauga Lake, but the third train was used for parts at Kings Island because it would not increase the coaster's capacity. Amazingly, *Firehawk* opened right on schedule on May 26, 2007, only about seven months after planning began.

Other changes for the April 21, 2007 opening included dropping Paramount from the park's name, a new logo, five new live shows, and an increased focus on cleanliness, a Cedar Fair trademark. "There was a big impetus to clean up the parks," said Jeff Gramke. "We had kind-of gotten away a little bit from the core business and were getting more into theming and a lot of stuff like that, so they pretty much emphasized the basics—keep everything safe, keep everything clean, do everything right."

Licensing from the Paramount days continued for the most part. The waterpark lost Crocodile Dundee, *Paramount Action Zone* dropped "Paramount," and *The Paramount Story* reverted to its previous *Tower Gardens* name. "We're looking at a lot of licensing agreements," park spokeswoman Maureen Kaiser told the *Cincinnati Post* in February 2007. "We have about twelve to eighteen months to make the transition." The park's marquee sign also retained its Paramount's Kings Island logo.

CEDAR FAIR CHANGES

The relatively slow transition from a Paramount park to a Cedar Fair park was a far cry from the rapid American Financial Corporation to Paramount changeover, but it was done on purpose. "We took it very slow," said Dick Kinzel. "Kings Island was a good park. We had a little bit of a different strategy on staffing. We have four cornerstones that we lift off of [safety, courtesy, cleanliness, service]. It was a slow, gradual process. We didn't do much the first year, and basically we instilled the four cornerstones that [former Cedar Point executives George] Roose and [Emile] Legros left us, and then I put a fifth one in, integrity...It was really a slow transition, and basically if someone from the Paramount organization, or from any of the parks that we acquired, couldn't adjust to our work ethic and our philosophy on cleanliness and service and safety, they pretty well worked their way out of a job...The ones that stayed fit really well with the Cedar Fair philosophy."

Kinzel saw lots of opportunities and potential with adding the new park to Cedar Fair's portfolio. "We knew it was an outstanding park. [International] Street was beautiful. It was altogether different than Cedar Point. Cedar Point was basically a pure [amusement] park. We had our big midway, but we certainly didn't have the big *Eiffel Tower* at the end! All the buildings [at Cedar Point] were built in the 50s and the 60s and Kings Island was '72 and everything was brand-spanking new and they had the beautiful *Eiffel Tower* and everything revolved off of [International] Street, I think it was four different areas, so it was an entirely different park. We had a lot of different ideas to work with."

The sale meant a change in the capital investment strategy chain-wide for Cedar Fair. "We always had a rotation of capital investment," explains Rob Decker. "What I like to say is some park systems, everyone gets a big prize or maybe the same amount of presents under the tree at Christmas time. Cedar Fair is a little different in that we try to collect our emphasis where it's going to make the most marketable impact and economic sense for the company. Sometimes, parks wouldn't star, but they would go into maintenance mode or maintaining appeal, guest appeal. So I think [with] Paramount...everyone had something in a range of x to x invested in the parks every year, so they always had something. So it was a challenge to try to figure out where our biggest impact could be made and what that product might be, and what the guest is looking for and all the dynamics of pricing and season pass and the demographics of the area and growth areas [after the sale to Cedar Fair]...If everyone had a fairly equivalent amount of investment, you would have never reached that level that you would have to put in to get a *Diamondback* into the park."

The sale also meant increased standardization. "We had to adjust over to where Cedar Fair felt like we needed to be consistent," said Jason McClure, Kings Island's vice president of finance. "It could be as simple as changing the uniforms that the associates wear, it could be as complicated as...every Scrambler in the company needs to operate the same. So everyone needs to have the same kind of restraints, they need to have the same safety spiels and safety checks. That's a complicated thing to do with multiple parks, and I think it was hard. With acquiring several parks at the same time, it upped the challenge."

Jeff Gramke, who became Kings Island's manager of facilities, engineering, and construction following the sale, remarked on the big picture. "Overall, I think it was a good thing. It made us a big, big park group that gave us a lot more opportunity to buy things from manufacturers. It's definitely been a positive. We've done great since Cedar Fair bought us."

"It was taking the best of what the Cedar Fair parks did well and what the Paramount Parks did well and merging them together as I came in," said Don Helbig, who joined the Kings Island team in 2007 as public relations area manager. "Both were really good operators, but the Paramount Parks were somewhat ahead on the technology side with e-commerce platforms and things of that nature while there were things that Cedar Fair parks did operationally that were incorporated into the Paramount Parks."

"Cedar Fair had always been known as great operators and [with] very high standards," said Mike Koontz, who worked as an executive under both Paramount and Cedar Fair. "Paramount Parks, we felt like we were great operators and [had] high standards as well. A lot of similarities in the two companies; safety is always the priority. I think some of the differences is Paramount Parks had the ability to use brands like *Tomb Raider* or like *Top Gun, Italian Job, Face/Off* instead of *Invertigo, Drop Zone* instead of *Drop Tower*, Nickelodeon, etc. One of the differences is Cedar Fair did not see the value in paying intellectual property fees whereas Paramount Parks felt there was value to our guests in providing those branded rides...I think Cedar Fair probably pays more attention to...every ride is open every day, every food stand is open, every merch store is open, every hour, every day. I think Paramount Parks felt like, if the attendance or the demand for certain things [was low], they wouldn't necessarily operate it the same way...I think the other thing, Paramount Parks probably took more risks with some rides. Like *Italian Job* for example. That was a unique-type ride. Cedar Fair was more just, 'Build the ride,' but Cedar Fair also built bigger, faster rides. I think at the end of the day you forward to 20[20] and the company, whether it was a Cedar Fair park or a Paramount Park, I think Kings Island is better today in a lot of ways than it was under the Paramount days."

THE SON RETURNS

Following the investigation of the 2006 *Son of Beast* accident, the Ohio Department of Agriculture ordered the park to go through multiple changes with the coaster to address the issues found during the state's investigation. One of those solutions Kings Island implemented was installing new, lighter trains. Unfortunately, that meant removing *Son of Beast's* signature element—the 118-foot tall vertical loop. "If we took the loop out, we could have more comfortable trains and ones that could handle more dynamics," said Greg Scheid. The loop was removed prior to the 2006 holidays and taken to a steel recycling plant. *Son of Beast* reopened on the 4th of July 2007 without the loop and with two trains from the defunct *Hurricane* roller coaster at Myrtle Beach Pavilion.

One of Son of Beast's new trains and the coaster's missing
loop can be seen here shortly after the ride reopened in 2007.
Courtesy of Paul Bonifield.

The ride's image had been damaged so greatly by the heavily publicized 2006 accident that the *Son of Beast* name almost didn't return. "There was a lot of controversy if it should [still] be *Son of Beast* or not, but that was what we decided on," said Dick Kinzel.

HALLOWEEN HAUNT 2007

For 2007, the park's Halloween event was renamed Halloween Haunt, the same name used for Halloween events at other Cedar Fair parks. It also featured a new maze in Action Zone, *Club Blood*, and two new shows, "Dead Awakening" in the *International Showplace* and "Torture Chamber" in *The Paramount Theatre*. Several existing mazes were expanded, renamed, and re-themed, including *Headless Hollow*, now *Tombstone Terror-tory*, *Death Row*, the former *Asylum*, *Trail of Terror*, the former *PsychoPath*, *Red Beard's Revenge*, the former *Cowboy Carnage*, and *CarnEVIL*, the former *Circus of Horrors 3D*.

Halloween Haunt ran from September 21 through October 31.

2008

After spending over a year pouring over licensing agreements, Cedar Fair ultimately decided not to spend the money and cancelled their contracts with Paramount. The single largest change to the park for 2008 was the removal of nearly all Paramount film properties.

- *The Paramount Theatre* was renamed the *Kings Island Theater*
- The *Paramount Action FX Theater* became *Action Theater*
- *Face/Off* was renamed *Invertigo*
- *Drop Zone* was renamed *Drop Tower*
- *Days of Thunder* was renamed *Thunder Alley*
- *Top Gun* was renamed *Flight Deck*
- *Bubba Gump's Shrimp Shack* was renamed *Outer Hanks* and *Lieutenant Dan's Back Porch Bar* was renamed *Outer Hanks Bar*
- *Happy Days Diner* was renamed *Juke Box Diner*
- *The Italian Job: Stunt Track* was renamed *Backlot Stunt Coaster*
- *Tomb Raider: The Ride* was renamed *The Crypt* and had

nearly all of its theming and effects removed, but with a
new, more intense ride cycle.

*A literal sign of the times from July 2007. Courtesy of Paul
Bonifield.*

"Paramount was a studio-based theme park, and I never bought
into that philosophy, I have to tell you," admitted Rob Decker. "I'd
never expected, if I went to the park, to run into Tom Cruise or Nick
or anyone, or to be discovered, or to be an extra in a movie scene or
anything along these lines. It was just all marketing. All marketing, all
promotions to support the studio. My friends in the industry would
argue back and say, 'But, it was relevant. The content was relevant. It
was populist-based, it was what people were doing that loved these
action films. They loved the characters, and we just wanted to bring it
to [be] more tangible, more personal.' Immersive might be going a
little far, but engaging in the marketplace, where they can go to the
Days of Thunder theater, or fly *Top Gun* off the flight deck and make it
relevant.

"So I think that worked for a while, but I think it ran its course and
CBS saw that. So the big challenge was de-branding the parks. In de-
branding the park with the urgency that had to happen, [there were]
some successes, some less so. The parks that had attractions the

people grew up with or loved or came to respect, etc, etc, were defaced. It was so abrupt. So that's the sad part of it."

Ed Dangler, who was promoted to vice president of maintenance and new construction at Cedar Point in 2007, added, "That was a real issue with the Cedar Fair upper management team to pay licensing fees on these products, these themed rides, and it's not the way Hollywood thinks. Hollywood thinks everybody owes them everything, the Cedar Fair people think, 'Why are we paying you to keep people aware of a movie that's fifteen years old?'"

"It was like, 'Who could find the most Paramount stars?'" said Jason McClure, Kings Island's vice president of finance at the time. "It made us realize how good we had done at branding the park for Paramount, because we found stars all over the place in the most unsuspecting places. And they all had to go! From the employee cafeteria, to people's offices, to letterheads, to everything. That was a really, really big change. Going through an acquisition like that is one of the most challenging things in my career. From the big problem-solving issues that we had to work through, to you throw on top of it that the branding had to change. It wasn't just a sale of the park, but the whole Paramount brand had to go away. That was a very intensive project to work through."

"What came out of that was trying to find the real soul, I think, and identity of the park," Decker continued. "And where it could be more relevant, and with my background in urban design, architecture, I always believed, especially in city design, that creating a stronger sense of place, that was something—identifying really what the park represents, going back into its past. Not necessarily recreating the past, but taking a reflection of its legacy and its heritage, and then making it relevant today was, I think, the opportunity that came out of having to change the park to get out from under the intellectual property and keep the lawyers off of us!

"And that became a new passion of mine. I really enjoyed trying to understand what the communities felt about their parks, how they related to it. And I'd have to say, Kings Island probably, and Cincinnati—I lived there seventeen years with a passion about it—have some of the most loyal fans to their community. It was always the Reds, Bengals, the Zoo, and Kings Island...And so, when people would come to the park, for parents, it's a right of passage to pass on to their kids. And to the family, they felt safe, they recognized what they did as a kid, they knew this as a place for fun. And so trying to respect and reflect that in a way that's relevant as generations would grow and other entertainment options come into the scene was all part of that transition from a movie studio park to Kings Island."

In addition to the de-Paramounting, *The Racer* was also turned forwards in a decision that has been surrounded by rumors for years. The truth is not as dramatic as many believe. "The ride was designed to go forwards and not backwards," explained Greg Scheid. "At that point we needed to clean up some safety things." Kings Island opened for the 2008 season on April 20.

LIKE FATHER, LIKE SON

One of the most well-known events in Kings Island's history was Evel Knievel jumping fourteen Greyhound buses in the parking lot in 1975. For 2008 the park brought Knievel's son, Robbie, back to the park. General manager Greg Scheid would later recall the jump date, May 24, as "One of my most memorable days in the park ever!"

"I'm sitting here in my office and my phone rings, and this guy says, 'This is Robbie Knievel,'" remembered Don Helbig, public relations area manager. "My dad did a jump there in 1975 and I want to honor his legacy. He just passed away and I want to replicate all his jumps and Kings Island's one of the places I want to do it.' Well, the first thing I thought is this is my brother having one of his friends play a joke. I asked, 'What's your number, I'll give you a call back. I'll look into it for you.' Then he gives me the number and it is a Butte, Montana number. So I go down the hall and I ask [marketing vice president] Matt Shafer 'If we can get Robbie Knievel to do a jump here, are we interested?' He asked Greg Scheid and he's interested. So I call back and it is, in fact, Robbie Knievel, and then we got in touch with his promotions guy. We discussed what would be needed from the park end. We didn't have a lot of time. He [Robbie Knievel] jumped on May 24th and this was already early May, so we didn't have that much time!

"We agreed to meet Robbie, Matt and I, over at Great Wolf Lodge, and we're sitting down, talking to him about it, and he would get side-tracked real easy. We'd be talking to him and he'd say, "You know..." and he'd just start [talking] and it was like, 'Okay.' We're trying to talk about what you need to do for the jump. He said, 'My dad did four-teen buses,' and we're like, 'How about breaking it by ten? We can go to twenty-four.' And he said, 'That sounds great! I'll do that!' And Matt's talking about, 'We can get Coke Zero, a sponsor,' and all this stuff, so they're talking about it, and Robbie's all excited and he agrees to twenty-four [buses] and everything. He goes back and tells his people what he's doing and they tell him, 'Robbie, you can't do that. That's longer than anything you've ever done before.' And he says, 'Yeah, but I want to beat my dad by ten.' They tried to explain to him just how far this jump was going to be, and Robbie told them, 'Well, I already did the contract!' So Robbie's committed to something he's not done before. So that created a little nervousness on our end."

"Robbie was quite the character, and we had to basically hold his hand for a couple weeks prior to the jump," Scheid said. "He was a true showman."

"Robbie probably wasn't as high-maintenance as his dad was said to be, but he was still a handful," Helbig continued. "It would be things like, 'Robbie, we have a live interview, we've got to get going, we've got to be there in ten minutes,' and he'd say, 'Ah, they can't start without me!' I'm like, 'Well, it's live at 5:10, they can and will start without you!' He's still over at Great Wolf Lodge at 5:05 and he's got to be in the Kings Island parking lot where the ramp for his jump is at 5:10! So it was those kinds of things. He made it, but it was still one of those, no concept of time or anything. So to make sure that we got him where he had to go, that was a lot of work. But a lot of fun, I mean, I wouldn't change it. It's probably the most memorable thing that I've ever been involved in."

"It was probably the day the Paramount people and the Cedar Fair people came together and really made it work," Scheid said. "If you go back and talk to a lot of the people that worked at the park back then, they would tell you it was one of their favorite days ever, most memorable. I will say I was ready to puke when he started to go, thinking 'What happens if he doesn't make it?'" Knievel ended up successfully and spectacularly jumping the twenty-four trucks in an event that drew a large crowd. "It turned out to be a fantastic day," Scheid concluded.

Crowds gaze as Robbie Knievel jumps over 24 trucks.
Courtesy of Paul Bonifield.

"The biggest thing about that was to pull that jump off, how every department here at the park had to come together to make that happen," added Helbig. "We always talk here about the One Team effort, the One Team concept, and that exemplified it 100% with that. With everybody chipping in, it turned out to be a great, great event. But we could not have done that without a buy-in from everybody. Everybody had to pitch in and be a part of this. I think that's probably, when I look back at my time here, that's the one event that stands out because it touched everybody…That was probably the turning point [of Paramount to Cedar Fair ownership] where everybody's on the same page now and working together as one team."

Robbie Knievel still keeps in touch with Helbig, twelve years after the jump. "He'll call me out of the blue sometimes and he'll say, 'I'm driving through St. Louis, do you know where a hotel is where I can check in at?' I'm like [lost]. He's just a random guy! He's come back here a couple times as a guest. Just comes back, and Guest Services will call and they'll say, 'Some guy named Robbie Knievel's here to see you.' Unannounced, shows up, just passing through. I think for him, this is probably his most memorable place to jump. It was his dad's...most successful [jump]...and that would be the same thing with Robbie. But he was definitely a character, and it brought the Paramount and the Cedar Fair groups, it brought everybody together as one."

Celebrities also made an appearance during Labor Day weekend. Carmen Electra, who got her start at the park as a dancer in 1990, returned on August 30 as part of the "Flashback: Totally 80s" show. A day later, three stars of *The Brady Bunch*—Barry Williams, Susan Olsen, and Mike Lookinland—came to the *Kings Island Theater* to celebrate the 35th anniversary of the "Cincinnati Kids" episode filmed at Kings Island.

"I'd mentioned to Matt Shafer and Greg Scheid that we should bring in *The Brady Bunch*," Helbig reminisced. "I remember Greg just shaking his head, saying 'Why?' And I told him, I said, 'When I was riding *The Racer* in the 80s, there wasn't a day I wasn't in line that multiple people wouldn't be talking and say 'This is the ride that was on *The Brady Bunch*.'' I said, 'So I heard that over and over again, people keep referencing *The Brady Bunch*. I think we should bring them in!' 'Okay, whatever,' Scheid and Shafer sighed dismissively.

"We got in the 2008 season, and we were about midway through or whatever, and we were having a pretty good year, and Greg and Matt, they came down, and they said, 'Okay, you can bring out *The Brady Bunch*. We'll go in and watch in the theater with you and your family and about ten friends.' They're dismissing it! In a fun way, in a friendly way. They were just like, 'Okay, we can bring them in.' So I reach out and get a hold of the agent for Barry Williams, and we're able to get Barry Williams and Mike Lookinland and Susan Olsen to

come in. I remember that morning, Jerry Niederhelman was the operations director, and he's looking over at me and he's like, 'Man, look at
all these people dressed like the 70s! This is kind-of odd.' Then they
had their first show at noon, so around 10:30 the line's already
formed and it's going past the front gate. So I take a picture on my
phone, and I send it to Greg and I say, 'Here you go, naysayer!' We had
such a great time, joking back and forth all the time. He walks out,
and he's looking at it, and he's like, 'Well, okay, that's one show.' The
next show, same thing, standing room only. Third show, standing
room only. After it gets done, we're standing in for the fourth show,
and we're back at the back of the theater, and I say, 'Well, looks like it
worked out pretty well, Greg,' and he's like, 'Yeah, you were right
about this one!' And I said, 'So when I suggest *The Partridge Family*,'
and he grabs my tie, 'Don't even go there! We got lightning in a bottle.
We're good on that.'"

HALLOWEEN HAUNT 2008

A new maze was installed in the *Action Theater* building for Halloween
Haunt 2008 and was called *Urgent Scare*. A new show, "Ghouls Gone
Wild," was produced in the *Festhaus*. Halloween Haunt ran from
September 28 through November 1, and the park closed for the
season on November 2.

2009—YEAR OF THE SNAKE

"As soon as I got here, talking to people and knowing what *Son of
Beast* was and what *Beast* was and even *Vortex* at that point was a
bumpy ride," said Greg Scheid. "I wanted to bring in something very
smooth that any family member could ride, but still get thrills."

Cedar Fair's corporate office also had similar thoughts. "They
[Paramount] didn't put in a high-thrill steel ride," said Dick Kinzel.
"The one that they had right before we bought the park was that crazy

thing [based] on the movie Italian Job! My God, they bragged it up, and I went there and rode it, and I thought, 'Okay, where's the meat?' This was what they were promoting as their big ride, and it was pretty obvious that they needed a big steel coaster with a lot of thrills."

Kinzel continued, "We had so much success with the *Magnum XL-200* and *Millennium Force* [at Cedar Point], and we knew, in fact, one of the selling points I made to the board when we made our presentation on buying [the Paramount Parks] and why we were going to pay a premium price was they concentrated more on family attractions than they did on thrill rides. And we felt that all of the Paramount Parks needed at least a 200-foot coaster, and we felt that that would really jumpstart the attendance at all of the parks."

Cedar Fair turned to their frequent partner Bolliger and Mabillard (B&M), a Swiss firm that's one of the world leaders in steel coasters. "I think at the end of the day we needed a big new attraction; I think that's what Cedar Fair brought to the table," said Russell Flatt, Kings Island's vice president of maintenance and construction. "They [Cedar Fair] did big coasters, they had worked a lot with B&M, and I think it was an appropriate product with the appropriate manufacturer."

The park began planning for the coaster in 2007, selecting a site in Rivertown. "You look at the numbers [of] the general store and the arcade, Rivertown in general was really just a highway, more like a byway, to get back to *The Beast*," said Rob Decker. "There really wasn't an anchor. I mean, *White Water Canyon*, sure, [but] you need a hot day for that, not into the marginal seasons, you're not going to be on that ride. *The Crypt*, that was not operating [consistently], and when you look at the revenue side of things, there was really a gap...So when you look at all the areas of the park that are generating revenue, where there's foot traffic, where there's excitement, Rivertown wasn't that. So I thought, by putting the station in Rivertown, you would start to activate that area for sure."

Initial ideas called for a straight out-and-back design. "If it's going to be 230 feet tall, the math will tell you it's got to be running out pretty far," Decker continued. "We got into the planning mode and I was just looking for a corridor to send the ride out pretty deep toward the river. As it turned out, the ride had to be such a scale that the last foundations were really going downhill at rapid rates. Those [would be] very difficult to build, but we knew from building prior hyper coasters about what scale it would be, so I just found a place that could be opened up, to be able to get the station, queuing, and a direction of travel and plotted that out onto the site." Instead, the coaster would take the L-shaped path that the ride currently takes.

Diamondback's 215-foot drop under construction in November 2008. Courtesy of Paul Bonifield.

"We walked Walter Bolliger, who is the head of B&M, through the woods," said Scheid. "We had a couple ideas in our plans, and Walter said, 'No, if you do this, let me do that. I can deliver you a great coaster.' I'm not going to second-guess that guy! So I said, 'Go for it.'"

"Kings Island has something a lot of parks don't have and that's beautiful topography," Flatt proudly claims. "That big woodlot back there didn't make it easier for construction, but the setting Kings Island has with the valleys and the woodlot and everything, it was a beautiful ride that fit back in there very nicely and B&M did an excellent job...It was challenging with all those grade differentials, to be able to get concrete in to get into the valleys, to get the cranes in and out. So I think it [the design] was twofold: one is how to use the topography to the best of your ability, and to use it in such a way that it doesn't overcomplicate the construction of the ride, and I think they did a good job doing that." Coincidentally, about ten years earlier Dave Focke walked Bolliger through the same patch of woods to get him to build a coaster for then-Paramount's Kings Island. An exclusivity clause with Cedar Point prevented that coaster from being built at the time.

The hills and valleys of Kings Island led to a hyper coaster design like no other, as this August 2008 photo shows. Courtesy of Paul Bonifield.

"One of the interesting things, being at Kings Island, being at Cedar Point [as current general manager], is just the feel and vibe of the parks," added Jason McClure, Kings Island's vice president of finance at the time. "As you walk Kings Island, so many of the coasters leave the midway and go out into the woods and/or into the back areas, and it creates a really neat coaster experience. It creates a different vibe when you're walking the park because there's nothing overhead. Whereas at Cedar Point, you're surrounded by coasters. Flat, there's not a lot of interesting flow to the park there. Just flat. So the topography is a little boring, but it means coasters are everywhere. So it was neat to bring *Diamondback*, a big ride, and take it over a guest midway, introduce it into the center of the park, and it wasn't necessarily a no-brainer decision either. A lot of people were worried that that would change the charm and the feel of Kings Island by bringing that type of experience into the middle of the park like that. Eventually, that location won out for that ride, and I think it's worked out very well."

The station's placement in Swan Lake in Rivertown led to the coaster's signature element. "Dick Kinzel said, 'Why don't we have that ride run through the water?'" Scheid recalled. "The entire time, Rob Decker and I were standing looking at each other and going, 'We don't want that pond there [Swan Lake] because it looks really bad.' We decided we were going to build the concrete thing of water and Walter Bolliger says, 'I can put water brakes on there and it will be really cool.'"

"There was that whole area over by *Italian Stunt Job* that was a pathway, which just created a natural bowl and an arena," Decker said. "[It's] another thing that you see, just a visual to build the excitement for the day as you're walking by when the train comes by and does this huge rooster tail."

At 230-feet tall and eighty miles per hour, the final design would have the coaster be the tallest and fastest roller coaster in the park. It would also be the longest steel coaster at Kings Island with 5,282 feet of track.

The coaster's name came naturally. "Greg Scheid let everybody on the team know, he said, 'We've got this big ride coming, we need a name,'" said Don Helbig. "So I suggested *Diamondback*, he came down the hall a couple hours later, and he's like, '*Diamondback*, I like that.' He goes, 'Let me talk to Rob Decker.' He came back a couple days later and says, 'Looks like we're going to go with *Diamondback*.' For me, the reason when he was asking everybody for name suggestions was I just thought it represented the characteristics of a diamondback. It was big, fast, mean, aggressive, those kinds of things, and it's in Rivertown so you're thinking okay, it fits like a western kind of thing and it could be diamondback snakes and all that. So that was my thing with it, was just being able to have that opportunity that Greg gave everybody to throw out a name idea, and it just happened to be that the one I picked out he liked."

The $22 million *Diamondback* was announced on August 6, 2008. "That was my first big ride that I got to be a part of from the beginning," Helbig said. "To be up there and be the one that's part of announcing it and seeing how excited everybody was. That was fun for me too, because I was always on the other side of that fence before; being a guest that's hearing this stuff for the first time. So for me, that was always the thrill before of learning what it was going to be. Now the thrill for me was watching everybody's expression and seeing how excited they were. I can tell you, I liked the side of watching everybody else a little bit better. To see what that was going to mean for everybody. Then you open it, and you hope everybody's going to like it and hope it's going to live up to the hype. Everybody builds it up in their own mind differently, and then you open it, and it meets and also exceeds everyone's expectations."

Don Helbig (left) and Greg Scheid announce Diamondback on August 6, 2008. Courtesy of Paul Bonifield.

Because the track and supports for B&Ms are fabricated in nearby Batavia at Clermont Steel Fabricators, construction of *Diamondback* went very smoothly. "They [Clermont Steel Fabricators] had a hard time keeping up with some of our erection. We wanted to go a little faster than they wanted to go at times," Scheid said. The last piece of track was installed on January 26, 2009, and the coaster started testing in February. "We actually had to put it to sleep for a couple of weeks because we had all of our testing done, and we just felt so good about it," Scheid commented.

Diamondback's track was locally manufactured at Clermont Steel Fabricators. Courtesy of Paul Bonifield.

Diamondback opened to tremendous acclaim on April 18. "I thought it was a great ride, especially the water element," Kinzel said. "It was something entirely different [for the park]."

"It turned out to be exactly what the park needed at that point," Scheid said. "We really needed a dependable coaster that ran very well and delivered great capacity."

Rivertown also got a makeover for the 2009 season. Asphalt was replaced with pavers for *Diamondback's* entrance plaza, the old *Trading Post* building was repurposed into the exit gift shop for *Diamondback*, a new restaurant, *Rivertown Junction Dining Hall*, took over the previous *Wings Diner*, and *The Beast* and *The Crypt* received redesigned entrance plazas. New fencing and light fixtures were added throughout to tie the fresh new Rivertown together.

SON OF BEAST CLOSES (AGAIN)

On June 16, a 39-year-old woman told Kings Island officials that she had suffered a burst blood vessel in her brain when she rode *Son of Beast* on May 31. The park closed the ride and contacted the Ohio Department of Agriculture to inspect the ride and investigate the incident. Investigative reporters discovered that state inspectors had been called to the park six times in nine years to investigate *Son of Beast*, more than any other ride in Ohio in that period.

Six weeks later the state cleared *Son of Beast* for operation after finding no irregularities in the ride. Park executives took a test ride. "I got off it and said, 'That's too bumpy, let's shut it down,'" said Greg Scheid. Kings Island management had had enough with the problematic coaster. Officials decided to review the coaster and find solutions to the poor ride quality, large maintenance cost, and low ridership.

"I didn't know that day I was closing it for good, but that's what it turned out to be," Scheid said.

THE WALLENDAS

The high-walking Wallendas made appearances at Kings Island in 2008 and 2009. For the 4th of July, 2008, the park brought in Rick Wallenda, Karl Wallenda's grandson, to break his grandfather's 1,800-foot tightrope walk record that was broken at the park back in 1974. Wallenda traversed 2,000 feet from the roof of the fifty-foot platform of the *Eiffel Tower* to the flagpole just outside the park's front gate.

"Rick called the park after he saw all the Knievel coverage on the news," Don Helbig said. "He's sitting at home and he's like, 'I could do something like that at that park.' He called and said he wanted to do it, and I went to Matt Shafer because he knew the Wallenda family and it kind of evolved from there."

On August 15, 2009, Nik Wallenda, the great-grandson of Karl Wallenda, made a tightrope walk at the park. "Nik is friends with some of the people at the park," explained Greg Scheid. "He is always wanting to perform in Cincinnati; he loved Cincinnati. He worked down at Coney Island quite a bit. Our marketing VP at that point, Matt Shafer, he knows Nik pretty well, and Nik would call him up and say, 'What can we do, what can we do?'" What Nik Wallenda ended up doing was a 262-foot high highwire walk at the park, a height three times that of any other Wallenda walk at the park. "That was a tough one because he was 300 feet up, the wind was blowing that day, it was rainy-ish," Scheid continued. "Even his wife was nervous prior to the walk! That and Robbie [Knievel] were the two that made my stomach turn." Wallenda successfully completed the walk and drew a large crowd in the process.

"After Rick did it, Nik wanted to do a walk at the park. He said, 'I can beat what Rick did! I can go higher,'" Helbig elaborated. "Rick was lower, at the fifty-foot level, and Nik was 230 feet up! Nik was phenomenal to work with. When you try to compare Robbie and Nik, Nik's the consummate professional. He knows what you need to do your job. He gives you everything you need to do your job. He's just very accommodating, just super easy to work with. Robbie [Knievel], on the other hand, he's a handful! So they were totally different characters, both unique in their own way. Nik was just that consummate professional where Rick Wallenda, he was in-between those two. He hadn't been out there as much as Nik and done as much and everything, but it was a big opportunity for him. To see him go from mostly being a part of the family things to having his own individual high-profile walk was exciting for him. Everything else he had done was part of a group with the family. Everything was done together. There weren't any solo acts up to that point for him."

HALLOWEEN HAUNT 2009

Haunt made national news in 2009 when skeletons made up to look like dead celebrities, including Steve McNair, Michael Jackson and Heath Ledger, were included in the decorations. Public outrage was considerable, so the display was pulled before Haunt opened.

A new maze, *Slaughterhouse*, was added in Action Zone in the *Stunt Crew Grill*. Another new maze, *Cut-Throat Cove*, was added on the

Outer Hanks Bar patio. A new show, "Hot Blooded," debuted in the *International Showplace.*

Halloween Haunt ran from September 25 until October 31. The park closed for the 2009 season on November 1.

Å

2010—PLANET SNOOPY

The Nickelodeon license was set to expire in 2010. Cedar Fair had gained rights to the popular Peanuts characters when they bought Knott's Berry Farm in 1997. For 2010, Kings Island, Kings Dominion, Carowinds, Canada's Wonderland, and California's Great America all received makeovers of their Nickelodeon areas, turning them into Planet Snoopy.

- *Nick-O-Round* was turned into *Character Carousel*
- *Backyardigan's Swing Along* became *Charlie Brown's Wind-Up*
- *Jimmy Neutron's Atom Smashers* became *Joe Cool's Dodgem School*
- *Plankton's Plunge* was renamed and re-themed to the *Kite Eating Tree*
- *Swiper's Sweeper* became *Linus' Beetle Bugs*
- *Phantom Flyers* became *Linus Launcher*
- *Nick Jr. Drivers* became *Peanuts 500*
- *Go Diego Go!* became *Peanuts Off-Road Rally*
- *Timmy's Air Tours* became *Sally's Sea Plane*
- *Blue's Skidoo* became *Snoopy vs. Red Baron*
- *La Aventura de Azul* became *Snoopy's Junction*
- *LazyTown Sportacopters* became *Woodstock Whirlybirds*
- *Rugrats Runaway Reptar* became *Flying Ace Aerial Chase*
- *The Wild Thornberrys River Adventure* became *Race For Your Life Charlie Brown*
- *Avatar: The Last Airbender* became *Surf Dog*
- *Little Bill's Giggle Coaster* became *The Great Pumpkin Coaster*

- *Fairly Odd Coaster* became *Woodstock Express*
- *SpongeBob SquarePants Bikini Bottom Bash* became *Snoopy's Splash Dance*
- *Scooby-Doo and the Haunted Castle* became the more generic *Boo Blasters on Boo Hill.*
- *Nickelodeon Theater* was renamed *Peanuts Playhouse*

Cedar Fair's planning and design team contemporized the familiar Peanuts graphics into a more pop-art style, aiming to make the transition from the award-winning Nickelodeon branding to Snoopy as seamless as possible. "We really took a page out of Nickelodeon, and so the transformation of that, we were able to keep whole buildings colored in red, keep blue ice cream that's left over from two and three properties earlier, the Smurfs, and do a lot of things like that, because we already kind of had the palette worked out," Rob Decker said.

"It was a good transition. It's familiar characters, everybody knew who they were and if you'd gone to any of the other Cedar Fair parks you had seen them in the parks," agreed Don Helbig. "So it was something that was a seamless transition to them...I think it was a smooth transition. We gave it a fresh new look in the kid's area and the guests, they loved the Peanuts characters."

The Peanuts gang was also featured in live shows, with "Charlie Brown's Hoedown" in the amphitheater, "Snoopy Rocks on Ice" in the *Kings Island Theater*, and "Snoopy's Starlight Spectacular," a light show behind the *Eiffel Tower.*

On March 18 the park announced that *Son of Beast* would not operate for the season. "The park will consider the *Son of Beast* ride for the future but at this time is not prepared to operate it in 2010," Don Helbig told the media.

Kings Island opened for the 2010 season on April 17.

HALLOWEEN HAUNT 2010

A new maze, *Wolf Pack*, was added in the *Son of Beast* station. A new show in the *Festhaus*, "Half-Pint Brawlers," was also added to the attractions lineup. Halloween Haunt 2010 ran from September 24 through October 30, with the operating season wrapping up October 31.

♈

2011 GOES *REALLY* TALL

For 2011, Cedar Fair got a package deal with Mondial for four *Wind-Seekers*, a new model of ride from that manufacturer. The four 301-foot tall rides, each costing $5 million, were installed at Cedar Fair's four largest parks: Cedar Point, Canada's Wonderland, Knott's Berry Farm, and Kings Island.

"*WindSeeker* is one of those products that, it gives you the statuesque aspect of it, being a landmark, and I think also being a bit of a thrill to get up that high and spin around," said Rob Decker, senior vice president of planning and design for Cedar Fair. "A very efficient ride at a great price point, a big thrill, a lot of height, and it doesn't take up a big footprint."

All four rides were announced the same day, August 24, 2010, but Kings Island advertised that theirs would be the first to debut on the park's opening date of April 30, 2011.

And then on April 28 the park announced that *WindSeeker* would *not* open with the rest of the park after all because of construction delays.

"Weather was a big part of it that year because of the height of it," explained Don Helbig. "You couldn't go up if there were high winds. There was a lot of high winds, a lot of freezing rain, a lot of snow. So that just delayed getting it ready to go at the beginning of the season... As we got into March and April, a lot of rain. So you couldn't go up when you were doing that either, those kinds of heights, they do things. So it just kind of pushed it back and then it finally opened in June that year." *WindSeeker* opened more than seven weeks late on June 21.

DINOSAURS ALIVE!

One of the more unique attractions Kings Island has housed throughout the years was *Dinosaurs Alive!*, the world's largest animatronic dinosaur park, which also opened for the 2011 season.

Greg Scheid explained the inspiration behind the attraction. "[Marketing vice president Matt Shafer observed], 'Anytime you go down to the museums or you go to a zoo that has dinosaurs, they draw huge numbers.' We were originally just starting to look at a couple week event. It grew very rapidly." Soon, park officials were looking at the world's largest animatronic dinosaur park, covering 12.5 acres with sixty animatronic dinosaurs.

To compliment *WindSeeker* for 2011, *Dinosaurs Alive!* was installed at the end of Coney Mall, with a path stretching into the woods behind *The Racer*. Construction ended up being a huge challenge. "It was probably the hardest single project we ever pulled off because of where we located it and the rain kept falling," Scheid continued. "We were getting stuck in mud every day trying to pour concrete. We had elevation changes that were ADA issues. It was just a nightmare."

Dinosaurs Alive! was announced on March 18, 2011. Just two days before it opened, one of the dinosaurs was destroyed by a fire started by a construction worker tossing a lit cigarette onto the ground near the animatronic. The dinosaur was destroyed, but the attraction still opened on time on May 26.

The walk-through attraction appealed to guests of all ages. "We were marketing that to smaller kids and grandparents who may bring their grandkids to the park who weren't coming without dinosaurs," said Scheid. "As I stood at the front gate every day, kids came in and people said, 'We're only here for the dinosaurs.'"

In addition to *WindSeeker* and *Dinosaurs Alive!*, Coney Mall got more attention in the way of new pavers and repainted buildings. *Son of Beast* remained idle for the 2011 season. "No decision has been made concerning the ride's future," Don Helbig told the press. "It would be inappropriate to speculate on when a decision might be made."

HALLOWEEN HAUNT 2011

New additions included the *Holiday Horror* maze in the *Peanuts Playhouse*, the *Nightmare Alley* scare zone in Planet Snoopy, the refurbished *Mysteria* maze—formerly *Death Row*, and the newly relocated *Cemetery Drive* scare zone on International Street. *CornSTALKERS* was moved into *Cemetery Drive's* former location in Tower Gardens. Halloween Haunt 2011 ran from September 23 through October 31.

A NEW LEADER FOR CEDAR FAIR

Dick Kinzel had originally planned on retiring as Cedar Fair's CEO in 2007. After the Paramount Parks acquisition in 2006, Cedar Fair's board gave Kinzel a five-year extension on his contract so he could oversee the transition of the parks.

But as his time wound down, the Cedar Fair board began looking for a new CEO—preferably someone from outside the company, following Kinzel's failed attempt to sell the debt-laden company to Apollo Global Management. On June 20, 2011, they announced Kinzel's successor—Matt Ouimet. Ouimet began in the amusement park industry in 1989 with Disney. He spent the next seventeen years at Disney, eventually working his way up to president of the Disneyland Resort, where he focused on restoring the park following the disastrous tenures of Paul Pressler and Cynthia Harriss. Ouimet left Disney in 2006 and joined Starwood Hotels as president of their Hotel Group. Two years later he joined Corinthian Colleges as their president and chief operating officer. Ouimet took over as president of Cedar Fair on June 20, 2011 and became CEO in January of 2012.

"It [Kings Island] was a beautiful park, but it's an entirely different experience than Cedar Point," reflected Kinzel on his time with Kings Island. "We marketed Cedar Point as a thrill park; we marketed Kings Island as a family park with thrill rides. You still had the idea it was themed more than an amusement park. That's what we did with all the Paramount Parks that we bought, Kings Dominion, Kings Island, Carowinds. We kept the theming that they had and basically just instilled where we could a thrill element...It was just a great park, a beautiful park, so we had a lot to work with."

GHOST HUNTERS

Kings Island is well-known for appearing in episodes of *The Brady Bunch* and *The Partridge Family*. It is less well-known for appearing in an episode of the SyFy Channel show *Ghost Hunters*.

Don Helbig recalled "When I first got here, I thought that would be one of my things I wanted to do. So, I wrote letters to *Ghost Hunters* every year; never heard back from them. Then I just stopped doing it, and then like two years later, not because of the letters, but they reached out and were just looking for places that would be unique to them. The producers, they were watching a Scooby-Doo episode and they said, 'It always seemed like they were at an amusement park.' So they thought, 'Let's find an amusement park.' They start doing a search, and they find that Kings Island comes up a lot. So, they just reached out to be able to do it." The paranormal investigation group looked into some of Kings Island's ghostly tales in November of 2011. "They spent several nights here at the park. We still had security on property, but they had to stay in their places and stuff to give them what they needed to do their investigation without any distractions or disturbances," Helbig continued. "Great people to work with."

The group captured supposedly unexplained voices in the *International Restaurant*. "Whether you believe in it or not, I don't know when I came here, but I just know that through the years there would be a lot of people that did not know each other, that had the same descriptions of things," Helbig added. "So that gave, in my mind, a little credibility, because someone's describing this little girl in a blue dress exactly the same as someone fifteen years later or whatever, so it gives it a little bit of credibility. When they did their investigation, in the episode the thing that had the most—if there was any kind of activity whatsoever, that gave them reason to say possibly, they didn't confirm that there was, would've been up in the *International Restaurant* with that. When you're listening to their tapes and you hear some noises and things, it kind of makes the hair raise on your arm a little bit." The episode, titled "Roller Ghoster," aired on January 11, 2012.

Has Helbig himself ever encountered a spirit at the park? "My favorite ghost story was my first year here in 2007, and a TV station was at the park doing a disadvantaged kids story, and there's a group shot that they're getting ready to do. This shot was back near where the *Diamondback* first drop is now, where the *Potato Works* is. So they're getting ready to do the shot, and the camera guy looks at me and he asks, 'Don, is that girl over there in the blue dress, is she part of this group?' Because he's trying to get them all in there. I'm looking and I'm like, 'I don't see anybody,' and he says, 'Nevermind. She's gone.' So the closest thing that I ever encountered would have been right there!"

40 YEARS OF FUN

For Kings Island's 40th anniversary, most of the attention for new additions was focused on the waterpark. Stripped of its Crocodile Dundee licensing, the area was given new life for 2012 and renamed Soak City. A new, more welcoming entrance building was constructed to take the place of a former season passholders-only gate.

The genesis of the 2012 investment really began all the way back in 2006, with a single observation from Rob Decker, Cedar Fair's former senior vice president of planning and design. "The waterpark was connected [to Kings Island] by a pathway, but it was a separate experience," Decker said. "From my observations in 2006, if the guest chose to only visit the waterpark, the access point from the parking lot was an opening in the chain link fence. It looked like a back entrance and a way to slip through directly into the water park. It looked like, 'You're going to come to the park, right? And then we have this waterpark that's an added amenity that's built into your price. Thank us for that!' Was it convenient, yes. Welcoming, absolutely not! So we created a new entrance experience and embellished the waterpark with the recognition that its user base isn't necessarily the theme park guest hoping to cool off at some point during the day.

Guests were visiting the waterpark as a destination and we responded by making that experience more like their version of a summertime country club, without the high end fees."

In addition to the new entrance, the rebranded Soak City would also include a new 39,000-square foot wave pool, *Tidal Wave Bay*, an expanded *Crocodile Run*, turning it into *Splash River*, and new sand volleyball courts and personal cabanas. Additionally, existing water-slides and attractions were renamed and repainted to fit in with the tropical theme.

- *Tasmanian Typhoon* was renamed *Mondo Monsoon*
- *Coolangatta Racer* was renamed *Rendezvous Run*
- *Awesome Aussie Twister* was renamed *Tropical Twister*
- *Bondi Pipeline* became *Pineapple Pipeline*
- *Sydney Sidewinder* became *Thunder Falls*
- *Down Under Thunder* became *Paradise Plunge*
- *Snowy River Rampage* became *Zoom Flume*
- *Jackeroo Landing* became *Splash Landing*
- The expanded *Crocodile Run* became *Splash River*
- *Kookaburra Bay* became *Coconut Cove*
- *Wallaby Wharf* was renamed *Castaway Cove*
- *Koala Splash* was renamed *Aruba Tuba*
- *Kangaroo Lagoon* was renamed *Lookout Lagoon*
- *Great Barrier Reef*, the old wave pool, was renamed *Breakers Bay*
- *The Outback Shack* food stand became *Coconut Cove Cafe*
- *Mic's Seaside Supplies* and *Matilda's* gift shops became *Seaside Supplies* and *Sandals Beachwear*, respectively

For Decker, Soak City was a huge success. "The telling moment for me was, and this is definitely Cincinnati and definitely a Kings Island thing, that when they opened up the park, we were able to get a couple of sand beach volleyball courts in there on the wave pool side of things. A group of young people came up and said, 'Hey, do you mind, can we reserve the court?' I said, 'No, it's open, you can just play. You don't need to reserve it, it's generally open.' They said, 'No, no, no, we mean like,' and I'm making this part up, but 'Tuesdays at 6:00. Can we reserve it Tuesdays at 6:00? We want to start a volleyball league.' And it's like, Bingo! They really adopted, they embraced it. And I kept telling the park, I said, "You have a great waterpark.' In a community like Cincinnati where it's close to every-body, you don't have to travel twenty-five miles to get to it or more, like Cedar Point, it's going to be like everyone's country club. 'We're going to take the kids after work or Saturday or whatever,' but they're going to own it.

"If you take care of them, create a great environment, don't gouge them on the food but give them a quality product, give them shade, a private deck chair, deck space galore so they can feel comfortable, they will own this like it's their own private country club. And they sure as heck did. I thought that was a huge success, it went well beyond what I had ever dreamed for the park. But it just started with that gate, it started with that terrible fence, and this gesture to welcome a guest into the park because you let them park within 150 feet of the waterpark. It wasn't enough, and it wasn't going to last."

Over on the dry side of the park, Kings Island received four new shows including "Ed Alonzo's Psycho Circus of Magic and Mayhem" in the *Kings Island Theater*. Multiple new food options were intro-duced, and *Invertigo* received a new blue paint scheme. Kings Island opened for the 2012 season on April 28. Soak City opened May 26.

THE CRYPT CLOSES

In February 2012, Kings Island announced that *The Crypt* had given its last rides. "I didn't like seeing all those tons flipping upside down and knowing the stress [on the supports]," said Greg Scheid. "When you're personally saying, 'I'm going to keep people safe,' that one made us nervous."

"At some point, with some rides you get to the point where you say the maintenance cost, the downtime, is not worth keeping it operat-ing," added Mike Koontz, the park's vice president of finance at the time. The $20 million ride did not even last ten years. Tellingly, it was the only Giant Top Spin that HUSS ever sold.

With nearly everything already planned out for 2012, it was decided to turn the building into a Halloween Haunt maze while management determined what else would occupy that space in the future. "The good thing about making it a maze is it could become a ride tomorrow," said Scheid. "We can go in and do anything with it instantly. There's enough square footage in there that it was easy to make the transition into a maze and keep it up year-round."

Years later, the giant, ugly building still sits vacant except during Haunt. Putting something in the building is on the list of priorities for the current general manager, Mike Koontz. "As not only the general manager of the park, but I like to look at things through our guests' eyes as well, and I do think it's definitely a waste of a building to just have it as a Haunt maze. I would love to see something done in that building that doesn't involve a Haunt maze. What that is right now I don't know. I will say this, there's been conversations about it, what we can do."

THE FINAL DECISION FOR SON OF BEAST

In 2012 Cedar Fair and Kings Island finally came to a decision on *Son of Beast*—demolition. In the three years since shuttering the ride, management had considered numerous options. "We had met with many companies, and we had looked at going over to the steel track that's up there now [at Cedar Point], the hybrid track," said Greg Scheid. "We had two companies pitch that idea to us. We had a redesign of the coaster, taking out some of the more dynamic parts, taking the height down about 30 feet was going to do a huge plus for the ride."

"The case with *Son of Beast*, we looked at a lot of different ways to modify it, but we couldn't come up with something that we thought was uniquely compelling and, after modifying, would be what we want it to be," said Richard Zimmerman, who Matt Ouimet hired as Cedar Fair's chief operating officer in October 2011.

Ultimately, it was decided to demolish the ride and start over anew. "It had become too much of a PR piece in Cincinnati that even though we thought we could run the ride without any incidents, one little hiccup became front page news," Scheid continued. "That's why we finally made the decision, just, 'It's time to kill it.'"

Son of Beast was demolished over the course of several months. Courtesy of Lelia Andrews.

Demolition lasted two months and was completed on November 20, 2012. *Son of Beast's* station was kept to house the *Wolf Pack* maze for Halloween Haunt, but the remaining acreage was cleared for an exciting future.

HALLOWEEN HAUNT 2012

As planned since the beginning of the season, *The Crypt* building became home to a new maze, *Madame Fatale's Cavern of Terror*. Additionally, a new scare zone, *Nightmare Alley*, was added on the path between International Street and Action Zone. Action Zone itself received a new scare zone, *Grimm Blvd*.

Halloween Haunt 2012 ran from September 21 through October 27. The 2012 season ended on October 28.

☩

2013

As is typical the year before a major addition, 2013 was relatively quiet in terms of investment. A new restaurant, *Reds Hall of Fame Grille* in the former *Rivertown Junction Dining Hall* space, was the big attraction for the year. Also new was the world's largest animatronic dinosaur, which was added to *Dinosaurs Alive!* The sauroposeidon was 118 feet long and fifty-six feet high.

Kings Island opened for the season on April 27. To commemorate the 40th anniversary of *The Brady Bunch* episode, the park had Barry Williams, Susan Olsen, and Christopher Knight back for four shows in the *Kings Island Theater* May 19. "The next [Brady Bunch event] just ended up being an anniversary year and we had the success with it [from the 2008 event] and we knew people would want to see them," Don Helbig said. "But it was a fun event, guests loved it, and...Brady Bunch fans from all over came to see them."

HALLOWEEN HAUNT 2013

Halloween Haunt 2013 ran from September 20 through October 26, with the park closing for the season on October 27. Additions included two new mazes, *Board 2 Death* in the place of *Mysteria* and *Delta Delta Die* in the place of *Massacre Manor*, and a new scare zone, *Backwoods Bayou* on the path from International Street to Rivertown. "Ed Alonzo's Psycho Circus of Magic and Mayhem" also ran during Haunt.

☩

2014—THE SHRIEK HEARD 'ROUND CINCINNATI

After the success the park had with *Diamondback*, Greg Scheid wanted Kings Island's next coaster to be another Bolliger & Mabillard. In particular, Scheid focused on a new model B&M had developed, the wing coaster. "I went to Dollywood and rode theirs and I got off and said, 'Man, that was great,'" Scheid said. "I really liked it, it was short, I knew ours would be longer, but I knew Cedar Point was going to put in *GateKeeper* the next year. I said, 'Let's just stick with the basics and do an inverted coaster,' but we wanted it to be as many world records as we could."

Scheid's pitch for an inverted coaster resonated with Cedar Fair's corporate office. Richard Zimmerman, Cedar Fair's COO at the time, recalled, "When Matt Ouimet came on and became our CEO in 2011 and 2012, we sat down and looked at the whole portfolio and wanted to identify two different things. First, where in our portfolio, where were the markets that were under-penetrated and had the most opportunity? And then within each park, if we looked at the product they had, what were the gaps in their product? And we quickly identified Kings Island, an important park for us. They didn't have an inverted coaster which is, as you know, a favorite of everybody."

While the decision to demolish *Son of Beast* was made independently of the decision to add an inverted coaster, the timing worked in that it, and the *Thunder Alley* go-karts plot, would open up a perfect spot for the ride. "Action Zone is another place where you can bring just a nice, complementary mix of attractions through there and it's simplistic," Cedar Fair's former senior vice president of planning and design, Rob Decker, said. "It's the Action Zone, right? So you just need a lot of action. You need loud, noisy, energetic, frenetic and kinetic activity in that area. That was the movie studio area of the park, so it really was kind of empty once the studio props and everything moved out. At that point in the investment cycle, it just seemed like the right place to put it and place it."

As with *Diamondback*, the park flew out Walter Bolliger to walk the land and get an idea of what the coaster would be. "There was a go-kart track in the position of the queue and the station for *Banshee* at the time," Decker said. "That little oval track, and that was really the only real estate that we thought we could just get a foothold into to develop a station and a queue, and then drop off the edge [of the steep hillside]. When we walked the site, we had somewhat of a layout that we forwarded to B&M, and then when he came to the site, Walter's eyes just opened up really wide. He was so excited. And he said, 'Do you realize what we can do down at the bottom of that hill? Because just the typical lift hill would create x amount of inertia. But once you go over the hill and you gain that much more speed, the elements down there can be enormous.'"

"We worked with B&M to produce a layout that would take advantage of the terrain where *Son of Beast* had existed and try and make it really unique," Zimmerman recalled. "We wanted to stretch it out; we wanted to get a lot of elements; we wanted it to be both eye-popping and eye-catching, but also have enough length that it was truly memorable."

"You have the real estate, so you need to work on that, and B&M is terrific in doing a layout and using all the things you want to do," said Russell Flatt, vice president of maintenance and construction. "And a lot of issues go into it; we wanted to put the station here, we wanted the lift here, we wanted a loop there. You work together, and Walter [Bolliger] puts it all together. He's just amazing and you tell him a bunch of the criteria and he puts it together. And you work together but you say, 'The station should go here and yeah, that's good, once you come out of the station and go up the hill, oh, that's looking out over Coney Mall, that's really good.' At the end of the day you're putting all these things together—a drop right there where you're right by the queue line; all these things add to not just the ride that you're going to ride, but you're also trying to appeal to the non-rider or the people waiting in line, and I think that was one of those rides that you could see even if you're a non-rider."

The final design was the world's longest inverted coaster at 4,124 feet of track, the fastest inverted B&M coaster at sixty-eight miles per hour, and would be tied with *Montu* at Busch Gardens Tampa for most inversions on an inverted coaster with seven. It would be the most expensive investment in Kings Island's history at $24 million, ironically narrowly edging out *Son of Beast*. In a unique twist, the ride achieves its top speed not at the bottom of the first drop like most coasters, but instead between the fourth and fifth inversions due to the changes in the terrain.

The next big question was what to name it. Scheid turned to personal experience from his time at Cedar Point, when the *Mantis* stand up coaster was originally going to be named *Banshee*. "A lot of Cedar Fair GMs really wanted the name *Banshee*, and we always joked about it, and Dick Kinzel would say, 'It will never happen!' Well, after he retired, I said, 'This has to be *Banshee*.' It's perfect with everything you have with *Son of Beast*, bring a little spiritual thing going. It became an internal fight, who was going to get *Banshee* and we won that one!"

Throughout summer 2013, Kings Island's marketing team employed an extensive teaser campaign, using shifting props and audio around the construction fence and cryptic clues posted on social media channels. "That was a lot of fun to do different things," Don Helbig recalled. "Have people, as they were in Action Zone, hear the scream from behind the fence, and we had scarecrows back there. People would peek through the fence and have the scarecrow looking back at them. It was a lot of fun. It was an open area, so you could see it from the *Eiffel Tower*. I thought it was going to be out there much sooner with what we were doing than it was. You would think that the media would have picked up on it a lot quicker than they did, but it was almost right around the time we sent out the invitations that they were like, 'Oh, you guys are building something.'"

Banshee was announced August 8, 2013. The park took a non-traditional route and chose to do the announcement at night. "[W]e thought the theming of the ride led to a nighttime announcement," Helbig said. "Ideally, you never want to make your announcements at night because that's not a good time for the media. They're getting ready to go on air for the 10 p.m. and 11 p.m. newscasts, and you're not leaving them with a lot of time to turn the story around. So when I sent out an advisory for a 10 p.m. press conference, every outlet called back and said, 'Is this a typo on the invite? It says 10 p.m. You meant a.m., right?' 'No, p.m.' They're like, 'That's going to be tough to get somebody out there.' And it is, it's extremely tough for them. We appreciate they realize the magnitude of the story, and it was a big story so they found a way, but it's not ideal for them. But what we wanted to do with this one is, we wanted it to be for our guests because they were so interested in what we were doing. What can we do to make it an event for them? Something they can be a part of, and they're just not reading about it in the afternoon when they're at work, but instead have the announcement at night so our guests can take part. We thought we would take that risk and do it at night knowing that if, for some reason, it didn't work out for the media, we had almost eight months to get the word out about the ride. It wasn't like if you didn't get it then, you were never going to get it. But it worked for everybody, and the media found that it was an electric atmosphere too and everything, so it was just good across the board. We did that again with the *Mystic Timbers* and *Orion* announcements because the themes of those rides fit doing it at night and provided an opportunity for our guests to be a part of it."

The first section of track arrived shortly afterward on August 16, and the park continued working on *Banshee* through the fall and into the winter. "It was the weather, [it] was just a challenge," Flatt said. "Just like *Diamondback*, the topography once it's all said and done is great, but from a construction point of view, going up and down these hills is challenging. I think the topography is challenging, and the weather was very cold that winter. But it went together and the thing that's nice about B&M, you work hard, you schedule these things out and on *Diamondback* and on *Banshee*, to have the construction done to give ourselves a lot of time to run the ride and to work through all the startup procedures. It was very nice. Both of them worked out very well that way. But the weather was a challenge!" Trackwork was completed on schedule on January 23, 2014.

Banshee debuted on April 18, 2014 and proved to be everything *Son of Beast* was not. It was smooth, re-rideable, high-capacity, and dependable. It quickly became known as one of the best coasters in the park.

"You go up and down into the valleys, down to the ground, and again I think it places in there beautifully just like *Diamondback* did,"

Flatt said. "I think it was the right ride for the right location, so I think it was a good replacement for *Son of Beast*."

"From what we had at *Raptor* at Cedar Point to all the other versions that we've done with B&M, that one is the most successful, I think, of these inverted coasters because you gained all that speed [from the terrain change], and he [Walter Bolliger] wasn't going to waste it," said Rob Decker. "His challenge was to get enough elements in there to satisfy that speed and then not over plan, and then come back up to the top. But it was interesting how he just grasped the concept right away, and then took it a thousand yards down the field and made it so much more terrific than what we had ever imagined."

Was the $24 million price tag for *Banshee* worth it to Kings Island? "Absolutely," said Scheid. "It brought us a different ride for the park."

The twisting loops of Banshee leave guests screaming for more.
Photo by the author.

In addition to *Banshee*, Action Zone received a long-overdue overhaul. The water tower, unused since the first few months of the area's original opening in 1999, was removed and the plaza transformed into a pleasant shaded seating area. The *On Location* gift shop was repainted and renamed to *Coaster Connection,* and *Stunt Crew Grill* was transformed into the *Chicken Shack. Ice Scream Zone, Xtreme Skyflyer,* and *Delirium* all received new paint jobs. *Flight Deck* was repainted and renamed to *The Bat,* paying homage to the fabled suspended coaster that ran at the park from 1981-1983. The games booth in the front of the area was demolished, which allowed for an expansion of the *Festhaus'* back entrance into a pleasant patio. The Action Zone overhaul finally made that section a nice place to be in the park.

"A park should be a park first," Decker said. "It should be a place of beauty and respite, a place of relaxation and pure enjoyment. Even if you don't ride a ride, it should still just be a place of beauty...It was a passion of ours to try to bring more trees, soften this big concrete area in Action Zone. You walk in and it's just windswept...Softening the edges of it, bringing in new trees, seating areas, it's a start. It's definitely a start."

HALLOWEEN HAUNT 2014

Two new mazes were added for Halloween Haunt 2014. *KillMart* was added in the Arcade in the back part of Coney Mall, and *Slaughterhouse* was relocated and expanded from its previous Action Zone location to a new purpose-built building next to *The Beast's* station. Haunt 2014 ran from September 19 through November 1, and the park closed for the season on November 2.

2015

For 2015, the focus was shifted across the park from Action Zone to Planet Snoopy. *Snoopy's Splash Dance* was removed and replaced with two new rides: *Snoopy's Space Buggies,* a Zamperla Jump Around, and *Woodstock Gliders,* a Larson Flying Scooters ride similar to the park's classic *Flying Eagles.* The *Peanuts Playhouse* amphitheater was also transformed into a petting zoo.

"The Gliders install, I think bringing that back, was another good attraction for the park," said Jamie Gaffney, Kings Island's vice president of maintenance and construction from 2014 to the present. "It's not the original [Bisch-Rocco set] that went to Carowinds. We would have liked to have had them back, but Carowinds wouldn't give them back!"

New tenants were also added on International Street. *Starbucks* moved from the French building to the Swiss building, making it one of the largest *Starbucks* in the Midwest. The old *Starbucks* location became home to *Yogurt Plus*, a frozen yogurt stand. *International Street Funnel Cakes* was expanded and enclosed. *International Street Candy* got a complete interior renovation to transform it into *Sweet Spot*. Even the *Picnic Grove* got a makeover by ripping out the asphalt and adding landscaping and LED signage.

Kings Island opened for the 2015 season on April 18.

HALLOWEEN HAUNT 2015

Halloween Haunt's 2015 run ran from September 25 through October 31, and the park closed for the 2015 season on November 1. A new maze, *Blackout*, replaced *Club Blood* in Action Zone.

PLUNGING INTO 2016

Tropical Plunge, a WhiteWater West, seven-story waterslide complex, was added to Soak City as the major addition for 2016. It was the first waterslide complex added to the waterpark since 2004 and featured three tube slides and three trapdoor "aqualaunch" slides.

Additionally, the two toll gates, fixtures at the park since 1972, were demolished and replaced by one large, modern toll plaza in the northern end of the parking lot.

Kings Island opened for the 2016 season on April 16. *Tropical Plunge* opened with the rest of Soak City on May 28.

HALLOWEEN HAUNT 2016

Halloween Haunt 2016 ran from September 23 through October 29. A new outdoor maze, *Field of Screams*, was added behind *The Racer*. The *Backwoods Bayou* scare zone became an outdoor maze and was added to Tower Gardens. *Tombstone Terror-tory* and *CornSTALKERS* were removed. The park closed for the 2016 season on October 30.

GENERAL MANAGER #11: MIKE KOONTZ

Immediately following the 2016 season, Greg Scheid was promoted to regional vice president of Cedar Fair. He continued to be based out of Kings Island until his retirement in 2018. Spanning ten years, Scheid was general manager longer than anyone else in the history of the park. Greg Scheid was inducted into the Kings Island Hall of Fame in 2017. "I'm very proud of what we did during the years I was there," he reflected. "Being that it was my chief competitor when I worked at Cedar Point for so many years, it was nice to come down here and just enjoy it."

Replacing him as general manager of Kings Island was Mike Koontz. Koontz started attending Kings Island in 1974 and began working at the park in 1999 as the vice president of finance. A few years later he was promoted to CFO of Paramount Parks. Koontz lost his job following the Cedar Fair acquisition, but returned to Kings Island in 2011, once again as the vice president of finance. He was moved to Cedar Point and became vice president of finance for that park for late 2015 and the entire 2016 season. Koontz came back to Kings Island as the vice president and general manager after the 2016 season, and he remains in that position as of the time of this writing.

Å

2017—WHAT'S IN THE SHED?

After the success of *Banshee*, Kings Island and Cedar Fair began looking for the park's next coaster shortly after *Banshee* opened.

"We started looking at possible product for the park, you know, what do our guests want?" said Jamie Gaffney, Kings Island's vice president of maintenance and construction. "Do we want another wooden coaster, do we want a dark ride? What does the attraction need to be? It all boils down to what the guests want, really. What is really going to drive them to want to visit the park? So we were looking at different concepts, different types of attractions, and we landed on a GCI [Great Coasters International] wood coaster."

"I was really thinking, 'Could I go with a good wooden coaster that would hold up and do well?' and the cost for GCIs are a lot less than a B&M," said Greg Scheid, who was the park's general manager during the development and early construction of *Mystic Timbers*.

"One of the things that we always focus on when we talk about attractions [is] we want a very clear target of what we want the experience to be and who gets to experience that," explains Cedar Fair's Richard Zimmerman, who was COO at the time. "We think in terms of age demos a lot and in terms of types of product. A large coaster that's [a height requirement of] 50 or 52 inches and up means less of our patrons can experience it. The push behind...*Mystic Timbers* at Kings Island was all about a family coaster, multi-generational, bigger age range that could ride it, and we wanted it to be family-friendly and family fun, and we got that."

The next question was where the coaster would be built. "There seemed to be some space over behind the old *Funnel Cake* building in Rivertown and with the way the [nearby] *White Water Canyon* entrance was built originally, it was not as desirable [for guest use] because of the stairs, having to go over the top of the train tracks," said Gaffney. "We looked at that area [and] we also thought that it would be kind-of neat to go over top of *White Water Canyon* in several places to get some more interactive feels between *White Water Canyon* and *Mystic [Timbers]*."

Meeting with representatives from GCI in 2015, Scheid and the Cedar Fair/Kings Island team began working on potential layouts. "I'd ridden the *Prowler* [at Worlds of Fun] and *Gold Striker* [at Great America] prior to us making that decision so we were able to sit down and say 'These are the parts of the ride we really liked for each of those two,'" Scheid explained. "I said, 'Keep it as low to the ground as you can because that makes you feel like you're going faster and it keeps our construction costs down, so keep it moving fast through the woods.'"

"We had a lot of confidence in what they [GCI] could come up with, and so we gave them a shot," said Rob Decker. "Running off into the woods, low, terrain-hugging, close to the ground, saving the trees and just darting through, crossing *White Water Canyon*, just seemed like a viable concept."

Adam House was Great Coasters International's design engineer for the ride. "We wanted to fill in that gap for a modern-day thrill machine, but not take anything away from the already great collection of wooden coasters that Kings Island already has...With *Mystic Timbers*, we wanted a ride that is smooth and would be perfect for kids to ride with both their parents and grandparents, but thrilling enough to make thrill seekers rejoice."

The location also provided several unique opportunities for the coaster. "The ride actually has seven bridges, so there's one over the lake and six over the trough of *White Water Canyon*," Gaffney continued. "With the wooded area that we had just around the *White Water Canyon* old queue line and the proximity it was to the park gave us the opportunity to build a lift that could be visible from the park, unlike *The Beast* which is off the beaten path, you can't really see the lift hill or much of the structure from the park. So it gave us an opportunity to do that."

The final layout would have a 109-foot-tall lift hill, a top speed of fifty-three miles per hour, sixteen airtime moments, and a track length of 3,265 feet. The addition of *Mystic Timbers* allowed Kings Island to reclaim the title of having the most wooden coaster track of any park in the world at 18,804 collective feet, a record that the park previously held until 2009 when *Son of Beast* closed.

A strong layout was not the only marketable key to *Mystic Timbers*. Kings Island and Cedar Fair began thinking of ways to make *Mystic Timbers* more than just a coaster, by creating a story-driven experience. "We wanted to do that because both me and Matt Ouimet say this, we want to be a place that's more than to ride rides," Zimmerman said. "We want people to come to do other things with us, so we want to make our experiences unique. *Mystic Timbers* at KI, *Copperhead Strike* down here at Carowinds—there's great appeal to 300-foot coasters like *Orion*, and the story gives you a backdrop but the ride experience is phenomenal, and there's other attractions where you try and tell a story and just create a much more fun atmosphere and environment. *Mystic Timbers* was our start into telling stories and thinking about the experience differently."

Rob Decker knew just who to turn to for a heavily themed project: Greg Crane. Crane was a set designer for stage shows in various entertainment facilities and amusement parks. As creative partner and chief of design with Alterface, he had been designing various amusement park dark rides, including some for Cedar Fair. In early 2016 Decker hired Crane as Cedar Fair's corporate director of planning and design. Greg Crane recalled Decker saying, "'The ride is currently being designed by GCI, but we don't know what to do with it.' He opened the opportunity and said, 'Let's explore what those [theming] options are. If it works, it works and if not, we have a great coaster, and it's themed.'"

Crane needed to start drafting story concepts and presenting them to corporate and park executives, but he also needed to prove that a storytelling coaster not based on an existing intellectual property could work on a regional park level. "I knew, right off the bat, I wanted to make sure that it was engaging to the guests as far as it told a story, leave a lot of layers there, make it repeatable. This was going to be a family coaster, so I wanted to make sure that there was something that was relatable on a marketing edge, because it's not the biggest, not the tallest, not the fastest. So it was creating, what is the catch? And the story all based off of that."

Crane's overarching strategy with Cedar Fair as a whole was to create a mythos that tied the group of parks together. "My whole goal was to be able to build a mythos that would allow us to tie Kings Island with Kings Dominion with a few of the other old Paramount Parks, and start expanding upon the story, start introducing characters, start telling people why these attractions are. Because I know there are a lot of coaster fanatics, but I also wanted to start bringing in and engaging them in a different way, and give them additional tidbits and let them start to create their own mythos of the attraction itself. So instead of laying it all out there, I wanted them to explore, give them pieces, but also allow them to go on their blogs and their YouTube accounts and start creating what they think is going on in the story, and then seeing how that would start affecting the other aspects of where we go in the future. So, sort of crowdsourcing! You always want to give them a surprise, but then you also want to give them what they want, so I was like, is there a middle ground?"

It was imperative for executives to be fully sold on the story ideas every step of the way. "I had to pass numerous auditions, presentations, with Matt Ouimet and Rob Decker and basically convince them we can tell a proper story and with marketing and the Kings Island GM, and basically lay it all out there," Crane said. "'I promise you, this is going to be engaging and fun and repeatable,' because I wanted to make sure that we got three different experiences, and then for the holidays, we can overlay additional storylines that are maybe a little more aggressive for Halloween, and then something that is still mystical and mysterious for Christmas and the winter holidays."

Crane started with the heavily wooded location and the out-and-back layout for his first concept: guests venture into the woods, the guests are frightened by what's there, and they hastily return back to the station. "We were looking at putting a series of mirrors [in the trees] and creature silhouettes...so that when you get out there, it's like the woods almost don't make sense," Crane describes. "Your brain starts to scramble the farther out you get into the woods, because the woods are all of a sudden looking fragmented and twisted. So there was going to be a tunnel—and there is still a tunnel halfway through—but the main show space was actually going to be halfway through the ride, and that's where you were going to see these effects with the trees...We started playing with the scenic [design] with that, trying to figure out if the trains are going too fast and if you are actually going to be able to take all that information in, and as we were sort of studying that, we realized that that really isn't the greatest location for a show moment to be front and center."

The spot that seemed like the natural placement for the show moment was, instead, at the end of the ride. "For me, what I like about roller coasters is the highly visceral aspect of when you're about to ride," Rob Decker said. "It started with me at *Millennium Force. Millennium Force* starts and ends in the bowl of the next riders. The next riders see the train coming back, everybody's screaming, and then they come into the brakes, then everyone cheers, and they go into the station and you're next to board. Somehow, with the layout of this and the mechanics of it, this ride would have ended in the brake field and the transfer section, and then it had to travel. I was just trying to time it, and all those cheers would have been way back there. Maybe it's just me, but when you come back into the ride, then the ride operator says, 'Welcome back, how was your ride?' Then riders might think, 'We were excited about it back there!' And so we were really trying to keep the excitement of the ride, keep the rider engaged through that process of getting from point A, B, C, back to the station and so we said, 'Well, we can put a structure in there and something could happen in there.'"

That idea led into the story's second iteration. "The second iteration was having this be an old coaster that used to be a part of the park years ago, and then something happened on that tract of land or in the woods to where they just had to shut the coaster down, and they hid it and acted like it didn't exist, took it off all the maps, and they had a desire to try to bring this coaster back and to fix it and to start operating it," Greg Crane explained. "You were basically getting a first look at the coaster before it was operational, where everything is overgrown, the woods are overgrown; if you're walking into the queue, the pathways are disheveled and it's like you're wandering onto that property like, 'I don't know if we should be back here! Is this actually a legit ride, is this a Haunt [maze]? What exactly is it?'"

The mysterious atmosphere would be the key component in this treatment. "We need to...allow people to come in and explore," Crane said. "Don't tell them what's there, and that was the [idea] behind, okay, let's open up this plot of land, let people realize as they're crawling through the bushes that there's this old coaster that used to run through the property, or still does, but it's overgrown and parts of the track are broken, and there's piles of wood on the ground from the old structure. But then as you get closer, through the show elements, the lights in the area would start to flicker and it was like the ride was trying to turn on. When you get to the load station, you get a show moment of an empty train rolling into the station as the lights are flickering and turning on, and then you have this carnival music, and the seats open up and you load in, and it takes you across this track that literally looks like it's in pieces. I wanted to make sure that we were engaging with the raft ride [*White Water Canyon*] that goes in and out of the structure below, and so as you're on the raft ride, you would see the structure crumbled where the raft ride goes through the structure...creating a tunnel out of the timber. It would also add show elements to the raft ride, so we're doing double duty and expanding the show of the raft ride, and then being able to build a mythos based on the coaster, which the mythos then carries over to the raft ride itself."

What would be at the end of the ride? "We started looking at different ideas and one of the ideas we thought, because we were in the proximity of the steam train station, is to maybe have a tunnel that, as you entered the tunnel, it looks like there's a train coming and a loud noise, and then dive underneath the light like you're going to have a collision with the train," Gaffney said. "We started with that concept [for the finale], then we built on the theming concept from there."

"Rob's concern [for that specific thematic treatment], rightly, was that if the coaster looks disheveled, destroyed, then when they [the park] do their regular maintenance on it, they're of course sitting there going, what's scenic and what's for real?" Crane said. "Then I tried creating a system for that, and then it was like, how can we tell a similar story to that, but not affect maintenance and operations? Because we don't want people walking by and going, 'You need somebody to go out there and check the coaster, because these pieces have fallen off,' and for that to be an everyday operations issue, when in reality, it's just scenic."

The next concept utilized the overgrown, natural aspect of the second iteration with an old lumber company. "The woods are taking over, something happened in the woods...we don't know what it is, but I think Mother Nature is starting to take things back," Crane explained. "So it's like the flora and the fauna are fighting back."

Interestingly, this concept originated not with Kings Island's history or area, but actually with a place closer to Planning and Design's headquarters at Cedar Point. "I lived maybe a mile or two away from this dilapidated greenhouse in Huron on the corner of 61, and I think Greg [Crane] as he came into the office, he would pass it as well," said Mark Schoelwer, senior corporate designer for Cedar Fair. "And it was really spooky, it was on websites like 'Spooky places in the US.' It's finally been knocked down, but the vines totally taking over the building was in part, some of the inspiration, I think, for *Mystic Timbers*."

The name of the lumber company, though, would take inspiration from the Kings Island area. "This is all about the time when the parks were under Matt [Ouimet] and challenged with, who are we...what are we trying to portray?" Decker said. "What's our identity, what is our sense of place? Where do we belong and where do we fit...For us, we own who we are. And who we are is either our heritage, the lineage of the park and where it started, or a new narrative to engage the guest, like a quest. If repeating or reflecting on the past gets too dull, how do we embellish it, or those types of things. You can start to take your local cues and different things and that's where the team went."

"I just penciled 'Miami River Lumber Company' on an elevation that I was working on with Greg because I knew the area, I grew up in the area," Schoelwer added.

The overgrowth story was the iteration that was being used at the time of the *Mystic Timbers* announcement on July 28, 2016. There was still not a solid shed/finale concept. "When we were getting ready to announce, we were still working on that," said Don Helbig, the park's public relations area manager at the time. "So 'What's in the Shed,' that was a legitimate question! We had an idea, but we didn't know what that was going to look like. As we're getting the [on-ride] animation and stuff done, we're like, well, we can't release anything because we don't know, how are we going to do this? So we're like, we'll just make it a cliffhanger. We'll say, 'The story continues!' One of those kinds of things. Greg Scheid's the one who came up with, 'Let's call it 'What's in the Shed.'' I was like, 'What's in the Tunnel,' we didn't know if it was going to be a tunnel [or a] shed, 'Well, let's make it 'What's in the Shed.'' So when Greg and I were up there announcing this, we did #WhatsintheShed, that was a question for us! We didn't know what was going to be in the shed. We knew it was going to be some kind of animation things or some characters coming out, monsters, creatures, but we didn't know what that was going to be."

Ultimately, Crane felt that that version of the story was too contrived. Still wanting to have a secretive shed finale and still wanting to keep the Miami River Lumber Company at the heart of *Mystic Timbers*, Crane reached out to Holovis, a visualization technology firm that had previously worked with Cedar Fair on the interactive *Battle For Cedar Point* virtual reality game. Holovis would not only show produce the ride and shed element, but also help to further flesh out the storyline in conjunction with Crane and Planning and Design.

"The Miami River Lumber Company [in the new storyline] became this thing where it opened, it produced lumber, and then it shut down," Crane said. "And nobody knows why it shut down, because that's the part where we just decided, you know what? Let's put out the Easter eggs of, there's a calendar in the shed, and then one day all the detail on the calendar just doesn't exist anymore. It was like deadline, deadline, deadline, and then it was like somebody picked up and left...But then at the same time, there's another overlay of video cameras, monitors, because another company comes in, we don't know who this company is, it's a dark company, and they're watching the place. It's potentially a government facility that is watching over the plot of land. They know that there is something there, they're trying to capture it, so we wanted to place different monitors throughout the queue, walkie-talkies that maybe are on backpacks that maybe the person that once had the backpack is not there anymore, and somebody's calling out for them. Every once in a while, you might see a shadow on one of the video feeds of something running through the woods, or you think you might see something. We were basically creating something where we could go, okay. There's *something* there. What do *you* see? And then let people [the guests] build upon it. My pitch to marketing was basically, let's not tell the story. Let's just say there's this place and there's something in the shed, but we don't want to tell them what's in there, because we wanted it to be a surprise. So let's just leave it with 'What's in the Shed' and from the get-go, tell everybody, 'Don't go in the Shed,' and of course, we have to end it in the shed. And we want people to leave the shed and say, 'We were attacked by a tree.' And then for somebody else to be like, 'We didn't see a tree. We saw a snake,' or 'We saw a bat.'"

"The whole idea with *Mystic Timbers* was we're going to try to get guests to come out to the park because of the shed, and we know the ride's going to be what sells them, because we think the ride experience was going to be incredible," Scheid added.

Crane's initial idea for the shed's three resident monsters was a sentient tree, a humanoid bat, and a gigantic ant. "I wanted to tell a sci-fi overlay, which was the giant ant, and then I wanted to tell more of a scary, horror overlay, which was the bat, and then I wanted to have a fantasy overlay, which was the tree. Depending on which version you got, you got a completely different mood, completely different intent [of the story]. The sci-fi would have been more laser beams a la *Godzilla*. Some sort of toxic sludge might have spilled on the property and went into an ant nest, and now the ants have grown into epic proportions and now they've turned the land into their colony. The bat was going to be, when you first pulled into the shed, you saw all these cocoons hanging up throughout the shed, and then the cocoons started cracking and opening up. You assume it's a bug, but then it opens its wings and you realize this cocoon is this bat that's being hatched, and it's this hybrid horror bat. And then the tree was going to be more like *Lord of the Rings*. This tree that could just pick up and just relocate, and he wants you out of his woods. So there were a lot of fireflies and mystical elements within that storyline."

Through internal discussions, the focus shifted to a much more general theme of flora and fauna striking back. This allowed the ant, which executives felt stood out too much compared to the other two creatures, to be replaced by a monstrous snake. "My last pitch to them, I [Crane] was walking into the conference room with Rob [Decker] and Matt [Ouimet] and [Cedar Fair chief marketing officer] Kelley [Semmelroth]...She ended up being the final approval on the characters, because she kept going, 'Okay, what is the story?' I said, 'We're on a piece of mysterious land, and we wander into a shed, and we wander into a bat, a tree, and a snake. And we have a situation that happens in conjunction with each one of those.' She said, 'Okay. Well, those are three things that can definitely be found in a shed. So I say we go with that.' I think the comment really came from a place of, we had been working hard with sci-fi, trying to work some of that in there, but what it came down to was we're all basing this around a shed or an old lumber mill. There has to be some believability in it, so it comes down to, okay, those creatures would actually be here, so let's build upon that."

"In designing those with Holovis, my main directive was, 'Okay. Each one of these things has to be noticeable as a bat, a tree, or a snake,'" Crane continued. "But they have to have a something about them which [makes people go], 'Oh, we don't know that species.' Like you see the snake, and when it opens its mouth, Holovis had this brilliant idea of taking the upper portion of the mouth and flaying it open. They originally had that with the bottom jaw as well, where it opened up a lot like the demogorgon in *Stranger Things*...If that had popped up, it would have been great for an older demographic and people would have been like, 'Sweet!' We would have had water or some sort of goo effect to coincide with it, but it honestly felt too scary. We also had babies of all these characters as well, so not only did we design the Big Bad, but also their minions or their babies that are slithering around on the side walls or scurrying out of some other location. Each one of those was designed slightly different to emulate the fact that there's a lot of them, and it's only going to get worse. The bat, looking at the bat, it was a bat/human-esque hybrid. Then the tree, the tree is just a walking angry tree that spews bugs from its mouth and eyes. That was the one that felt like it needed to be the front and center logo character; [it] ties in with the [coaster] structure itself."

An elaborate theming package immerses guests in the story of Mystic Timbers. Photo by the author.

"There was a lot of conversation with the trains," Crane added. "They're based on the truck that's at the entrance, but they're also in three different colors, and we wanted to make sure that people didn't catch on and go, 'Oh, the green car has this specific scenario in the shed,' or 'The blue car has this scenario,' and so people are waiting for a different car. So we worked on randomizing the scenes in the shed, so that no matter which car you took, you still didn't know what the outcome was. It's a tiny little detail that we realized, if we're running three trains or two trains or one train, how do we make sure that the guests aren't trying to decipher the code, just so that we could keep it as random as possible. Therein lies the fun."

The randomized features and assorted details would also help keep guests engaged the entire ride. "The audio changes, and so that audio could be randomized, so even if you have a snake scene, it might be different audio at the beginning, or the animatronic elements that are built into it are triggered differently, so maybe the lights sway and bang around in one scene, but the next one, they don't," Crane said. "Or the lockers tip over in one scene, and then they don't in another. Make it so that every time they ride through it, they go, 'Oh, I didn't know that did that,' or the Coke machine lit up and you saw a silhouette inside of it of one of these creatures. Because that's a big hold depending on how busy the park gets. If they're running three trains and there's a hold in that area, it allowed us to be able to tell a show and entertain for a little bit of time."

Holovis brought on Daniels Wood Land, a California-based custom theming and treehouse company, to produce the physical props for the project. "They [Cedar Fair] had [the idea of], it was very much stuck in the '80s. Everybody got up and left one day, something scared them away, and so that was always the story that fit," recalled Andy Dauterman, custom and theming projects manager for Daniels Wood Land at the time. "The calendar on the wall is 1983 and has dates circled, and there are lots of hidden Easter eggs and stuff that guests on the ride will never see, but it all plays into putting you in that time and place. The music, the effects, the Coca-Cola machine couldn't just be one off the shelf, it had to be one from the era. It was presenting that sort of look and style to keep it true [to the story] that nothing after 1983 was new."

Other props lent an air of authenticity. "One of the things that Daniels Wood Land does is we reuse a lot of old equipment, old machinery, old parts and stuff and just really bring that authenticity to it," Dauterman said. "In this case, it was that lumber mill processing facility, and we happened to have in our possession at the time an old walnut processing factory that we tore down, and conveyor belts and machinery and hoppers and all that stuff are universal. When it came along to that [*Mystic Timbers*], I more or less started sending them [Cedar Fair] pictures of all this essentially junk that we had in our possession, and we started looking for creative ways to use that stuff. We started photoshopping some things together, and we'd be like, 'We want to do something over on this wall, that would be pretty cool, the guests can go under it,' and we were like, 'What if we did this neat conveyor belt into a hopper, you can see where maybe it's processing lumber shavings into something or going to a furnace, or who knows what it's doing underneath the floor, but we can do that and then we'll have vines growing up through?' It was just a very dynamic process where we showed them a lot of stuff that we had in-house that we could utilize and repurpose, and that's kind of how it continued to grow in-tune with the story that Cedar Fair and Holovis had put together."

While the projections from Holovis are fun, many guests overlook the propping that reacts to the shed creatures. "Not only do we do sets and theming, we also do animatronics and interactives and all sorts of things, so we started bringing a lot of interactivity into it," Dauterman said. "The lights overhead sway, the sawblades on the wall rattle together, and the lockers swing out and the radio turns on and the Coke machine goes crazy. There's a lot of practical and animated effects that go along with it and that was all part of the stuff that we brought to life."

The story extended from the shed and encompassed the entire area. "The truck that's at the entrance, that's actually my voice that was doing the narration for it," Crane said. "If you listen to the [audio], it talks about *Flight of Fear* and a few of the other parks, and certain things happening in those other attractions. That was ultimately my goal, was just make sure everything is consistent, yet ties in…We also have, going up the lift hill when you leave the station, there's audio going up the lift hill…and in order to make a lot of that work and to feel like it is a story, the train slows down at a certain point and then it speeds up at a certain point on the lift hill. Just trying to accentuate bits of the story and add additional beats and a rhythm to it, or a cadence."

To tie it all together, Holovis contracted IMAScore to compose a soundtrack for *Mystic Timbers*—the first IMAScore track in the U.S. "From the get-go, I had a piece of music in mind, where every time I watched the ride-through, I went, 'I want this sort of vibe,'" Greg Crane said. "I sent them a piece of music and I said, 'This is what I like'...Music-wise, the main piece of music was the *Gravity Falls* theme song. It was popping in my head constantly...I was watching the ride-through and stuff like that, and it's really upbeat and it has a sense of mystery to it. Then as we started embellishing the characters, it had to take a little bit of a darker, more mysterious tone and a little less poppy and upbeat. It rightly so diverted away from something with that sound aesthetic. We wanted to have a different soundtrack so that depending on where you are in the queue as well, it starts taking on a different tonality. There's a different track for the queue versus the load station, versus obviously the shed. That's something that to me was very intriguing, to try and tell a story, just by tweaking the audio just a bit."

Overall, the thematic design of *Mystic Timbers* invites the guests to be a part of the story. "There is a really solid backstory [written for *Mystic Timbers*], but going into it, I don't want to really ruin what people have created for themselves," Crane said. "I wanted to make sure that, let's say you were to wander in there and you started reading a bit of information, like they have their business cards that are laying around that you might read one of those and go, 'Oh, that's interesting.' But then you read maybe a little too much into it, and maybe you start creating your own little mythos about it, and I wanted to make sure that that was always an opportunity...No matter what story I laid out there, I felt like somebody's always going to come back and go, 'That's cheesy!' But if I allowed you to fill in the blanks and create the story that pops into your head, then you're going to create something that you think is cool. I think people are going to inevitably nitpick on anything, but the goal was to try and give everybody something that they can get behind and feel like they have a part in bringing it to life."

Construction moved through the fall and winter. "Even though we had a fairly mild winter, the weather is always a bit of a factor," explained Adam House. "I think we had twenty-four days of rain in January, so you can imagine that there were some hurdles there. Ultimately, designing and working out the construction logistics of the lake/lagoon crossing was a challenge. At the end of the day, everything [was] well worth all the blood, sweat, and tears."

There were more issues on Kings Island's end. "The topography of the land and the proximity and interfacing of *White Water Canyon* really restricted us a little bit and access to the site because we had to work around the other ride that's already there," said Gaffney. "The scheduling was, some of the timber deliveries and those type things for the station and all, became a challenge. The other challenge that we had was to interface the show system with the ride itself and make sure that we hit schedules and install every one of those."

The new general manager, Mike Koontz, gave a fresh take on the project, especially in regards to theming. "That [the storage track section of the shed] originally had no theming, no props," said Koontz, who was vice president of finance during the coaster's early planning stages. "It was just going to be blank. It was still a building, [but] it was just an empty room. One day, Jamie Gaffney and I were walking through it as it was being built and I said, 'What's going in here?' He said, 'Nothing.' I said, 'Huh, well that's not good! That's boring.' So Jamie Gaffney got with our sign shop people, our creative people, and a few days later they were putting up more props and theming in that storage area section. That's where sometimes a general manager will stop and say, 'If we just do a little bit more, it's going to make a big difference.'"

As a Bowling Green, Ohio, native, the project took on a special meaning for Daniels Wood Land's Andy Dauterman. "I went for the two-week install and helped along with the crew. It's always a joy to be back in Ohio. Kings Island and Cedar Point were the parks I went to growing up, so it was cool to actually be working on my childhood parks. And this was our first roller coaster themed project, so to be able to do something that, yeah, it's not the lift hill and the banks and the curves and all the fun parts of the coaster, [but] it's still a memorable part. That was really cool."

Trackwork was completed March 6, 2017, and *Mystic Timbers* took its first test run on March 20. Park executives took their first rides soon afterward. For Mike Koontz, it became his favorite ride in the park.

Opening weekend for Mystic Timbers drew huge crowds.
Courtesy of Will Herrmann.

"I was surprised because I knew all the stats, I knew what the speed was, I knew all the banking, and I knew the ride layout, but what I didn't expect was the feeling of how fast you felt like you were going. The elements of the banking and the airtime, I didn't realize how exciting the ride was going to be until I rode it the first time. The other thing, I'm not going to go out and ride a ride four times in a row. It's like one day we were doing something at *Banshee* the year it was built, and there were a lot of full-timers out, and we were riding *Banshee*, and I rode it the first time, and I loved *Banshee*. I thought it was a great ride. I rode it the first time, I rode it the second time straight and we came back in the station and it's like 'Let's go again!' And I said, 'Nope! I'm done!' With *Mystic Timbers*, I think I've ridden it four times in a row."

Mystic Timbers opened to the public on April 15 to wide acclaim. "I think the other thing and the thing our guests love, it's very re-ridable," Koontz continued. "It doesn't beat you up; it's not so intense. And what I like about it is it's very broad. I'm a little bit older, not super old, but a little bit older and I've got an eight-year-old grandson. I could ride it with him. I thought that was really cool. There's not a lot of big coasters that you can do that. I thought the 48-inch height requirement for *Mystic Timbers* was perfect."

"*Mystic Timbers* is a great wooden coaster, but it's a great wooden coaster because such a big percentage of our guests that visit us can ride it and want to ride it and experience it," concurred Cedar Fair's Zimmerman.

Adam House appreciated the coaster's variety of fast-paced elements. "I think *Mystic Timbers* does a great job at capturing some typical GCI elements, but still throwing in several new and unique elements. We were excited for the double camel back trick track which is two back-to-back bunny hops that switch directions up and over each element. There is also a quadruple S-turn going back into the mid-course tunnel that will catch everyone off guard. All of that being said, I think my favorite aspect of the ride is the sheer speed that the ride unleashes on you. It literally feels out of control from start to finish."

The mysteries of the shed were also revealed to mixed reviews, even among park executives. "We tried to do the shed well, but we found out why people don't do animation inside," commented Scheid, who was regional vice president of Cedar Fair at the time *Mystic Timbers* opened. "It's just tough because depending on where you're sitting in the train, the experience is totally different. You try to time it for everybody, and you can't."

Mike Koontz has a brighter outlook on the shed. "I know a lot of people were speculating that the floor was going to drop out, or it was going to do something wild and crazy, go backwards, but what it accomplished was to give the guests something to do other than just sitting in the brake area waiting on the next train in front of them to leave the station. Out of that we got the video walls, some of the theming, the noise, the lights, just all the stuff that goes on...It just added another element to the experience."

Amy Steele of Holovis has wise words for first-time riders. "If you go in without an idea of what you want 'What's in the Shed?' to be, I think you'll see that the story, or, more correctly, stories, plural, we are telling is a lot of fun. The team and I at Holovis had a lot of fun making the show, and I hope that people who ride *Mystic Timbers* have as much fun as we did."

Perhaps most importantly of all, *Mystic Timbers* signaled a new beginning for Cedar Fair as a company. "I think all the pieces really fit, and I think Rob [Decker] was pleased with it, marketing was pleased that they were able to say 'What's in the Shed' and it seemed to catch on like wildfire," Greg Crane concluded. "We knew, that being our test module [for themed coaster experiences], if that works and it becomes marketable, and we knew it was going to be a solid ride minus all theming, but we knew with theming, if that pushed it over the edge, then that was a way we could continue to tell story and push out additional attractions that are similar.

"The other thing I'm proud of is the fact I knew we went in there going, 'Okay, this is the first time that we're attempting to do this,' really at Cedar Fair, and trying to make sure that everybody from Rob to Matt Ouimet to Richard Zimmerman, just making sure that everybody saw where [it was going]—you know, because it's additional money, obviously. You build a coaster and that has a very definitive price tag, but the moment you start adding story and soundtrack, theming, animatronics, video, it has an additional price tag to it for sure, but trying to prove out that by adding these elements, it's actually going to engage the guests better in the queue, on the attraction, even after they get off the attraction and they're hashtagging 'What's in the Shed,' letting people know that they saw whatever creature...The moment that you start marketing something other than a coaster but more of an experience, I really wanted to show them that it could be done, that by spending a little extra money on an attraction, or a considerable amount of money on theming and everything associated with it, story, that it does have a payoff and longevity to it."

HALLOWEEN HAUNT 2017

For Haunt 2017, the park added two new scare zones. *Wasteland* replaced *Nightmare Alley* on the path between International Street and Action Zone and *Dance of the Macabre* was added underneath the *Eiffel Tower*. *Sorority House* did not return, as the *Attitudes* building, across from *The Racer*, it was housed in was in the process of demolition. Haunt ran from September 22 through October 28. After a successful six year run, *Dinosaurs Alive!* closed for good on October 29. Cedar Fair's contract with Dinosaurs Unearthed, which produced the attraction, was up and the company opted not to renew it.

WINTERFEST TRIUMPHANTLY RETURNS

The other significant change at Kings Island for 2017 was a reintroduction of WinterFest after a 12-year hiatus.

"It's funny, when I moved to Cincinnati and Mason in '06, probably the number one question I kept getting was 'When are you bringing WinterFest back?'" Greg Scheid said. Officials realized that bringing back the popular event and offering it free to passholders, just as the original event was, would extend the season, make more money, and add more value to the gold and platinum season pass. "It allows us, a park like Kings Island, [which easily draws teenagers to ride coasters]...but how do we get a 25-year-old or a 30-year-old to go to Kings Island? We had to reach a different demographic."

"When you're out in the public, outside of the park, and somebody sees 'Kings Island' on your shirt, they say, 'Oh, wow, you have that WinterFest event, is that coming back this year?'" said Jamie Gaffney. "It's one of the most requested events to return by our guests. That was one of the primary reasons we brought it back. Just to keep the name Kings Island out there and give an offering of lights and a special event like that to our guests, I think is one of the things that we like about the event and wanted to bring back. It's really unique with the visuals that we can produce with International Street and the fountain and those types of things you can't produce anywhere."

To test the waters, Cedar Fair introduced WinterFest in the milder climate of California's Great America. "I went out to Great America the year they opened in '16 and experienced WinterFest there, and I thought, 'Man, this is going to be a great event,'" said Mike Koontz. "Because I think Year One for Great America it felt that they had been doing it for several years. Just like here it was very immersive. All the lights, all the shows, *Mrs. Claus's Kitchen* and things like that. I knew it was going to be a big success [at Kings Island]."

The new WinterFest includes breathtaking lighting technology.
Photo by the author.

Transforming the park from Halloween Haunt closing on October 29 to the opening night of WinterFest on November 24 proved to be a huge hurdle, and prep work for the event began even earlier in the 2017 season. "With what we were trying to do with WinterFest with all the lights, we had to add a lot more power," Koontz said. "The ice skating rink was a challenge, designing that properly. Man, I could go on and on! Changing out all the merchandise stores from what it is during the regular season to WinterFest merchandise. Changing the end of *Emporium* to the ice skating shoe pick-up place. Converting the other end of *Emporium* to *Mrs. Claus's Kitchen.* Some of it was the infrastructure, the wiring, the electric, the sound. Some of it was the short time period between the end of October and Thanksgiving to get everything done. Putting lights on all the buildings. It's a tremendous amount of work."

"[T]he first run of it in 1982, you didn't have Halloween Haunt," said Don Helbig, who became area manager of digital marketing in 2017. "So you had a lot more time. You weren't taking something down and putting something up at the same time. So just how involved that had to be to flip the park over. Probably the number one challenge was just doing that. We knew what we wanted it to be and everything, but it was just so labor-intensive to get the park ready to go, put up five million lights, and you've got three weeks to do it. And we get better at it every year in terms of doing that, but in terms of the timeline and stuff, you're looking at it and you've got to run that fine line where you don't want to start putting everything up during the Haunt season, and we have to do it a little bit to a degree where there's a little bit of a crossover, but you want to keep each event as separate as possible with that. That's the biggest challenge for us, and I'm sure it's going to be a lot different if you ask some operations people, but just being able to flip the park from a Haunt to WinterFest in three weeks. Whereas in the 80s, that wasn't—you had six, eight weeks to get it ready to go."

New technology allowed for incredible illuminations. "The old Winterfest events, they didn't have as much control over the lights and that's one of the things we brought into the event in 2017," Gaffney said. "There's a lot of controlled lights. On Coney Mall, each individual light down the center of Coney Mall is controlled. It can go on and off or different colors and not have to repeat with the whole strand of lights. Just like the *Eiffel Tower.* The light strands that create the Christmas tree effect, those are all individually controlled and individually color controlled. So really, we map the programs to adjust those colors and brightnesses and those types of things individually. So the data infrastructure and computer power that's required to do that and the communication around the network is a lot greater than what it ever has been before."

The new WinterFest would bring back classic traditions, like ice skating on the *Royal Fountain* and an improved *Eiffel Tower* Christmas tree with new and expanded materials. New live shows and experiences were introduced, and the park ran seventeen rides, including *Mystic Timbers*. In total, 180 acres of the park were open for 2017, more than any other WinterFest prior to that time, and five million lights decorated Kings Island, more than ever before.

"We spent millions of dollars, millions of man hours to produce it, but...there was a lot we learned as a company, as a park, and when guests came through the gate on the first day and they oohed and aahed, it really made it worth it," said Rick Belhumeur, director of park operations.

The new and improved WinterFest drew large crowds and praise, including from Kings Island founder Gary Wachs, who visited the newest incarnation of WinterFest in 2018. "If that [International Street] isn't the most gorgeous sight in America in winter. It was gorgeous! [While we were] ice-skating, I told Mike [Koontz], 'You've done such an incredible job.' I didn't get a chance to really study it...but every shop it seemed like there was specialized Christmas merchandise. I thought it was out-of-this-world."

"I think what Cedar Fair has done for [that] event...took it to such a level that we could never even imagine it back then," said Ed Dangler, Kings Island's manager of rides maintenance from 1992 to 2007. "They have the big resources and the knowledge and things, and Cedar Fair has made it a tremendous event in [that] park."

Just as with the original Winterfest, the newest incarnation has appeal for all ages of the family. "If you think of our parks as a platform and programming on top, the winter holiday event gave us programming that had multi-generational appeal," said Richard Zimmerman. "So what we've seen, and what we thought we would see, and what we have seen is grandparents come with grandchildren. It's truly a multi-generational event, and we really think for the health of our business, broader appeal—appealing to more different age ranges, more demographic groups—is very good for us and keeps us healthy."

STILL GOING STRONG

O n January 1, 2018 Matt Ouimet took on the role of executive chairman of the Cedar Fair board of directors. Succeeding him as Cedar Fair's CEO was Richard Zimmerman, Ouimet's COO. Zimmerman joined the amusement park industry in 1993, when he was transferred from the master planning division of the Paramount-owned Madison Square Garden to Paramount Parks corporate headquarters as their vice president of finance. In 1994 Zimmerman became vice president of finance at Carowinds, and the following year he took on the same role at Kings Island. He was promoted in 1998 to assistant general manager of Kings Island, then soon became general manager of Kings Dominion, a position he remained at for nearly a decade. Shortly after the Cedar Fair sale, he was promoted to regional vice president of Cedar Fair. In October of 2011, Zimmerman became the chief operating officer for Cedar Fair.

"Through all those things [ownership changes and promotions], we have great people, we have great culture, and the reason I keep staying is because of the people I work with and the culture we've created," Zimmerman proudly stated.

CONEY BAR-B-QUE

After two significant investments in one year with *Mystic Timbers* and WinterFest, 2018 would focus on the smaller things, namely the food scene. Kings Island hired a new executive chef, James Major, a two-time winner of the TV show *Chopped*, and opened up a new restaurant, *Coney Bar-B-Que*. The *Attitudes* and *Coney Potato Works* buildings were demolished and the large *Coney Bar-B-Que* was built in their place, with outdoor seating facing the *Scrambler* and *Grand Carousel*. Kings Island opened for the 2018 season on April 14.

HAUNT 2018

For Haunt 2018, the park replaced *Board 2 Death* with a new maze, *C.H.A.O.S.* Additionally, they added two new scare zones with *Pumpkin Eater* on the path between Rivertown and Coney Mall and the return of *Coney Maul*. *Freak Street* did not return, as most of the *Freak Street* props and characters were relocated to *Coney Maul*. Haunt 2018 ran from September 21 until October 27 and was ranked the #1 Halloween theme park event by USA Today.

IT'S BIG, IT'S GONE

Firehawk, that last-minute, frantic transfer from Geauga Lake, had come to the end of the line. Kings Island announced on September 27, 2018 that the flying coaster would close on October 28. Greg Scheid was general manager of Kings Island when the coaster opened and regional vice president of Cedar Fair when *Firehawk* closed. "I was sad to see it go because a lot of people liked that ride. But the issue is that we could only put about 400 people an hour through there when both sides [of the station] were running, which was really a low number… [T]he price of [spare] parts is so high. The cost per rider goes way up and sometimes you just go, 'This is cost prohibitive, and let's do something else with that land in the future.'"

Once the decision had been reached to remove *Firehawk* from the park's lineup, executives still had one last decision to make—what to actually *do* with the removed coaster. "We had two options," said Mike Koontz. "One was demolish it, two, sell it. There's only [three] of that type of coaster in the entire world. There's one at Carowinds, there's one here, and one at Six Flags America. Because we do consider Six Flags to be, in some ways, a competitor and because that's such a unique ride, we said, 'We're not going to sell it to Six Flags.' In addition, even though Carowinds has that ride, and we did send some parts and pieces to Carowinds, but the ride vehicle itself, the trains, are not the same. There's some differences in how they operate, the way they were made. So we said, 'Not Six Flags; we don't want it to be anywhere in the United States,' so the only places it could be sold would be in China or somewhere like that. We tried selling it. The cost to take it apart was three times as much as just demolishing it, so nobody was willing to give us the amount of money that would cover the difference in the cost. At some point we just decided it's cheaper for us to demolish it."

Firehawk was dismantled in January of 2019. The land could now be used for one of the most significant additions in the history of the park.

Firehawk's final crew on its closing night. Courtesy of Abigail Highley.

WINTERFEST 2018

WinterFest 2018 saw more of the park open than ever before. The back half of Coney Mall was open as *Tinsel Town* and the path between Rivertown and Coney Mall was open as well. Two rides were added this time around: *Flight of Fear* and *Shake, Rattle & Roll*. Carriage rides, a tradition from the original Winterfest, started up again, this time carrying guests up and down Coney Mall. WinterFest opened on November 23 and concluded with a gigantic New Year's Eve celebration.

A NOSTALGIC SEASON

For 2019, the park would restore many charming aspects of the park's identity that had been stripped away through the years. "We have found every time we really dive into and understand what the brand [of each park] is and invest behind the brand in each of our markets, it resonates; we see a reaction from the market. So when you think about Kings Island and the heritage it has, soon to celebrate its 50th anniversary, when we touch things that touch the core of what people remember, there's always a great reaction," said Richard Zimmerman.

One of the keystones for the 2019 investment strategy was the return of the *Antique Cars* as *Kings Mills Antique Autos*. "The reason we decided to put *Antique Cars* back in was it's always been one of the most requested rides to bring back, just like *Flying Eagles* was," said Mike Koontz. "Now, I've tried a few times because Carowinds has them and they took them out for a short period of time as they were remodeling a section of the park. I begged and pleaded, I offered whatever to get our *Flying Eagles* back. But, no good! The best I could do, then, was bring back *Antique Cars*. Plus if you think about that area of Coney Mall where we're putting them, where the old *Flight Commander* pad was and the *Dino* tent and the dinos have gone away, they're extinct, they're not coming back, so it's like, 'What are we going to do with that area to improve it and make it look better, and bring back a ride that people are going to enjoy?'"

An original concept rendering of Kings Island's original Antique Cars. Courtesy of Tom Kempton.

Bringing back a nostalgic classic like the *Antique Cars* helps families relive memories and make new ones. "When you talk about the *Antique Cars*, one of the first things is, 'Oh, I used to love to drive those when I was a kid!'" said Jamie Gaffney. "There's so many people that talk about those types of memories that you have to consider bringing those types of attractions back for sure."

"I think it was a good fit to put it over there [in Coney Mall], but it was also positioned with the restoration of the fountain, International Street pavers, new trees, landscaping, and the *Festhaus*, and a broader initiative to restore and rejuvenate and reflect back into Kings Island's past and just make it a better place," said Rob Decker, former senior vice president of planning and design.

Charming billboards and intricate details helped to bring a new level of fun that wasn't on the original car ride. "I've grown up with this park, so adding specific Kings Island history Easter eggs among the designs comes naturally," said Paul Bonifield, graphic and scenic designer for Cedar Fair. "I made the billboard and license plate designs; people ended up really loving those license plates on social media! I think that's what makes that ride more fun and re-ridable...I had a lot of freedom for that attraction. Since it wasn't the 'biggest' attraction, they were just letting me run with it."

All of the logos and graphics throughout *Kings Mills Antique Autos* have a purpose and add a touch of realism. "That's the actual logo...from Peter's [Cartridge Company]," Bonifield continued. "I found it in an old newspaper. The one that's about the animal safari, the animals on there are actually from a 1970s safari monorail coloring book that was sold at the park. So I combined the graphics from the old coloring book to create the billboard design."

Tim Fisher, who became Cedar Fair's COO in January of 2018, sparred with Koontz, thinking it to be an unwise idea to bring the attraction back. After it opened, however, "I could not have been more off-base," Fisher said. "The appeal that that ride had to families and loyal Kings Island fans was huge. I'm pleased to say that ride was a big success for Kings Island."

International Street was also completely transformed to bring it closer to its 1972 glory, while simultaneously adding fresh and modern updates.

"Previously being a visitor to Kings Island from 1974 until I started [working] here in 1999, I remembered what International Street used to be, used to look like," Koontz said. "We went through, I want to say it was 2017, we went through a process called brand positioning. It was a process for us to stay focused on certain pillars, certain things that were part of the Kings Island brand. One of those was the nostalgia and the importance of International Street. So when you step back and look at International Street, over many years, we had removed all the things that really made International Street international. Everybody always knew we had the Italian Building and the French Building and the German Building and the Swiss Building and the Spanish Building. That was well-documented. But you looked at those buildings and there was nothing that said German or French or Spanish."

Nondescript buildings with ghastly '90s paint jobs weren't the only issues with International Street. "The trees that were inside the fence around the fountain created a lot of issues for the [WinterFest] ice rink," Koontz continued. "The type of trees those were, the leaves tended to fall off the trees later in the year. When you have ice and leaves, not a good mix. In addition, the pavers needed to be redone, we needed new tables. And at one point in time, I had had a conversation with Gary Wachs. I said to Gary, 'Tell me about your inspiration for International Street.' He told me the story about how before Kings Island was built, he was on vacation in Europe and he visited these countries. He said, 'Mike, it really is about three things: flags, flowers, fountains.' So when you stepped back and looked at it, the entire look and feel of International Street needed an upgrade. So we knew we wanted to redo the fountain and modernize the fountain effects with the water features. We knew we wanted to put new pavers down International Street. We knew we wanted to take the old trees out. As part of that, we knew we had to repaint the buildings, freshen it up, and we wanted to put the flags [back] on the buildings. Ultimately, that's where I got to, was bringing back some of the original nostalgia of International Street in a different way. You've probably seen pictures of the white rock and the shrubbery that was originally around the fountain. The problem with white rock is white rock eventually turns brown and dirty. I didn't want to do things that were going to be maintenance nightmares."

The project also took on a special meaning for Rob Decker, who had been coming to the park since 1972. "It's just the enchantment of being in the village and being caught up in the moment and the beauty of it, and with all of the little shops along the way, they need the love," Decker said. "Things change over time, and in my heart of hearts, I wish it looked just like it did when I was twelve, and walking through there [in 1972], but it has to take on a life of its own...[It took] a lot of money to do that and a lot of focus and energy and commitment by a lot of people to make that work, because a refurbishment is not a marketable improvement like a new ride or attraction. International Street is the first impression for a guest, an entry portal to a day at the park and should be a transformative experience. Capital allocations only go so far, and typically funding allows you to paint a building or one quadrant in one year, and then the opposite side of the street the next, and then replace a few pavers over here and there, and you never really get the credit for it. You have to just stop, maybe put all that away, all those other allocations, put them away in a piggy bank until year five and then say, 'We're doing the whole thing.' And that's when you get the credit for it."

A benefit to removing the trees, walkway planters, and seat wall around the fountain was restoring the open and sweeping feel that Gary Wachs originally envisioned. "If you look at old pictures of the park, International Street was wide open," Jamie Gaffney said. "You could really see the buildings and everything from anywhere on the street really good and you could actually appreciate, get a good feel of what each one of them were. That's one of the things, we wanted to open it up a little bit more so you could actually see and appreciate the decor and some of the lighting and stuff that takes place on International Street."

The herculean transformation came with its share of difficulties, from finding the twenty-two new trees to encircle the fountain to getting the right umbrellas for the new tables. "The trees we selected, you can't go out in the woods and find twenty-two trees the same height, shape, and all that," Koontz said. "We bought the biggest trees we could find. I think they were twenty-five, thirty-foot high trees, autumn blaze maples. Some people would say, 'Oh, those are nice little trees.' Five, ten, fifteen years from now, they're going to be huge. Then we thought about the tables around I-Street and the umbrellas. One of the pictures from the past showed all these colorful umbrellas on I-Street. So we knew we wanted to add umbrellas and picking the different colors of umbrellas was a challenge. We picked the colors to distinguish, again, 'This area is the Spanish Building' and the color matching of the buildings with the umbrellas."

Paul Bonifield helped to restore the thematic murals and stenciling on the buildings. "I took a bunch of old reference photos from our archive and I redrew the graphics on the buildings. The Swiss

Building has that Swiss text, it's the same logo that used to be on the side of the building. I retraced the design in [Adobe] Illustrator...Also, the graphic on the corner of the Spanish Building, that one used to be on that building back in the day, too."

The original Swiss logo was returned to the building for 2019.
Photo by the author.

The three F's of Gary Wachs once again took center stage in the decision-making process. "The two flower carts on each side of the fountain, that was one of those extra touches we did because years and years ago, there was a flower cart on International Street and they used to sell paper flowers," Koontz added. "It was a merchandise cart. So we said, 'We don't want to sell paper flowers, but let's put the flower cart back on I-Street and make it part of the flags, flowers and fountains experience.'"

Unlike Kings Island's other off-season projects for 2019, work could not begin on International Street until after WinterFest ended on January 1, 2019. With an opening day set at April 20, the top to bottom transformation had to be completed at a relatively breakneck pace. "All of the area around the fountain was torn up and it was a pretty brutal winter," Koontz said. "When you're putting that many new pavers down and trying to get the trees in the ground and irriga-

tion and get all the buildings painted, it was probably more complicated in some ways than building a new coaster!"

Unfortunately, the new *Royal Fountain* was unable to make its full
debut until Memorial Day weekend. "One of the suppliers was out of
Canada, and they just got behind on production of some of the
components," Koontz said. "I wasn't very happy about it, but it was
what it was."

International Street was a busy place in early 2019 as it was
reimagined from the walkways to the Royal Fountain. Photo
by the author.

Ultimately, the revamped International Street continued the Cedar
Fair strategy of placemaking. "Our marketing is telling us guests want
more placemaking," said Mark Schoelwer, the senior corporate
designer with Cedar Fair Planning and Design. "They're not so much
into the big coasters anymore; they want a place where they can hang
out with their family and a place to spend time with their family."

"That's definitely one of my favorite projects," Bonifield said. "I
think the guests really took on to it positively. One of my goals
moving forward is to continue to restore the charm of our Cedar Fair
parks by respecting the park's history, but also not being afraid to do
things a bit differently. As we've seen, all these older things the parks

did are almost always way cooler and more detailed than things are today. Like all these paint styles and the painted murals, why did we ever get rid of that? I see the park as a big canvas, and we're creating the artwork with everything we do within it."

Over in Rivertown, *Reds Hall of Fame Grille* was replaced with the *Miami River Brewhouse*, continuing the overhaul of Kings Island's culinary scene. For *The Beast's* 40th anniversary, the trains were repainted to a similar color scheme as they were in 1979, and the iconic pawprints returned as well.

Finally, the *Festhaus* animated glockenspiel and clock, removed before the 2014 season, was beautifully restored and returned to its place above the building's entrance, along with the return of much of that building's exterior stenciling. "We were just going to do International Street," Bonifield said. "But then I showed the team the current status of the *Festhaus* facade, which at that time was just a blank canvas because the clock was gone. But working in the Entertainment Department in 2012, I remembered we used to climb up within the clock and see the glockenspiel components inside there. I knew everything was still there, so I knew it wouldn't take too much to bring the clock and glockenspiel back. I subtly nudged that project to the right people, and we got that into the International Street renovation scope. I redrew all the clock and grape facade graphics and then passed that off to the Kings Island sign shop and they made it happen."

"It's the soft touches, it's the Easter eggs, it's the things that [make] you say you have such a strong heritage in your park," Decker concluded. "It has such a great following, what if we revisited this that was either then or could be contemporized to now, or could be something similar. Like bringing back a glockenspiel or the floral clock, or something. The GM of the parks will go, 'Yeah! That's great.' But I mean, to do all of that in a package where it starts to make an impact just takes time."

"[The 2019 additions are] nostalgic, but it's more focused on investing behind the brand and those elements of the brand that people find value in," Richard Zimmerman concluded.

GOODBYE TO A CLASSIC

On September 27, 2019 Kings Island announced they were closing *Vortex* at the end of the fall season. "It's a 33-year-old Arrow coaster, so you have to look at a lot of things," said Mike Koontz. "You have to look at, one, the ride itself from the guest perspective. If you compare it to *The Beast*, which is a wooden coaster, *The Beast* is a lot more intense ride, but *Vortex*, for a steel coaster, is a very, very uncomfortable ride. Looking at it that way, and then the second piece is the future cost of maintaining a ride like that. You combine things like, in the next couple years it's going to need a paint job and it's going to need a control system upgrade, and then it's still going to be the same ride. To modify a ride like that is very, very expensive."

Vortex's entrance sits quiet as it experiences its last employee riders. Photo by the author.

Koontz remembered they discussed closing the coaster for several years. "When we started talking about *Orion* before it was *Orion*, we started looking at various rides that potentially we wanted to take out. Both *Firehawk* and *Vortex* were on that list. Obviously, with a ride like

Orion, that was not going to fit in the *Vortex* space. It's been on the list [of rides to close] for I'd say a couple years."

As the conversation began again in 2019, it seemed the ideal year to close the ride. "We closed *Firehawk* last year [in 2018], we got *Orion* coming on, and with *Orion* coming and opening in 2020, we got another coaster that could easily take the place of *Vortex* and help with the crowd sizes and capacity of rides for the park," said Jamie Gaffney. "Because *Orion's* coming is not the reason that we are taking it out; the timing just worked and it just makes more sense to do it in the year *Orion* was going to be new."

Koontz said, "I hadn't ridden *Vortex* in a few years, so one Sunday afternoon [in September 2019] I was walking by and I said, 'Yeah, I'm going to hop on it before the final decision is made and just see what I think.' So I rode it, I got off, and I was like, 'Yeah, that's the right decision.'" It was final—*Vortex* would be retired October 27.

Shuttering an iconic ride like *Vortex* may have been the right decision for management, but it was not an easy one. "Ultimately, we want to provide our guests value, and taking a ride like *Vortex* out was hard," Koontz continued. "I don't get excited about that. I get excited about building new rides. One way to look at it is like '17 and '20 we put in two new coasters, '18 and '19 we took out two coasters. People always want to look at 'more,' but we've got to look at the footprint of the park and what makes sense."

After the closure was announced, ridership increased by 20% as guests arrived to take their final ride on a Kings Island staple. "I think people have fond memories of that ride from when it was maybe brand new, or the first ten years, but the last five years or so, especially when you compare it to the newer steel coasters—*Diamondback*, *Banshee*, and soon to be *Orion*—it's not a comfortable ride," said Koontz.

Will *Vortex* be replaced in the coming years? "We're always [looking] two, three, four, five years out and saying 'What can we do to the park over the next four or five years?' There're conversations about what we can do with that area. But nothing is on the drawing boards right now. We want to do something in Snoopy, that hasn't had anything new since 2015, Soak City hasn't had anything new since 2016. Coney [just] got *Antique Cars*."

"Building new stuff is a lot of fun," Koontz concluded. "Taking things out? Not so much fun."

Vortex saw a significant increase in ridership in the weeks before it was retired. Photo by the author.

REACHING FOR THE STARS

For the 2020 season, Kings Island unveiled the largest investment in park history. *Orion*, a Bolliger & Mabillard giga coaster, drops guests 300 feet at ninety-one miles per hour over 5,321 feet of track. The $31 million ride cost almost as much as it did to build all of Kings Island in 1972!

Strange as it may sound, *Orion* did not begin in Mason, Ohio—but rather in Santa Clara, California as a coaster called *Megabite*, an homage to both the local San Jose Sharks hockey team and the ride's Silicon Valley location. "That ride originally was destined to go to Great America," reveals Mike Koontz. "But it wasn't that ride [exactly].

B&M had designed a ride for Great America [for 2020] and like I said, it wasn't *Orion* specifically. In June of 2018 was when I received a phone call from Tim Fisher, our COO, who said, 'I'm moving the B&M coaster from Great America to Kings Island.' So that was the first time I had any inclination that we were going to do a B&M coaster [for 2020]."

Koontz elaborated, "The reason it was moved from Great America to here is the construction cost in California is just astronomical because of earthquakes and such...It's in Santa Clara, in Silicon Valley, so there's all these office buildings all around it [so you have to sound-proof the coaster]...Part of it was just the cost to build the ride financially exceeded what they wanted to do at Great America."

"They [Cedar Fair] had a contractual responsibility to B&M to buy that ride," Jeff Gramke, Kings Island's manager of facilities, engineering and construction said. "So rather than just backing out of the deal and having a bad relationship with B&M...[Cedar Fair] decided to move it here because the company felt that Kings Island could get it done and get all the design in, get all the permitting and everything done in time to be able to build it here."

"I think that Tim Fisher was very passionate about making sure that the people that were building it [at Great America] were not going to lose their jobs," added Rick Belhumeur, Kings Island's director of park operations. "He didn't want to terminate anything, he didn't want to cancel anything, he wanted to move forward to allow the people in Batavia [at track manufacturer Clermont Steel Fabricators] to have their jobs. So I think that's really cool."

As Cedar Fair CEO Richard Zimmerman further explained, "When we made the decision to move [Great America's *Megabite*], it really was centered on...how could we create another uniquely memorable coaster, and when we looked through the chain, Kings Island did not have a giga coaster, and back to having a gap in our product selection, we thought that was a gap that we could fill. The other thing that we looked at was we knew that we had a couple coasters that were getting long in the tooth. *Firehawk* was aging, and we had a perfect spot where we could put it in. So the combination of having the right real estate, being able to work with that real estate and create a design for a 300-footer that was compelling, and looking at Kings Island, the gap in their portfolio, it all came together very quickly."

With the location changed, the ride would have to be redesigned from scratch to fit Kings Island. "After I received that call in June of '18, we had some meetings with B&M to decide what this ride at Kings Island would be," said Koontz. "Walter [Bolliger]...loves Kings Island. He's built two great coasters here in *Banshee* and *Diamondback*. He said, 'Mike, I promise you I'll build you a great coaster.'"

"We already had a similar coaster as what was being planned for Great America here at the park [*Diamondback*] so there was no reason to build a duplicate," said Kings Island's vice president of maintenance and construction Jamie Gaffney. "It goes back to what our guests have asked for and over the years, it's been a giga coaster. We wanted to provide what was most requested and we thought would add to our arsenal of rides here at the park."

"California's loss was Kings Island's gain to be able to get a giga here, so that worked out pretty good for our advantage," Gramke chuckled.

The question then arose about where in the park to put what would become Kings Island's signature attraction. "We [Planning and Design] began the planning process for *Orion* by studying different areas of the park for placement of the new ride," said Rob Decker, Cedar Fair's senior vice president of planning and design at the time. "This analysis differed from previous master planning studies to add major attractions, namely *Diamondback*, *Banshee*, and *Mystic Timbers*, because each of those attractions had already effectively rebalanced the park dynamics. Not everyone who attends a theme park is a thrill-seeker, but roller coasters are a primary attraction for guests, and over time, each of those additions affects guest flow within the park. And although we knew the new ride could be so popular that it would undoubtedly have a major impact wherever we placed it, the ride site placement wasn't entirely strategic. We needed to carve out a huge chunk of contiguous land to accommodate such a massive ride!"

To do this, Decker relied on his prior experiences for master planning to maximize this once in a lifetime opportunity for Kings Island. "When planning for previous significant new attractions, *Diamondback's* layout followed a similar logic as the development of *Magnum XL-200* at Cedar Point," Decker continued. "The hyper coasters' height above 200 feet results in a lengthy footprint that could not consume a lot of park space displacing the park's core functions. Instead, the solution was to occupy a small-ish footprint for guest access to the ride station, nestled efficiently within the park boundaries. In doing so, and by aiming the lift hill outwardly, most of the ride track is sent dashing toward the park perimeter to utilize unoccupied areas before returning in a traditional out-and-back roller coaster style.

"*Banshee* and *Mystic Timbers* also followed this logic by minimizing the displacement of valuable land and taking advantage of huge variations in topography, dropping down outer perimeter hillsides to optimize steep terrain benefits, gaining greater inertia to enhance the ride. As for other considerations, giga coasters were not new to Cedar Fair, and I had the experience of working on *Millennium Force* at Cedar Point before developing *Intimidator 305* at Kings Dominion, *Leviathan* at Canada's Wonderland, and *Fury 325* at Carowinds. Each ride layout utilized the perimeter of the park to bolt-on the massively scaled attractions without much disruption to core [park] functions. The last consideration for ride placement was steered by Kings Island [management], who were contemplating future ride maintenance needs in the Coney Mall area of the park. *Firehawk* was viewed as a placeholder, and its ride maintenance needs were escalating while rider counts continued to drop year after year. *Vortex's* operating days were numbered as well. With these discussions, a site selection in the Coney Mall area became much clearer."

"We looked at some other locations, but we didn't spend a lot of time and energy on the other locations as we did with the *Firehawk* location, just because of the available land on that side of the park to build something that big," Jamie Gaffney added.

With the location selected, management at Kings Island, the engineers at B&M, and the team at Cedar Fair's corporate planning and design team worked together to develop potential layouts for the

2020 giga coaster. "Kings Island is a family park," Koontz continued. "Think about *Mystic Timbers* for example. *Mystic Timbers* is a great ride; it's my personal favorite. But it's very broad as far as the ages that can ride that ride. An eight year-old, a sixty year-old, it's a very good family ride. What we wanted with Orion was something that was broad enough that one, sixty year-olds would want to ride it, and those who meet the height requirements would want to ride it. So then we knew it was not going to be a world record breaker, but we wanted it to be the tallest, the longest, the fastest steel coaster at Kings Island, which it is, and we wanted it to meet the definition of a giga coaster...I've had guests stop me in the park and say, 'Mike, you could have spent a little bit more money and made it a world record breaker.' Yeah, we could have, but that's not what I wanted. The more tall it is, the more intense the ride is going to be, which narrows the demographic that's going to want to ride it. We definitely wanted it to be fast, tall, long, but we wanted people to say, 'I want to ride it again.'"

"The other thing Kings Island is known for, which Cedar Point is different, Kings Island is known for using the terrain of the land," Koontz added. "So you think about *The Beast*, you think about *Mystic Timbers*, even *Banshee*, we're using some of that terrain to make it a unique ride experience."

For *Orion*, B&M was able to use the hilly terrain to create the unique ride experience of a 300-foot drop with a lift hill height of 287 feet. Kings Island's management also wanted to make the giga something truly distinctive for this park. "We were looking for anything that was unique on it and I think taking advantage of the topography of the land and the wave curve or wave hill is going to be unique, the helix is going to be unique," said Gaffney. "We were looking for unique elements."

"To refine the planning process and relay the impact of a giga coaster-scale attraction to park management, I prepared conceptual ride plan layouts to illustrate areas where the roller coaster could potentially fit," Decker said on the design process. "These layouts reflected the required ride length and potential sensations a steel roller coaster with giga coaster stature could offer. Next, the concepts were vetted by the park before sending to B&M along with a list of specific objectives. For instance, we shifted a conceptual ride footprint around on a site plan to indicate potential site placement opportunities and limits. I mentioned B&M might recognize a few of the proposed ride elements from *Fury 325* [the B&M giga coaster at Carowinds] or derivations of what we built in another park. We granted their engineering team full liberties to come back with a different type of concept or ride profile, etc, etc. Still, it had to be 300 feet tall, deliver incredible airtime, fit within the defined area, and this would require guest access from Coney Mall.

"Two entry locations were considered. One was closer to the terminal end of Coney Mall to draw guests farther down its length, and the other site access indicated utilizing the current pathway leading to X-Base. At that point, B&M's engineers came back with three to four different concepts for review before we met internally as a team to have another round table discussion."

Orion's first drop is 300-feet tall at an 85-degree angle. Photo by the author.

The final plan that the park selected was 5,321 feet in length, the longest steel coaster in the park, but the shortest of the three B&M gigas, packing dynamic elements into a shorter track length. "We always like to see the ride coming back in high-speed form, hot into the station area with a lot of momentum to get that last pop of airtime before skidding into the brakes," Decker said. "Yeah, the ride could always be longer to add another element, but the inertia lost to that element could diminish the dynamic finish."

Interestingly, the coaster was initially planned to have trains in the same staggered seating style as *Diamondback*, as a holdover from the Great America plans. Wanting to differentiate the giga from *Diamondback*, Kings Island fought back, and Mike Koontz lobbied for floorless trains. Ultimately, capacity desires resulted in the selection of the standard four-across trains used on the other two B&M gigas.

Rick Belhumeur led his operations team to finalize the operational details of the coaster. "We put our heads together, operationally, to figure out what the queue line [has] to look like, how long the queue needs to be, what kind of fixtures and furniture that I needed to get for the area. And again, we try to do as much recycling as we can as far as, do I have benches that are somewhere else that I can paint and move over? Work[ing] with the manufacturer, they have certain specifications and guidelines that we need to comply with, so we take their information and accompany it with our standard operating guidelines and try to just make sure that we are compatible and consistent with those guidelines. It's just a lot of cooperation with maintenance, the designers, and the manufacturer to put out the final product."

With the layout finalized, it next came time for the name and theme of the attraction. "Naming a ride is not easy," Koontz said. "Internally here, our marketing team came up with a list of names. We engaged our corporate marketing team; they came up with a list of names. We engaged our outside advertising agency, they came up with a list of names. Our corporate planning and design team came up with names, and I came up with my list. I'm proud to say that *Orion* is my name. But it did not start there...Originally, we were thinking about some type of—you think about *Diamondback* and snake, we weren't

STILL GOING STRONG

thinking about a snake but we were thinking about a bird. A falcon. An eagle. That type, because it's soaring high and then it's swooping down into the area, hunting its prey. But when you start researching names of rides that other parks have all over the world, there's already falcons. Griffon was on the list, and there's *Griffon* at Busch Gardens. So all the good bird names were taken. Everybody loves birds! I started researching Greek mythology and there's lots of rides out there with Greek mythology-type stuff. One day, Rob Decker and I were having a conversation and he said 'I've got this idea.' There was still a semblance of this bird theme to it, but he said, 'What if we tie it all in to *Flight of Fear*, this ride, the area, X-Base. What if we made it all work together instead of having just this big coaster over here called *The Falcon?*' So I started thinking about it and I came up with *Orion* and *Polaris*."

Koontz pitched the two names to Decker, who loved them and came back with several potential storyline and theming ideas. "Quite honestly, when I first pitched *Orion* as the name, here's what I was thinking was Orion is the most prominent constellation in the sky. This coaster is going to be the most prominent thing in the skyline of Kings Island. You're going to see it from the interstate, from whichever way you're coming to the park, you're going to see *Orion*. So it's prominent in the skyline of Kings Island. But Orion was also the great hunter in Greek mythology. So going back to the bird theme, this falcon/hunter, Orion. And Orion or Polaris, nobody in the amusement industry has a ride with that name. So it's unique to Kings Island just like *The Beast*, just like *Banshee*, just like *Mystic Timbers*, so we wanted the ride name to be unique. Some people said, 'We need a two word name. Like *Orion Star*.' [I said,] 'No. Just *Orion*.'" Nearly seven months went by before *Orion* was finalized in early May 2019 as the name of Kings Island's giga coaster.

Kings Island once again decided to make their latest attraction a themed experience. Additionally, the location of the ride access point spurred a discussion about redeveloping the X-Base zone, and the Kings Island team became excited with the prospect of revitalizing the entire area. "I think that adding theming is a good thing to any ride that we do," Koontz said. "Sure, we could have saved more money if we had just put up a sign that said, '*Orion*,' and was done with it. But X-Base, which now is Area 72, because there's only two rides there in *Flight of Fear* and *Orion*, we just felt that we could make that story of that area a little bit stronger by doing some of the theming we do...It was important. Kings Island deserves something more than just a ride with a sign."

Mike Koontz introduces the world to Orion on August 15, 2019.
Photo by the author.

Movement on the ride's storyline began even before the name was finalized. "I always said I wanted this to be a sequel to *Flight of Fear*," said Paul Bonifield, Cedar Fair's graphic and scenic designer—and a former Coney Mall area ride supervisor, overseeing *Flight of Fear*. "I live and breathe *Flight of Fear*! I love the storyline of that ride, I can still quote the entirety of the pre-show video! Using the existing layers from the *Flight of Fear* storyline, I wanted *Orion* to fit into the same world and build a new story for the area."

"Planning and Design explored possible themes that might pique the guest's curiosity without fully revealing the answers to their questions," Decker said. "For instance, X-Base was not part of the park's original development, so why is there a futuristic flight/space themed area adjacent to the theme park? What is the relationship? From a contextual perspective, how did it all start? Could a new storyline weave into existing themes such as a cataclysmic event, an alien craft sighting, or an extraterrestrial visit related to *Flight of Fear* and *CHAOS* [Halloween Haunt maze]? Or possibly reflect a secretive agency exploring interstellar flight? Ultimately, we recommended concepts to convey a broader baseline of thematic context to loosely tie together a few park-related 'occurrences' with references to present and future content. The creative intent evolved to include storytelling with hints, and sporadic reveals by leveraging mysteries related to Kings Island attractions using the guise of the unexplained, mysterious occurrences, or mystic influences."

Cedar Fair Planning and Design continued bouncing around theming ideas. "I went to Rob Decker and suggested, 'Can we use under the coaster station as part of the queue?'" Bonifield said. "Because all these newer coasters have room under the station that's just dead space, so I said, 'Can we make part of the queue wind under a portion of the bottom level of the station building to where you'd be looking through windows that would showcase a control room or something before you go up the stairs to the station?' Rob said, 'That's an awesome idea. Let's do it even better and put a building that they walk through!' So that's how we ended up with the quonset hut as an additional queue feature."

Bonifield was even able to assist in securing IMAScore to compose another soundtrack for the park, only the second theme park track from them in the United States, after *Mystic Timbers*. "I'm glad we secured IMAScore to do *Orion's* soundtrack," Bonifield added. "I love their soundtracks. I pushed hard for it. I listen to their [IMAScore] content [from other parks] when I'm working on projects; I'll listen to their soundtracks such as *Helix* [coaster at Liseberg] and all the different coasters they've done in Alton Towers. I was really happy with how the *Mystic Timbers* soundtrack came out, so I was like, 'We need to do it for this. This is the perfect opportunity to do it. Let's do it, let's do it, let's do it.' And it happened!"

The story and theming opportunities soon spread across the entire area. The former X-Base "neighborhood" of Coney Mall would be redeveloped into its own distinctive theme area, Area 72, a secret government base that has been studying the effects of flight on man at Kings Island for decades. "[As *Orion* developed], our marketing team...started thinking about it, how we can tie it into *Flight of Fear*," said Koontz. "Then we ultimately said, 'Let's just rename the whole area.' It's like *Flight of Fear*, the history of that, it was like paranormal activity, kind of like that Area 51 stuff. So I said, 'Why don't we name it Area 72?' They were like, '[Huh?]' I was like, 'You know, '72 for the year the park opened.' It's the area where all this secret stuff has been going on. It kind of fit because we got the new *CHAOS* maze there, so that was how Area 72 came to be."

Like International Street, the reimagining would be top-to-bottom. "What's exciting about something like that is seeing the different parts and pieces come together," Koontz added. "Tapping into the creativity of whether it's marketing, food and beverage, merchandise, ride operations, and really just the excitement of being able to start with a clean slate and say, 'What do we want this to be?'"

"Mike was beating the drum on this, that we were really building a story and tying it back into the heritage of the park and of the region, with Wright-Patterson [Air Force Base] being just up the road and the connection with the paranormal activity already sort of developed and in the drawer that could be embellished," said Rob Decker. "Then from there, [it's] anyone's wildest imagination to take all these sort of cues and things from what's really going on, what's in the hanger and all the things, what's behind the closed doors...There's not a whole lot of that [redevelopment of specific lands] that was happening back in the day of *Millennium Force*, which was my first ride, but with *Steel Vengeance* [at Cedar Point] for sure, *Maverick* and *Steel Vengeance*, to try to depict the characterization of a Western town, FrontierTown. And then because you've got the capital investment to put in an anchor attraction, everything leading up to it has to be redone...A lot of the more contemporary attractions that we put in, we were able to give some love to that section of the park, whereas it would have been impossible to go in and revamp it and rebuild it without a new attraction. It would just have been, 'Well, that's nice, they changed this. Okay. Let's go back to the park.' So when given the opportunity, take it!"

Between the retirement of Cedar Fair Senior Vice President of Planning and Design Rob Decker in March of 2019 and the hiring of his replacement, Chuck Myers, in June of 2019, the thematic side of the project was guided by Kings Island's marketing department, who shifted the story's focus from paranormal activity to a coming meteor storm. Utilizing both teams of marketing and Planning and Design, the final *Orion* storyline came together.

To actually develop and design, as well as physically manufacture the theming, Cedar Fair and Kings Island once again tapped the talents at Daniels Wood Land. "We typically like to bid projects out...but that particular year, it was a lot of last-minute projects and so out of necessity and fast tracking this, we picked a group that we felt would be best qualified to work with," said Mark Schoelwer, senior corporate designer with Cedar Fair Planning and Design. "We felt like *Mystic Timbers* went off really well and the park liked working with [Daniels] Wood Land. So we decided to...go with them."

"They [Cedar Fair] have their P&D, their planning and design folks, but Greg [Crane], the creative director [from *Mystic Timbers*], had actually left and was working on his own," said Andy Dauterman, executive vice president of business development for Daniels Wood Land. "When they [Kings Island] came to me, they had an initial story, or at least an idea of what they wanted to do. They knew it was going to be this meteor strike and you're going up to save the Earth, essentially, is the idea...They were like, 'Here's money for design, here's money for build.' So it was a true design-build project. So what I did is I actually went out and hired Greg to work for us and he was my creative director! It was perfect because he already knew everybody on the other end of the call, it was basically like a high school reunion for him! He knew everybody, they're all his family, and I was the outsider who brought him in to really make it all pull together."

The design process for *Orion's* theming was a departure from the process for *Mystic Timbers*. "For this one, we got on the initial planning and then it was more or less Greg and I would just sit there and go back and forth several times a day on phone or Skype or Zoom or whatever, and just hash out ideas," Dauterman said. "You know, 'This would be neat, we could do this, no, that's going to be too expensive and we don't know how to figure that out.' It was really just that traditional 'throw a bunch of stuff at a wall and see what sticks' and start to make a story out of it! Weekly, we would be going back with P&D and saying, 'Here's what we're thinking,' and they obviously would have their input and the park would have their input, and then as it started to evolve a little bit, then the team grew and [Kings Island] marketing got involved and they had their own input.

"I would say we got it about 60-70% of the way and then the marketing folks came in to where it was like, 'Well, we need to do this because we're hashtagging or trending this, and so we've got to find a way to work that into it,' or 'Let's not do that and let's do this instead.' In most cases, they were wonderful, great ideas; in some cases it was like, 'Oh, darn it, I really liked that idea, I thought it was fun!' and we hated to see it go. It was more or less, from the start it was Greg and I, and then P&D and then marketing and then the GM until all the designs were approved and then it was fabrication time."

"It's a little different [than *Mystic Timbers*]," Greg Crane explains, "because when the story's laid out there, then it gives us a definite path to be able to build from. With this attraction, it wasn't like there was a Big Bad character [like the monsters of the Miami River Lumber Company], it was more or less a mission-oriented experience, or this event that's going to happen so many years in the future. They're more or less testing and going on a mission now to make sure that they're prepared for the day. It came down to, okay, that's our storyline, so what's the setting for it? Just drawing something knowing that there is going to be a show building in the queue, that there is going to be an entryway that we were going to repurpose to fit the theme, and then on the attraction there wasn't going to be a box or a show space per se. That became something for the guests to take on themselves. They were essentially assigned that role [as volunteers in the story] to fill in the gaps."

The quonset hut quickly became one of the focal points of the queue experience. "It's very ride-specific as far as you have your table in the center of the room which has the different plans and props," Crane continued. "Somebody's coffee mug, a stack of papers and a plan, and then your binders that coordinate to the project itself...[The initial idea for the lockers was] one locker was housed with clothes of people that are getting ready to go on the mission, the next lockers are minus the space gear because that's assuming they got into the space gear, and then the next set of lockers originally was going to be empty, because it's assuming that would have been yours to place your gear into. The previous group would have gone off on the mission. It was trying to tell a story within, okay, we have this much space, we go from here directly to the load platform, so what are the tidbits within the props that we can tell the story with?...We did have some nods to the mission and then to the other parks, and even to the park's history through the peg board walls...We knew we wanted to have nods to other attractions within the Cedar Fair company, but marketing wanted to reuse those posters that they used to announce the attraction...so those made an appearance on that wall. Paul Bonifield put a beautiful and often humorous spin on some of those elements."

Cedar Fair's in-house FUN TV, which is based out of Kings Island, produced the pre-show video for inside the quonset hut. "It's different from *Mystic Timbers* where the show's at the end," Koontz said. "In *Orion's* case, the show is before you ride the ride...It just became part of that ride experience. Kind of like how Disney and Universal does with that. We had that thought process, let's take some of the learnings from Disney and Universal and let's apply it here."

For Daniels Wood Land, Area 72 meant an exciting opportunity to not just theme the coaster like with *Mystic Timbers*, but to breathe life across a brand-new themed land. "It was cool because you got to spread it [the theming] all out," said Dauterman. "Any time we can do a larger space, that's always the goal. We got to create our own themed land, how cool is that? It plays well with *Flight of Fear* that's right there. The idea that it's an abandoned government installation already kind of worked into the story. Everything just worked between *Flight of Fear* and the captured UFO and, how does that make sense? How do we tie that to *Orion*? Well, let's do a meteor strike. Okay, we'll do multiple meteor strikes. But there's got to be a unique reason why this area is a hotbed. Well, it's because of the captured UFO.

New theming brings Area 72 to life. Courtesy of Paul Bonifield.

"Then you've got the podcast car who's out front who is telling you this is all a conspiracy and the aliens are coming for us. It just started to flow to where some of them turned into jokes, like 'We could actually make this work and be funny and interesting to guests.' To do it not only within a queue space, but within an entire land, it was a blast. The challenge is you have to spread that amount of money out now over a wider surface because they don't keep giving you more money! So imagine you have a bagel and only have so much cream cheese to spread on it, and then all of a sudden, people throw 300 bagels at you and the same amount of cream cheese, and you've got to make it work for everybody. Some parts of the bagel might have a little bit more than others, but that's really the only challenge was keeping it within budget and schedule to pull the whole thing off. I think we did a pretty good job."

"To me, it's great to start telling the story before you can actually get back there [to a coaster entrance]," Crane added. "The moment that you see, right before *The Racer* there's that pod[cast] wagon parked over in the grass and there's a No Parking sign. He's keeping an eye on this base and he's like, 'Something hinky is definitely going on over here,' and that audio that is in that car pertains heavily to the audio that's over at *Mystic Timbers*. That's our connection to *Mystic Timbers*, and then *Mystic Timbers*, in that truck where the audio is playing, it ties over to *Flight of Fear*. In order to tie the new *Orion* attraction into *Flight of Fear* in creating a plaza, we basically were like, this is an entire facility that we're going into, and *Orion* is the newest branch of that facility. That pod vehicle is...your pre-show to the land. Then you go through the gates and you step into Area 72, where they have the new food and beverage and then the revitalized *Flight of Fear* exterior, you see the meteor impact and then leading up to the actual *Orion* entry."

The focal point of the plaza is the meteor collision in front of *Flight of Fear*. "That was the element that I really wanted from the beginning was to take a light post that used to be there and knock it over, rest the meteor down there, and distress the building a little bit," Crane added. "Just so it's like there have been some [meteor] impacts prior to, and they're only going to get worse from here. Instead of just telling a story about this thing that's going to happen, we see that it's already started happening and we're at the front end of the story, because as they get onto the ride, they go into training. We're not going into the big final event, because that's not where we are in the timeline. It's interesting that this story is based around what is to come, and the Big Bad is not happening today in that storyline."

The Area 72 transformation redefined that section of the park. "When I worked there [in Games in the early '80s], it was back-of-house," Mark Schoelwer said. "When I worked in Skill 3 and I was behind the games crushing boxes or whatever, that was all woods or part of the carpenter's parking lot for their shops. But Kings Island saw an opportunity to wrap up a restroom facility and food service [as *Meteor Canteen*], so more amenities were offered...just so guests could spend more time there. Again, placemaking."

One cancelled plan for the plaza involved the *Orion* constellation set in lights in the ground. "You can't see the plaza from the *Eiffel Tower*, so putting those lights in the ground wouldn't make sense," said Rick Belhumeur. "You're going up the lift [on *Orion*] away from the plaza [so] you wouldn't see it, so it's best to save your money."

Construction on the ride moved right on schedule through the winter and towards an April 11 opening date. Chicago-based Sky High Coasters, LLC, did the erection. "They did a great job and with B&M's engineering, it's like when you lift that final piece in place and there's only about a quarter inch gap on each side, that tells you things went well, and that doesn't always happen," Koontz said.

Cedar Fair officials were excited for what the coaster would mean for the park. "That type of ride is a fabulous attraction," Cedar Fair COO Tim Fisher said in January of 2020. "Whenever...you have something of that scale, something of that significance, when you add that type of attraction to a theme park, you generally find that the market responds very favorably. I think it's time. I think you look at since the last major coaster went into Kings Island, it's been several years now. This will be well-received in the market, something of this scale and significance doesn't happen every year at a regional theme park...I think it's going to be very broad. It's going to be something people respond to very favorably. It will be a great experience for a teenager and it will be a great experience for someone that's older that still wants the excitement of that type of ride but doesn't necessarily want loops or inversions. I think it's going to be one of those rides that appeal to a very broad market segment."

For CEO Richard Zimmerman, *Orion* is the materialization of a long-time goal to add a giga to the park. "There had been [discussions about building a giga before], but Kings Island had other priorities in terms of investing behind the brand...But now we think it's time to play the giga coaster card there, and I think the reaction when people ride it will be phenomenal."

Orion is one of the most technologically-advanced rides in operation today. "It's new-style trains, so the anti-rollbacks are silent," Belhumeur said. "There's an eddy current system on there so as the train moves over the rail, it causes the chain dog to lift up so there's no clicking and clacking, so it's silent. There're magnets in the seatbelts that allow the receiving end of the seatbelts, both ends, to stick up so that when you get up, it's out of the way so you're not as inclined to sit on the seatbelt. The microphone for the operators is all hands-free, it's operated by foot pedals. There's a water fountain in the station, which is just a good idea for all of them to have!..From an entertainment perspective, there is uplighting on the support columns that's actually programmed into the park lighting control system so we can program that with the fireworks show or whatever we want to do. The load area gates...[are] all tied into the system so if there's one gate that's open or ajar, the ride won't go, so it's all tied in. The anemometers are tied into the system so if the winds are not in the appropriate parameter, it won't let a train dispatch. So it's a very smart ride, it really is."

Work soon began on installing the theming elements, including the centerpiece meteor collision in front of *Flight of Fear*. "For the crater area, we work with a great concrete sculpting company that we hired to do the actual crater depression," Andy Dauterman explained. "Cedar Fair went in and did the excavation work for us and put in all their utilities and plumbing that we needed in that area, and then we had our sub[contractor] go in and do the sculpted concrete area, broken concrete and dirt and the depression, and then we did the meteor out of fiberglass, and included the glowing internal effects and smoke and that sort of stuff. Really, it wasn't all brought together for the first time until it was on-site...It all worked out and the dimensions all fit, and the utilities were all in the right spots and everything to where we could really pull it off."

Mike Koontz was able to take his first ride on March 11, 2020, a moment he had been looking forward to since planning for *Orion* began in June 2018. "I was very, very happy," Koontz said. "It exceeded my expectations...It's kind of like when you have your first child and the excitement of the baby is finally here and you and your wife and your family are just so excited. You have this new coaster that you know is going to be there for years and years to come, millions and millions of people are going to ride it, so that was my excitement...We accomplished what we wanted to, which is give people a ride experience that's going to be repeatable, that people want to ride over and over again."

Just a few days later, the world suddenly came to a stop with the coronavirus outbreak—and the Daniels Wood Land crew was still on-site. "From L.A., I started talking with my project manager up here and saying, 'We need to start talking about getting our guys home because we can't have them get stuck in Ohio,'" Dauterman said. "'We need to start making contingencies for it.' We worked really closely with Kings Island, they were wonderful, they obviously understood the gravity of what was going on, everybody's health and safety is paramount compared to anything else. We had slated for I think about fourteen to sixteen days on-site, and I think they were there for about eight or nine when we finally...I mean, everything was shutting down. The restaurants were shut down, they literally couldn't even go eat. So we made the decision at that point that for the safety of everybody, we had to pull them out, get them all home, and this way everybody could be with their families during this time and not expose them any more than we had to. As I said, Kings Island was wonderful."

"The ride was built, but there was still a lot of testing and control work," Koontz added. "We had cycled it several times when we shut down, but most of the theming had not been completed. Some of the Area 72 work had not been done. It was hard to shut it down, knowing we were so close to being done."

Instead of staying put, Kings Island and Cedar Fair used the coronavirus lockdown period to re-evaluate the *Orion* site, adding new theming features that would not have been added had the coaster stuck to its original timeline. "I came in during April 2020, just to casually visit the site and see how things were going," Paul Bonifield said. "I was visiting my family here in Ohio at the time. I saw there were quite a few pockets of opportunity that could benefit from additional decor. Now that we had the time, I put together a design deck of these new prop ideas. I paired up with the decor team here at Kings Island; this is the team who creates and installs the Haunt and Winter-Fest events. I shared my huge 'wish list' with them and we tried our best to knock all my crazy ideas out!"

"Updating and blending *Flight of Fear* into the new world of Area 72 was high on my list and [everything but the facade] hadn't been touched at that point," Bonifield continued. "From restriping the exit hallways and the new control room scene taking over the former *Flight of Fear* photo booth, to simply adding signage and crates to the outdoor queue building, I wanted *Flight of Fear* to be a star in Area 72 just as much as *Orion*. We worked closely with the wonderful folks of the Kings Island sign shop to print and mount all the signage designs I had created. The sign shop team created the ID signage for everything other than the *Orion* ID around in Area 72. *Meteor Canteen*, restrooms, *Flight of Fear, Image Control, CHAOS*. They were inspired by Disney's EPCOT Center pavilion logos. You'll notice how the base icons reflect that style/vibe."

"I went on Facebook Marketplace and picked up that satellite that's on the *Orion* entrance," Bonifield continued. "It was in West Chester [Ohio], in some guy's backyard, and I borrowed the Games [department] truck to drive down there and pick it up. We put that on a flatbed and drove it back, and then our paint shop painted it up and put it out at the ride. Mike Koontz just so happened to be driving down Tylersville Road on his way home for the day. He told me he had a good chuckle after seeing me pass by in the Kings Island Games truck with the giant satellite strapped to the back!

"You might recognize the radio tower at the *Orion* entrance plaza...It was formerly in front of *Flight of Fear's* queue entrance before being removed around [the] 2010 Haunt [season]. Exploring the park over the years, I became very familiar with the various boneyards and random things laying around the park, and for years the tower had been sitting behind the sign shop. We had maintenance assess and see if it was still structurally sound. It was, so the paint shop freshened it up and it was reinstalled to the left of *Orion's* entrance. So it was a lot of in-house talent to make this project come together at the very end."

The transformation of the Skylab drive box into an Area 72
prop. Courtesy of Paul Bonifield.

Faced with a very small budget and a very large space, the Planning and Design team got creative and recycled numerous items from around the park's "boneyards" for the final *Orion* experience. The *Royal Fountain* pedestals that were removed in 2019 were repainted and scattered around the site—with one of them even bearing the name of Bonifield's first K'NEX Coaster as a kid, *Radium XL-200*. Metal fencing in the *Orion* entry portal planter and on the maintenance gate next to the entrance are bunk bed pieces reused from the employee dormitories. *Firehawk's* entrance greeter booth was saved from the wrecking ball and moved backstage, with a plan to install it as a security checkpoint prop in the queue. The idea was scrapped when it was discovered that it would require a permanent foundation, which was outside of Planning and Design's budget. Instead, they opted to use and repaint the former *Skylab* drive box to serve the same purpose—which did not require a new foundation.

While Planning and Design was busy adding new theming elements, Kings Island executives were discussing the reopening process. "We had as a company, not just at Kings Island but at every park, we had been working on our COVID reopening plans when we were shut down," Koontz said. "We wanted to be ready, whenever we got the opportunity to open, to get open as soon as possible. So all the behind-the-scenes stuff, the plexi barriers, all the stickers, the social distancing stickers, the hand sanitizer stations, cleaning supplies, masks, the health screening test. All that took a lot of time to document and get to the point where we felt like, 'Here's a document.' In Kings Island's case, it's a 400-page document that details out every food stand, every ride, all of our protocols on how we're going to operate during the pandemic.

"When we were able to come back to work, I can't remember the exact date now we came back, I want to say it was mid-to-late May. We immediately started work towards communications with the governor and his office on when we could open. We were working with the committees he had established. Travel and Tourism, I think, was the committee that amusement parks were in. Cedar Fair had a couple people in that committee, so we were pretty connected with conversations, what was going on. Both Kings Island and Cedar Point's plans had to be submitted to that committee, and as you know, that process took time. At some point, we felt like we were being ignored, and that we were seeing restaurants being able to open and retail being able to open, and [public] parks and other things being able to open...So a lot of things were being able to open and as a company, we decided to pursue a legal remedy, and that definitely got the attention of the governor."

The lawsuit worked, and in early June Kings Island finally got the green light to reopen from the Ohio state government. While this was great news for the park, this also prompted a new discussion. "We debated, do we open the ride this year? Or do we wait until next year?" Koontz said. "I always fought to open it this year because I think our guests would have been very disappointed had we not opened it."

With that decision finalized, the park invited the Daniels Wood Land installation crew to return and complete their work by July 2, when the park would open for season pass holders. Andy Dauterman explained, "We left it in the middle of installation, it was like 'Get home.' It involved a couple weeks of our crew going back and in some cases starting from scratch and cleaning some things up. And some of the things we had done just weren't working from a visual standpoint and so there was a little bit of, 'Let's move that over to there and let's figure this out,' and in many ways as much as it [the temporary closure] hurt, it also helped because what we would have done [with the original installation timeline] is installed everything and left, and then it would have been like, 'Ah, this just doesn't work.' We realized having that TV over there doesn't work or this thing against that wall just doesn't work or this doesn't look as good as it should have. By it being semi-done, you could walk in and go, 'That's not working,' you know, 'this needs to move,' and still have the reassurance that we were going to be able to come back and readdress those issues. It was chaotic, it was difficult, but like I said, in a small way, the positive is that it allowed us to reevaluate and make the attraction that much better."

Orion and Area 72 opened to passholders on July 2 and to the public on July 10, almost three months after the initially scheduled April 11 opening date. The months of hard work paid off to all involved. "That was a day I'll never forget!" Koontz said. "Always, the most exciting day for me is when we open. Every opening day is exciting, and you don't know what to expect during a pandemic! We were overwhelmed, I will say, for the first few hours, of people coming into the park. It was exciting and gratifying to see that all the hard work that our associates went through and the patience, and to see the Kings Island team do what they do best, which is take care of our guests, make sure that the guests are having a good experience, and then couple that with opening a world-class coaster at the same time, was just [amazing]. I have a lot of special days in my tenure so far as GM. My first year, opening *Mystic Timbers* and then opening Winter-Fest that year, that was special; re-doing International Street, bringing back *Antique Cars* was special. Doing [*Grand*] *Carnivale*, that was special, and this year, in the midst of the pandemic, getting Kings

Island open and opening *Orion* was definitely up there on the top of my list."

The entry plaza of Orion. Courtesy of Paul Bonifield.

The 2020 season might have been short overall, but it was meaningful to Mike Koontz and the guests that passed through the gates throughout the year. "Throughout the season, they've said, 'Thank you for opening. Thank you for giving us the opportunity to come and enjoy the park and have some fun. This has made this year feel more normal.' Mask-wearing and social distancing, it's hard. But I think we accomplished our mission, which was to get the park open, operate safely for our associates and our guests, and do the right thing. So, Mission Accomplished."

"I've been part of the evolution and understanding of what [*Orion*] was going to be [at Great America] and what we ended up with [at Kings Island], and I think what we ended up with is a great product for the particular location that it's at," Rick Belhumeur concluded. "I don't get really excited about the coasters; I like to provide a good guest experience, and I think that the cohesiveness now of that particular area really came out very, very well."

Andy Dauterman of Daniels Wood Land hopes that the theming

trend continues for Cedar Fair. "I'm hoping that they'll continue this progression in understanding the importance of theming and story-telling, and I think what they've done at Kings Island in particular has pulled off really well and fans are appreciating [it]...I think that it's an important part of the experience for guests. They're going to be standing in line only for so long to ride a minute, 28-second ride, but when you can entertain them with a podcast car or a meteor strike or some fun queue line stuff, I think that's what keeps guests entangled in the story...and it makes the payoff [for the coaster] worthwhile."

"In the end, the in-house teams at the park all working together is what made this new roller coaster and new land turn into something special and unique," added Paul Bonifield. "I'm proud of the hard work the team put in to pull it off. I was only planning on being on-site for about a week, and that turned into nearly two months once I was tasked with being the onsite scenic director! A project of this scale and one that just so happens to be at the park I grew up working at and visiting doesn't come around every day. It made the long hours I put in worth it."

For Mike Koontz, the opening of *Orion* means the completion of the largest investment in the park's history, a project that Koontz oversaw from the very beginning to the grand opening. "Not every general manager of every amusement park in the US or the world can say they've had a $31 million coaster," Koontz concluded. "But hey, I'm a guy who is like, 'Okay, we did that, we came in on budget, it opened, we were successful, let's move on, what's next?' I put the same amount of passion and enthusiasm behind every project, whether it's a million dollar project or a thirty-one million dollar project. So my job is to make sure that everything we do at Kings Island, no matter what it is, is to the standard of Kings Island and it's going to make our guests happy...It's part of my legacy, it's part of what I accomplished as my time as GM of Kings Island, and I'm very proud of that."

Å

LOOKING TO THE FUTURE

With Mike Koontz as general manager and Richard Zimmerman as CEO of the park's parent company, Kings Island's future is looking brighter than ever.

"My vision for Kings Island is that we continue to invest behind the brand," Zimmerman said. "We do a lot of consumer research, and we're really trying to pay attention to what our guests are telling us— what they want, what they like, what they'd like to see...Our key four strategies is broadening our guest appeal, broadening our guest experience, the events strategy, bringing things like *Grand Carnivale*, bringing things like WinterFest and Halloween Haunt, having key elements of an event strategy that appeals to different demos, we lean into that hard because our guests tell us they find a lot of value. They like the rides, they're there every day, but when you put programming on top of the rides, it creates a unique value proposition and really drives a lot of demand and has incredible appeal."

Zimmerman envisions a more complete park experience. "We're going to lean hard in events; we'll always invest in new attractions over the course of time, but what you'll see us do is invest heavily in the guest amenities—make sure there's enough shade, make sure we've got comfortable places to sit, more and more food and beverage is a very important part of what we do. Our guests tell us it's part of the decision of whether or not to come. We've invested heavily at Kings Island in their food facilities, their food program, and seeing great growth and not just great growth, but great usage and demand from our guests that visit Kings Island...Food and beverage, events, unique attractions, that's what I see as the future of Kings Island," Zimmerman said.

"I think some of my vision is what our guests [experienced] in 2019, to bring back some of the original feel of Kings Island, the way it was," Koontz said. "Quite honestly, one of the reasons we brought back *Antique Cars* is at the end of the day we're a family park. That's who we are. Kings Island will never be the Roller Coaster Capital of the World like what Cedar Point is known for. We have to know who we market...The area we live in has a lot of families with kids. We need to make sure we always focus on what's going to appeal to that demographic.

"Ultimately, the goal is to look at each area of the park whether it be Snoopy, Rivertown, Coney, Action Zone, International Street, waterpark, and say, 'What's going to appeal to the families?' We want to appeal to the coaster enthusiasts as well, but I think season passes are [a] very important component of our business model."

Koontz also wants to continue restoring the park's charm and theming. "As I look around areas of the park I see the opportunity to do more painting, do more landscaping. Those are just maintenance things that I'm not going to say have been neglected, but I use the term, 'Over the years, some aspects of what this park was have been neutered.'"

"My vision is that we don't forget where we came from," Koontz concluded. "We don't forget our heritage and history. We don't ignore what our guests are telling us that they want."

CONCLUSION

Through nearly fifty years of history, Kings Island has seen it all. The park is under its fifth owner and eleventh general manager, and has boasted twenty-two roller coasters throughout its time. The beloved playground has created lifelong memories for the hundreds of millions of guests that have passed through its gates as well as for the thousands of employees that have worked to create a memorable experience for them.

"I've always said, we don't make hubcaps or bottle caps," declared Dennis Speigel, the assistant general manager when the park first opened. "What do we do? We don't pollute the skies, we don't put pollution in the rivers. What do we do at the end of the day? We make smiles and memories; put smiles on people's faces...I still have a wonderful relationship with the Cedar Fair guys and Kings Island. There isn't a park basically on the planet that I can't go to, walk in, and see somebody I know and have fun with. It's been great for Kings Island. I mean, here it is nearly fifty years, I look back, it seems like it was five minutes ago and sometimes it feels like it was forty-eight years ago, but as I said at the outset, if we knew back then what we know today, we probably wouldn't have done it! We would have been scared to death. We just forged ahead and were in the right place in the right business at the right time."

"It takes a lot of guts and patience and courage and determination," said Rob Decker, Cedar Fair's senior vice president of planning and design from 1999 to 2019. "So I give full credit to Kings Island for believing in who they are and trusting the confidence of the community to continue the entertainment in a safe and fun way, and I think that's just the best part of looking back over twenty years, right? What happened and what are you proud of. It's just all of that. It's all of that and a Skyline Chili!"

"I think Kings Island has always been a great place to work and has always been successful," said Nelson Schwab III, executive vice president of the Taft Broadcasting theme park division and CEO of Kings Entertainment Company and Paramount Parks. "Not many businesses can say that over a long period of time. I think it's a real tribute to the people who work there who've kept the culture intact of doing what's best for the guest and having a lot of pride in what they do. I really admire everybody at Kings Island. There are a lot of folks who have started their career at Kings Island and have gone on to a lot of different places and spread that culture throughout the industry. It's really had a wonderful impact on the whole theme park industry."

"We found common ground, regardless of who we were owned by. We found good ways to steward the brand and build on the guest experience," remembered Craig Ross, general manager from 2002 to 2006. "I think at the end of the day, Kings Island is really beloved in the Greater Cincinnati market. You won't find many parks, there are a handful of them, but you won't find many that are as beloved by their local community as Kings Island."

"What I really loved about working there was discovering the local passion people would have," added Dave Cobb, senior creative director for Paramount Parks from 2002 to 2006. "I would basically live there for a couple of months out of a hotel while we'd install things. And I remember I'd go into town and I have friends in Ohio, so I'd meet up with them and I'd meet their friends or I'd be making some conversations with people in bars and I'd say, 'I work for Kings

Island,' and they would, without question every single time, tell me their entire life story of Kings Island. Going there as a kid, the first roller coaster they went on, their favorite ride, they worked there for a summer serving cotton candy, like, everybody. People who go to Universal and Disney, the big parks, people have stories about those too. But it's different for a regional park, and I didn't really understand that until I worked at one. The world of the regional parks and what they represent to people is something I learned working at Kings Island."

"I went to Coney Island when I was a kid, so the fact that when Kings Island was built and they so respected the Coney Island heritage, they so connected the community to Coney Island with moving and becoming Kings Island, I think it very early on had very loyal customers and followings," reflected Jane Cooper, CEO of Paramount Parks from 1995 to 2002. "Even for somebody like me, who went there and worked there as a teenager, as you age you want to share those same experiences you had with your children and your grandchildren, and I think that they have so nurtured that, that it will always be a really special place."

"The thing that I would mention is that bond it's developed with the community and the region," added Tim Fisher, general manager from 1997 to 2002 and Cedar Fair's current chief operating officer. "The other thing is the people. Not only the people in the marketplace, but the employees that have made Kings Island such a special place over the years. People like yourself [seasonal associates] and others that have grown up there and moved into management, and they've continued the traditions of the past. That's what's made Kings Island so special. You have the community that loves that park and employees that have loved it just as much, and that chemistry makes for a very special theme park. When you have employees that love it and you have consumers that love it, you can do something very special, and that's what's happened to Kings Island. That's what made it so special in the past, and that's what's going to make it so special in the future."

"It's definitely transformed, I think, into something all of Cincinnati and Mason is very proud of," Greg Scheid reflected. "It'll always be a part of the history around here for sure."

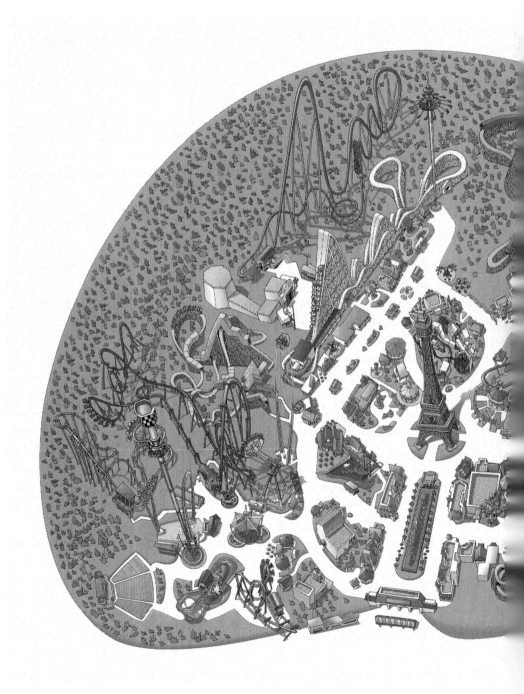

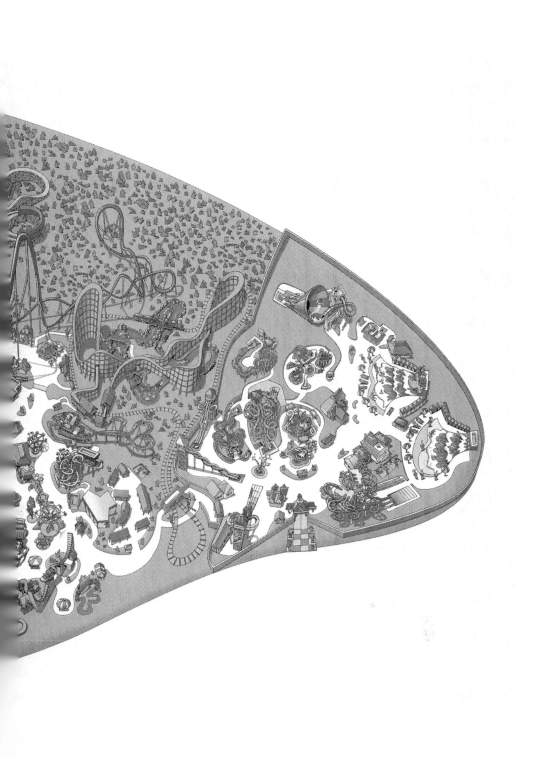

ACKNOWLEDGMENTS

First and foremost, I would like to thank everyone that contributed to this book with interviews and photographs. This project would not have been possible without Lelia Andrews, Rick Bastrup, Rick Belhumeur, Paul Bonifield, Dave Cobb, Jane Cooper, Greg Crane, Ed Dangler, Andy Dauterman, Walt Davis, Rob Decker, Perry Denehy, Anthony Esparza, Tim Fisher, Russell Flatt, Dave Focke, Mike Foley, Alfred Freeman, Richard Fussner, Jamie Gaffney, Jeff Gramke, Don Helbig, Will Herrmann, Abigail Highley, Adam House, Keith James, Josh Kellerman, Tom Kempton, Dick Kinzel, Mike Koontz, Jason McClure, Michael Meadows, Charles S. Mechem Jr., Bill Ossim, William C. Price, Craig Ross, Jack Rouse, Greg Scheid, Mark Schoelwer, Nelson Schwab III, Dennis Speigel, Amy Steele, Monique Gubser Strucke, Dudley Taft, Gary Wachs, Reggie Whitehead, Kirk Whittemore, and Richard Zimmerman.

A very special thanks to Paul Bonifield, for his incredible cover design, and Gary Wachs, for writing the uplifting forward.

Thanks to Emily Burrows, Michelle Dillon, Billy Goldfeder, Jamie Hawkins, Lisa Murtha, Tim O'Brien, Matt Ouimet, and Gretlyn Thomas for help with contacting sources and for helping to coordinate interviews. This book would not be the quality that it is without their help.

I also have to thank Jacob Tartabini for coming up with the book's wonderful title, Julie Herrmann for legal advice, and James A. Willis for publishing advice.

For their help finding archival material, I'd like to thank the staff at the Mason Historical Society, the Public Library of Cincinnati and Hamilton County, the Warren County Historical Society, and Paul Sarver of the Warren County Sheriff's Office.

A huge thanks to my advance readers: David Billman, Tyler Mullins, Dennis Speigel, and Kirk Whittemore. Thank you for taking the time to read through it and helping ensure that the final book goes above and beyond.

Many thanks to my editor and publisher, Barry Hill, for his countless hours spent proofreading, editing, and formatting. Thank you for turning my dream of this book into a reality!

Finally, I would like to thank my parents for their endless support and assistance throughout the research and writing process.

DEDICATION

This book is dedicated to all my family and friends for their constant support and help with this project!

In Memory of Richard Fussner.

SELECTED BIBLIOGRAPHY

Though a great deal of the information in the story comes from my interviews with the officials who built and ran the park, there were lots of other sources that helped fill it out. The complete list includes hundreds of newspaper and magazine articles; all of this is posted on the book's website at www.rivershorecreative.com.

BOOKS

Caudill, Sally Sherman, and Sherri Reed Federle. *Mason, Ohio: A Photographic History.* Print Management, LLC, 2014.

Jacques, Charles J. *Cincinnati's Coney Island.* Amusement Park Journal, 2002.

INTERVIEWS

Bastrup, Richard. Personal interview. September 30, 2020.

Belhumeur, Richard. Personal interview. November 5, 2020.

Bonifield, Paul. Personal interview. November 5, 2020.

Cobb, David. *Personal interview.* October 26, 2020.

Cooper, Jane. *Personal interview.* April 8, 2019.

Crane, Gregory. *Personal interview.* December 11, 2020.

Dangler, Edmond. *Personal interview.* October 1, 2020.

Dauterman, Andy. *Personal interview.* September 22, 2020.

Davis, Walter. *Personal interview.* January 8, 2019.

Decker, Robert. *Personal interview.* December 9, 2020.

Denehy, Perry. *Personal interview.* July 29, 2019.

Esparza, Anthony. *Personal interview.* September 26, 2019.

Fisher, Tim. *Personal interview.* January 3, 2020.

Flatt, Russell. *Personal interview.* February 5, 2020.

Focke, David. *Personal interview.* January 9, 2020.

Foley, Michael. *Personal interview.* November 13, 2020.

Fussner, Richard. *Personal interview.* October 23, 2019.

Gaffney, Jamie. *Personal interview.* December 9, 2019.

Gramke, Jeff. *Personal interview.* October 17, 2019.

Helbig, Don. *Personal interview.* January 13, 2020.

House, Adam. *Personal interview.* April 18, 2017.

James, Keith. *Personal interview.* November 3, 2020.

Kempton, Thomas. *Personal interview.* January 27, 2020.

Kinzel, Richard. *Personal interview.* July 10, 2019.

Koontz, Michael. *Personal interview.* March 13, 2019. Second interview session October 13, 2019. Third interview session November 23, 2020.

McClure, Jason. *Personal interview.* December 21, 2020.

Meadows, Michael. *Personal interview.* January 16, 2020.

Mechem, Charles. *Personal interview.* January 23, 2019.

Ossim, William. *Personal interview.* October 16, 2019.

Price, William. *Personal interview.* January 11, 2019.

Ross, Craig. *Personal interview.* April 22, 2019.

Rouse, Jack. *Personal interview.* November 10, 2020.

Scheid, Greg. *Personal interview.* February 9, 2019.

Schoelwer, Mark. *Personal interview.* September 29, 2020.

Schwab, Nelson. *Personal interview.* March 18, 2019.

Speigel, Dennis. *Personal interview.* December 27, 2019.

Steele, Amy. Personal interview. May 1, 2017.
Taft, Dudley. Personal interview. April 25, 2019.
Wachs, Gary. Personal interview. January 29, 2019.
Whitehead, Reginald. Personal interview. December 20, 2019.
Zimmerman, Richard. Personal interview. April 7, 2020.

INDEX

ABOUT THE AUTHOR

Evan Ponstingle has been a frequent visitor to Kings Island since he moved to Mason, Ohio in 2007. He has been working at Kings Island since October 2017 in the park's merchandise department, and in his free time Evan enjoys visiting amusement parks and playing the baritone. He is looking forward to attending Bowling Green State University and majoring in Resort and Attraction Management.

Photo by Bud Strudthoff.